Crisis Management in the Tourism Industry

Crisis Management in the Tourism Industry

Dirk Glaesser

AMSTERDAM • BOSTON • HEIDELBERG • LONDON
NEW YORK • OXFORD • PARIS • SAN DIEGO
SAN FRANCISCO • SINGAPORE • SYDNEY • TOKYO

ELSEVIER   Butterworth-Heinemann is an imprint of Elsevier

Butterworth-Heinemann
An imprint of Elsevier
Linacre House, Jordan Hill, Oxford OX2 8DP
200 Wheeler Road, Burlington, MA 01803

First published 2003

British Library Cataloguing in Publication Data
A catalogue record for this book is available from the British Library

Library of Congress Cataloguing in Publication Data
A catalogue record for this book is available from the Library of Congress

ISBN-13: 978 0 7506 6523 0
ISBN-10: 0 7506 6523 8

For information on all Butterworth-Heinemann publications visit our
website at www.bh.com

Typeset by Newgen Imaging Systems (P) Ltd, Chennai, India
Printed and bound in Great Britain

To those who dedicate their lives to tourism

Contents

List of examples

Preface

The tourism industry is like no other economic sector challenged by negative events. Its above average sensitivity towards these kinds of occurrences has given it such an exposed position that it already serves as an early warning indicator of critical situations for other sectors.

The destinations and businesses active in tourism have to face these challenges. Some years ago, companies could consider negative events as extraordinary and less likely. However, the developments of the last decade indicate the necessity to make crisis management a permanent part of the practical and scientific considerations. While doing so, organizations are confronted with the fundamental difficulty that despite the best intentions and highest efforts of prevention, risks cannot be completely controlled and therefore totally excluded.

Under these circumstances, besides the necessary implementation of measures which minimize risks, it is important to analyse negative events from every angle, to systematically identify critical success factors, to integrate them and take them into account when considering the strategic corporate orientation. Marketing is in this perspective very important. As many crises in tourism are causing impacts on companies and destinations whose products and services are objectively not affected or damaged – in other words subjective distortions of perception are taking place –, it is important to consider the store of knowledge of marketing for coping with crises but also for preventing them.

That is the aim of this book, which develops a general framework for crisis management and offers the basis for further analysis. It looks at the important area of prevention but also on how to cope with emerging crises; it discusses strategic dimensions but also operational techniques. It has one overall aim: To ensure a sustainable development for those working in the tourism industry and for those enjoying the services of this sector.

For the second edition of this book new chapters have been introduced, several restructured and the overall text has been completely revised and updated. New checklists, descriptive illustrations and additional representative case studies aim at giving a close and realistic insight into the practise of crisis management.

While preparing a book like this, which intends to offer a comprehensive approach to the topic of crisis management and which, above all, tries to connect the bits and pieces which are so important for understanding why some situations occur, in ways that no one would have expected, I had the assistance of an excellent team.

Firstly, I want to thank my wife Matilde for supporting me and having the time to discuss all the facets of this book. Prof. Dr. Peter Keller, a profound expert on the issues of international tourism policy was again a great help with his comments and advice. Ute Meyer, Stefanie Theuerkorn, Jens Oliver Glaeßer and Sarah Beswick helped me with plenty of comments to improve the script. Anika Mattheis, Maryen Blaschke, Tamara Nebel, Fabian Rütschi assisted me in the research. I also want to thank Prof. Dr. Guillermo Aceves for his valuable comments from a U.S. point of view.

1   Tourism in a changing world

Objectives

- To obtain an overview of developments which are influencing the tourism sector
- To understand the importance of the study of crisis management
- To understand the influence of climate change on the natural environment and the consequences for tourism

Key terms and concepts

- Technological progress
- Climate change
- Natural catastrophe

Nowadays, tourism is an absolutely normal part of our daily life. Even if there was travel to the Olympic Games or to the Knight Games in the ancient world, society's extensive participation in tourism started only a few decades ago.

The positive effects of tourism are varied. For tourists, a holiday means satisfaction as travel gives them the opportunity to bring their hopes and dreams to life. Furthermore, by holidaying outside their usual surroundings, tourists increase their knowledge of other cultures and ways of life, be it knowingly or unknowingly. This changed view of things helps to foster greater acceptance and tolerance among the human race.

As far as the national economy is concerned, the tourism industry has, in many countries, achieved such a leading position that it counts as one of the most important sources of income and foreign exchange. This growth will continue in the future and will contribute to make tourism the most significant industry in the world. Besides, tourism is, like no other industry, in a position to create prosperity and economic development opportunities even for places that would otherwise be considered as difficult to develop.

Leading position of tourism

However, the positive development of the tourism industry is gradually being threatened by negative events. Incidents, that have taken place in the recent past, had economic consequences which were previously unheard of in other economic spheres. The Terrorist attacks in Egypt, SARS, 9/11, Tsumamis in Asia, are a few prominent examples of crises that caused economic losses to the tourism industry in the millions or even billions of U.S. dollars. But also indirect effects have a considerable impact like, for example, the rise in transport and travel costs across the globe, which especially threaten the competitiveness of long haul tourism destinations. At the same time, a number of other effects are becoming apparent such as image damage and the limitation on entrepreneurial room for manoeuvre from which businesses are still affected in both the medium and long term.

The reasons for the increased appearance of crises are complex. However, a first analysis shows that there are different areas contributing to this rising number of negative events.

1.1 The living conditions of humans

Living conditions

Among the first ranking influences is the fact that living conditions in the most important source markets are changing at an increasing speed. These fast changes become especially clear when one looks at the social developments from a very early perspective.

Today's information indicates the existence of human beings on earth at around 2 500 000 years B.C. During the first one million years, human beings became accustomed to the use of stone tools. It took many generations for minor changes to occur. Man started to dominate fires some 500 000 years ago. Again, during many generations, he had the time to get used to these innovations and to its impact on his social environment. Man as we know him today, from his anatomy and physiology and especially from the size of his brain is only 40 000 years old. Even younger is the Neolithic revolution which is only 9-10 000 years old. Only at this moment, Man started to actively shape nature, to settle and to domesticate animals. Thus, life as we know it today only started some 9000 years ago.

Diagram 1: Development speed

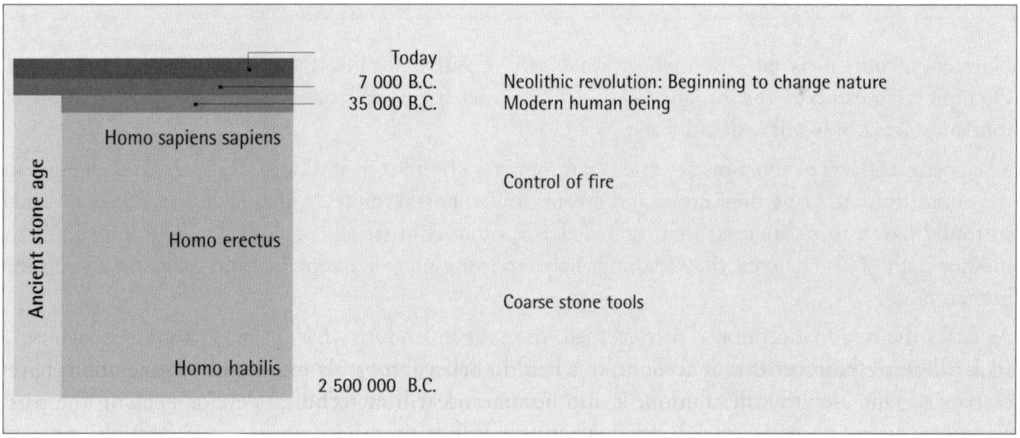

Average life expectancy

Age is another important factor of influence. 35 000 years B.C., the average life expectancy was around 20 years. As shown in the following diagram, changes over time in the average life span were only minimal. In fact, it only reached 35 years some 200 years ago. Since then, with the changes brought about by the Industrial Revolution and the ensuing developments in science and social structures, among others, life expectancy has more than doubled. Today, a woman in Western Europe has a life expectancy of some 80 years.

Diagram 2: Development of average age

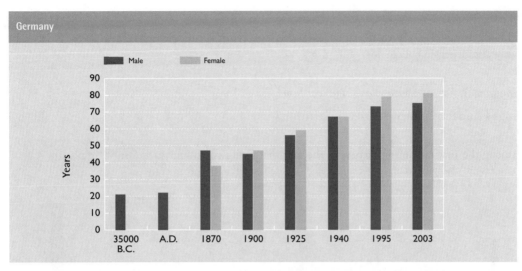

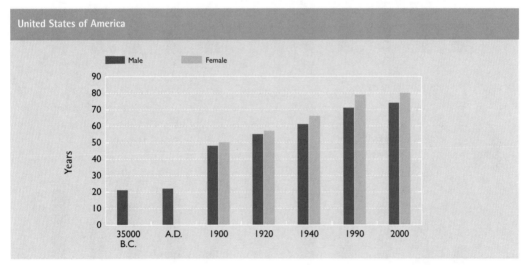

Taking these developments into account, it is hard to believe that only four hundred generations have passed since the Neolithic revolution. It also becomes clear how technical developments in the past several generations took longer to happen, whereas in this day and age several technical revolutions take place within one generation. Looking at telephone use since it was introduced, it took around sixty years before one could speak of wide dissemination. The personal computer on the other hand needed only thirty years to become part of our daily life. The cell phone achieved this in only twenty years.

However, these technical changes, which we consider to be positive developments, can also have negative impacts. The first PC virus appeared in 1993. Twenty years later we speak with normality about the existence of these damaging programs, which can change the overall social structures worldwide in seconds.

Demographic trends

The demographic trends of human beings are also changing. Looking at the development of the average household size over the last 100 years, we can observe that at the beginning of the last century, the majority of households, specifically 44 per cent, contained five or more people. At the beginning of the twentieth century, there was a clear tendency towards smaller households. In 1998, 36 per cent were already single households.

Diagram 3: Size of households (in percentage)

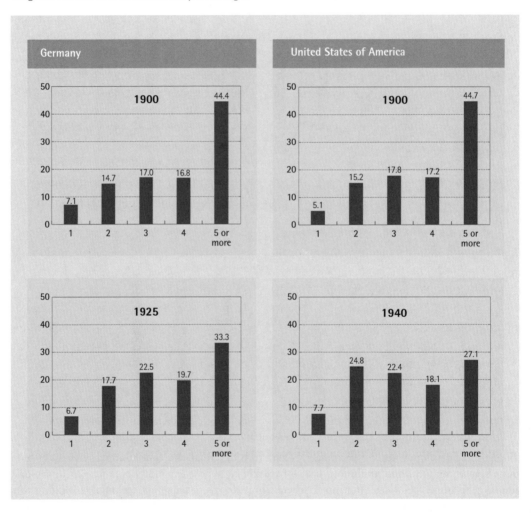

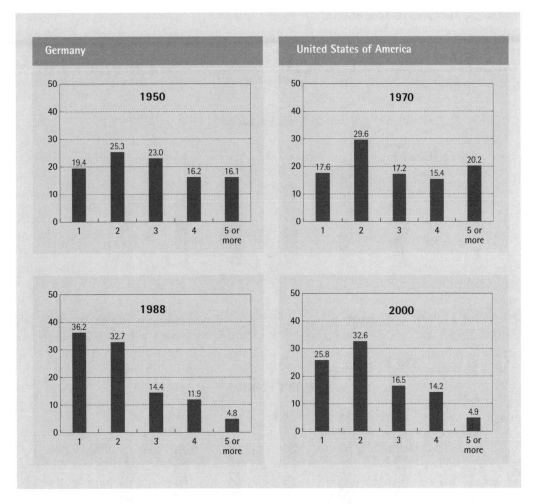

In addition to this, it can be observed that marriages are taking place at a much later age. There is a wider existence of unmarried couples and the average time of marriage is permanently decreasing. In the extreme case of the United States, some 40 per cent of marriages end in divorce after only 15 years. For younger couples, i.e. under 45 years old, this quota of divorces reaches 50 per cent. And, if a couple was already divorced, new marriages normally last much less.

Diagram 4: Marriages and divorces

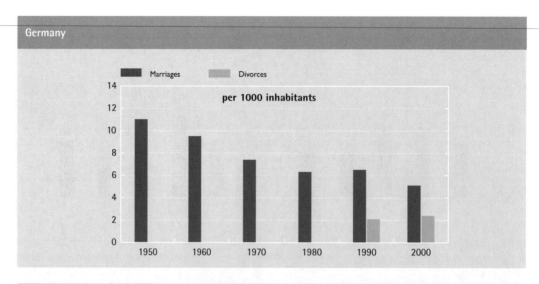

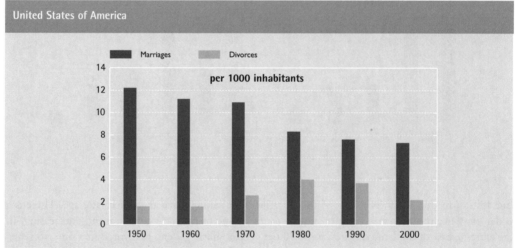

These are only some factors that describe the environment in which human beings live today and indicate the challenges they are faced with.

Supply of information

One of these challenges is the worsening supply of information. This might surprise at first as we live in an age where there is precisely no lack of information. In fact, there will be more data produced in the next three years than in the last 300 000 years in total. With the oversupply of information it can be difficult to filter that which is considered to be important. In addition, the changing family environment makes it more difficult to transmit information to the individual that is tailored to their individual needs. This is of crucial importance for an improved perception and processing of information.

Furthermore, demographic developments cause insecurities, which were previously dealt with by traditional family communities but are now resting with the individual. This represents an enormous challenge for the individual. Therefore, we can observe that more and more occurrences, which are normally considered as dangers are now labeled as risks. By this, the 'unavoidable' shall be made 'avoidable'. While dangers are sourced in the environment and cannot be influenced by man, risks are often traced back to decisions and are associated to individuals.

Secondly, individuals aim to find institutions, which can be used to cope with these insecurities. This includes the State, which is confronted with tasks and expectations which it has not previously been responsible for. But also private companies are affected by these changes. Increasingly, companies are made responsible for occurrences and situations which do not form part of any contract nor which have been considered in the past as part of their scope of responsibility.

It remains to be mentioned that human beings are creatures of habit. What Man has learned once, he aims at continuing. He tries to avoid changes that are too big or tries to postpone them at least up to such a moment that they are impossible to avoid. Man has difficulties in adapting and absorbing all the changes in the technical environment as fast as they take place. Large and small technical revolutions do not happen across generations any longer but rather within one same generation. Eruptive changes are the consequence and there is a natural defense reaction that needs to be overcome. This is very often only possible when situations are carried to an extreme.

Creatures of habit

1.2 Natural changes

Man has always attempted to become independent from the powers of nature. Technological progress has helped him in this effort; but this progress can be partly considered a result of this continuous effort of independence. Thousands of years ago human beings were seeking protection from natural adversities in caves and attempted to shield themselves from nature. Nowadays they are experimenting with natural environments such as the Biosphere experiment in Arizona (USA) and an increasing number of tourist attractions such as indoor skiing-arenas and fully climate-controlled leisure parks.

However, despite these intensive efforts, the powers of nature cannot be controlled fully. It seems that exactly the opposite has happened in the meantime. During the past 100 years, more than 50 000 natural catastrophes have been accounted for worldwide, which collectively claimed more than 4 million human lives. In the past fifteen years between 500 and 700 natural catastrophes have been registered annually. This does not take into account the unnumbered droughts and famines which cost the lives of many more millions of people. Interestingly, those

View of part of the fully climate-controlled Gaylord Opryland Resort in Nashville, USA. The inmense size, enormous number of attractions, exposition space, restaurants and more than 2800 hotel rooms, make it possible for tourists to stay inside the installation for several days without being in contact with the warm and humid weather.

catastrophes, which have geological origins such as earthquakes or volcanic eruptions, remain constant in numbers. Differently, those catastrophes, which originate from extreme weather conditions such as floods, windstorms, landslides, cold spells, forest fires, are increasing constantly. Even before the devastating Tsunami in Asia, the year 2004 was considered the most costly year for the insurance sector in terms of natural catastrophes. With insured losses of 40 billion US$ and economic losses of 130 billion US$, the insured losses of 26 billion US$ from the year 1992 were exceeded significantly. This trend will continue in the future.

Diagram 5: Great natural catastrophes

Decade	1950–59	1960–69	1970–79	1980–89	1990–99
Number	20	27	47	63	91
Economic losses in US$ billion (2003 values)	42.7	76.7	140.6	217.3	670.4

There are several important reasons that explain this increasing number of natural catastrophes. Firstly, there is the exponential increase in world population and the developments linked to it such as urbanization, water shortages and use of exposed areas. If the population continues to grow by 1 billion every 10-15 years, by mid 21st century, the density of the population will be 50 per cent higher than today. This will have an especially strong impact on cities, which have absorbed an above average percentage of the population growth in the last fifty years. While in the 1950s only 30 per cent of the world population (about 2.5 billion) lived in cities, this figure has changed to some 50 per cent of the 6 billion people of today. And this tendency is very likely to continue. Areas, which are exposed to a high level of natural risks, are increasingly used because of tourism interests but also because of the deficit of further areas of expansion, especially in those fast-growing urban zones.

Population growth

The strong tourism development of Florida, which is explained by the agreeable climatic conditions, the nice beaches, changed a mostly agricultural geographical area into one of the most densely populated areas of the United States. Despite the known tracks of hurricanes and their extensive damage, this is an area which is not avoided but rather looked for. The record of the most expensive natural catastrophe was caused by hurricane Andrew in 1992 with losses for the insurance industry of 17 billion US$. Other areas such as the Alps where there are frequent avalanches, demonstrate that the use of particularly exposed areas for tourism is extremely risky.

Climate change

Without any doubt, the climate change is also playing a fundamental role in the increase of natural catastrophes. As the following chart of the Intergovernmental Panel on Climate Change (IPCC), an institution of the WHO and UNEP, shows, the average global temperature increased by 0.7 degrees during the last 100 years. Taking into consideration that the average difference between the moderate periods and the ice ages was only 5 degrees, this is a value to be taken seriously. Today, we can observe some of its consequences: melting of glaciers, shortage of snow at traditional ski destinations, warming of the oceans and the resulting increase in the water level of the oceans, but also the increase of floods through extraordinary rainfalls and storms in areas which were until recently spared of these occurrences.

Diagram 6: Climate change

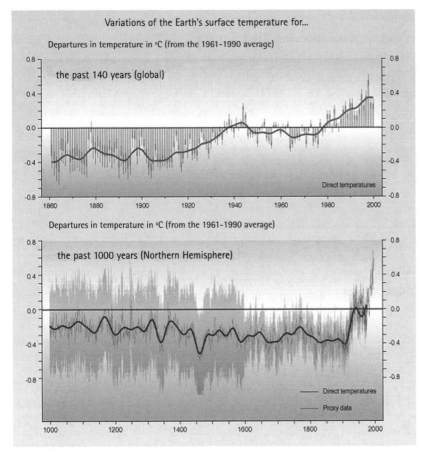

Source: IPCC

Our extreme confidence in technological achievements has caused natural events to trigger not only more often but also stronger damages than necessary. As most of the engineering measures help to protect us against floods or make buildings earthquake-resistant, they at the same time make us forget that these measures bring little to protect us against larger events. The absence of consequences from regularly smaller and medium-size natural occurrences gives us misleading confidence. Events which finally exceed a certain threshold like the earthquake of Kobe in 1995, Northridge 1994 or Mexico City in 1985, the flooding of Red River in the north of the United States and the south of Canada in 1997, the flooding in central Europe in 2002 or the devastating Tsunami in Asia at the end of 2004, is hitting largely unprepared populations and administrations.

Technological achievements

Questions for review and discussion

- Can all negative events be avoided?
- Why has the importance of crisis management in tourism risen?
- Which role does the family play in coping with insecurities?
- What are the driving factors of the worldwide population growth?
- How is the use of high-risk areas assessed by the tourism industry? E.g. construction in coastal or mountainous areas.

Suggestions for further reading

Intergovernmental Panel on Climate Change (2001), *Climate Change 2001: The Scientific Basis,* Cambridge University Press, Cambridge.

Luhmann, N. (2005), *Risk: A Sociological Theory*, Aldine Transaction, New Brunswick, N.J.

United Nations Population Fund (2004), *State of World Population 2004: The Cairo Consensus at Ten - Population, Reproductive Health and the Global Effort to End Poverty,* UNFPA, New York.

World Tourism Organization (2003), *Climate Change and Tourism*, WTO, Madrid.

Useful websites

www.world-tourism.org
www.ipcc.ch
www.unfpa.org

2   The basics of crisis management

Objectives

- To obtain an overview of the linguistic development of the term 'crisis'
- To be able to understand the scientific discussion on the crisis phenomenon
- To be in the position to define 'crisis' and to disassociate it from various other terms
- To learn the system and activity of crisis management in tourism
- To understand the role of mass media for information dissemination as well as influencing the recipient's opinion
- To name the dissemination influence variables

Key terms and concepts

- Crisis
- Negative event
- Crisis management
- Tourism, tourist
- System theory

2.1 What is a crisis?

2.1.1 The origins

The word crisis comes from the Greek 'krisis', which means differentiation or decision. Within the legal sphere, the term was used to describe the differentiation between just and unjust whilst, in theology, it described the separation of salvation and damnation. Medical terminology used the expression for the break in a development that had previously been continuous. In the sixteenth century, with the revival of classic medicine the word became part of everyday language. The use of the term 'crisis' became evident in all areas of politics, society and the economy and, by the mid-19th century, people were already complaining about its overuse.

The increase in the linguistic use of the term crisis was accompanied by a renewed scientific discussion of the 'crisis' phenomenon. Various scientific findings can be classed as either referring to

危机

The Chinese equivalent for the word crisis is 'Weiji'. It is formed from the first letter of danger 危险 'Weixian' and opportunity 机会 'Jihui'. This composition of the word clearly reflects the real characteristics of a crisis.

persons/institutions or as contributions to the individual/collective model depending on their focal points.

As a rule, the human being is the focal point of considerations concerning individual models. In this case, the individual experiences the crisis as an intensification of the actual situation, which, in extreme cases, can lead to his or her end. Contributions to the individual model come from medicine and psychosomatics, psychosocial development theory and crisis intervention (crisis intervention is a collective term for theories about human behaviour in exceptional circumstances and therapy concepts). For collective models, on the other hand, social systems are analysed under certain circumstances that could be described as a crisis. Economics, political science and communications research all contribute to the collective model.

Furthermore, by using the subdivision practised in political science, system-and decision-oriented approaches can be distinguished. Within the framework of decision-theoretic approaches, crisis is understood as a dangerous and extraordinary situation in which a decision must be made under time pressure. Investigations carried out from this angle concentrate on the state of an acute crisis and acquire knowledge on the workflow organization in a crisis.

In systemic approaches, crisis is seen as a critical change in important variables that endanger or destroy either parts of or the entire system. The majority of the contributions to this area come from political science and the aim is the development of early warning systems. Due to their analysis of actual use and overuse, the results are especially useful for the organizational structure of the company in situations of crisis. The following diagram shows the areas of knowledge within crisis research.

Diagram 7: Areas of knowledge within crisis research

	System-oriented approaches	Decision-oriented approaches
Individual models	Medicine: • Turning point is the decision between life and death during the course of an illness Psychology: • Perception of an occurrence or situation as an intolerable difficulty which exceeds a person's resources and coping mechanisms • Failure of behavioural patterns • Danger of identity loss	Individual cognitive problem solving qualities of decision makers in crisis situations

Collective models	Social sciences:
	• Crises as phenomena of societies: endangered national interests during conflict due to a threatening escalation towards war (e.g. Cuban crisis)
	• Crises as phenomena of societal subsystems:
	  - Politics: real changes to the patterns of political relations (e.g. coup, revolution)
	  - Economy: exogenous economic shocks; phases of downward trends in the economic cycle
		Collective decision behaviour in crisis situations

Source: Based on Linde (1994)

2.1.2 Decisive characteristics of the term 'crisis'

National economics was the first to look into crises. The approaches understood crises predominantly as cyclical economic problems. Business administration only started to take an interest later and this was prompted by the conditions that accompanied the crude oil shortage of the 1970s. The limitations that were, until then, unknown and the ever more frequent insolvency of companies prompted an economic investigation, the consequence of which was the emphasis on coping with crises.

Business administration predominantly terms crisis as a process that negatively influences the development of a company to a considerable extent (Krystek, 1987; Schulten, 1995). In this sense, the crisis either endangers or makes the survival of the affected company impossible.

To determine a crisis situation, the question must be asked as to whether the organization still has the ability to achieve important corporate goals. However, only those goals that exert considerable influence over the future survival of the company are of significance. The initial specifications of these high-ranking goals include solvency, that is, the ability to fulfil business payment obligations, and success expressed through minimum profit or return on investment. The advantage of this narrow version of the term 'crisis' was the simple definition of crisis conditions within a company. Its financial base allows the simple derivation from accounting through a target/actual comparison.

Important corporate goals

However, this advantage of a simple definition is confronted with the disadvantage that the actual causes of the deviation from corporate goals, which occur earlier, are not covered. For this reason, the inclusion of the company's success factors that form the basis of solvency and success as a further criterion is important. Defined by Porter (1998a) as competitive advantage, these factors determine the present and, more specifically, future success of the organisation.

From this perspective it is important for a prompt determination of a crisis situation to concentrate on the seriousness of events. It must be assessed whether actual or potential events within the company or its environment influence its competitive advantage or other important business goals. Advantageous in such a contemplation of crisis is the early opportunity to analyse these events within the framework

Seriousness of events

of preventive crisis management. Moreover, the crisis situation can thereby be better determined than through the previously demanded 'survival threat' to the organization. The objection to the latter is that, as a rule, it is only possible to determine this threat correctly when the crisis is already in an advanced state. It is then already too late for the introduction of crisis management countermeasures.

> **Intensity of the time pressure**
>
> The intensity of the time pressure can essentially be broken down into the following three components:
>
> - Limitation on the time available, i.e. the decision time;
>
> - Individual sensitivity of the participants towards external pressure;
>
> - The magnitude of the problem.

Furthermore, concentrating on the seriousness of events takes into account that certain areas never face a threat to survival. In tourism, for example, destinations are organizational units, which, despite a considerable number of negative influences, are not threatened in their existence. The risk of a threat to survival would apply to businesses active within the destination but it would not necessarily have to be so.

Another characteristic of a crisis is the development possibility over the course of time. This process character is marked, on the one hand, by its temporal limitations, on the other, by its ambivalence. The latter is a prerequisite for the actual crisis management, that is, the sensibleness of the use of

Process character

countermeasures. Only after the so-called turning point of the crisis can it be decided whether the previously ambivalent crisis situation will take a clearly positive or negative course.

In addition, the fact that it is not possible to determine the onset of a negative event implies immediacy in view of the prior warning time and the available reaction time. Because crises, considered as processes, progressively limit opportunities of action, a need for decision and action is triggered, which is perceived by the participants as time pressure.

Time pressure

Crises are also characterized by extremely badly structured decisions that can be traced back to information deficit or even too much information, restrictions on information processing, complexity, etc. The conclusion often reached in this context, that crises are unplanned processes, proves to be imprecise. As crises in certain areas can, with planning, be easily anticipated and, therefore, influenced, the term 'undesired development' in relation to the formulated corporate goals is more precise. Both exceeding and falling short of goals can be undesired. Activities described as demarketing, which are of use in the undesired exceeding of corporate goals, should not, however, be the object of further considerations.

Undesired development

At the same time, a crisis is an exceptional situation, the onset of which is uncertain. Consequently, all preparations with regard to negative events have only eventuality as a characteristic. The number of theoretically possible events and the accordingly considerable expenditure demand restrictions and concentration of the precautions. Even organizations such as armies or the police whose exclusive task is the identification and planning of such processes cannot prepare for every event. On the one hand, this has to do with the number of influential factors that contribute to complexity and, on the other hand, with their continuous change. The possibilities for companies are, in comparison, even more limited because the preparation for and the coping with crises are never seen to be corporate goals.

Exceptional situation

> **Definition: Crisis**
>
> A crisis is an undesired, extraordinary, often unexpected and timely limited process with ambivalent development possibilities. It demands immediate decisions and countermeasures in order to influence the further development again positively for the organisation (destination) and to limit the negative consequences as much as possible.
>
> A crisis situation is determined by evaluating the seriousness of the occurring negative events, which threaten, weaken or destroy competitive advantages or important goals of the organisation.

2.1.3 Catastrophes, turnarounds, structural changes and conflicts

The term 'crisis' should be disassociated from various other terms that are also connected with negative events or are used instead of it, in order to ensure its standard use within the framework of the rest of this book.

Catastrophes

Catastrophes are negative events, which, in contrast to crisis, have a clear inevitable outcome. Consequently, the catastrophe is missing the crisis' ambivalence towards development opportunities. A connection or a simultaneous occurrence of a catastrophe and a crisis can be found especially in tourism, where catastrophes that occur in the environmental sphere trigger a crisis for the affected organization.

Turnaround is understood as countermeasures used when an organization falls short of its goals. These activities, which concentrate, in part, on an acute crisis, aim for an abrupt reversal of the development. Thus, they concentrate on a particular part of the crisis, the object of which is coping with the crisis. Turnaround, consequently, portrays a special case within crisis management.

Turnaround

Structural changes are changes in the economic structure and take place in economies on a regular basis. They are not to be traced back on seasonal or cyclical influences but are a consequence of, for example, changing demand structures, technological progress, discovery of new products, raw materials or production technologies. From the viewpoint of a destination or a company, those changes of a so-far continuous development, i.e. the structural changes, require a process of adaptation. If this necessity of changes is not identified or handled in good time, the organization is more prone to crisis. Generally seen, the management of structural changes normally belongs, because of its principally long-term development, to the sphere of normal management activities.

Structural changes

Clashes between personal groupings, which can take place inside or outside the company, are described as conflicts. In contrast to crisis, conflicts can be of an unlimited duration and can even be desired. Thus, they must not necessarily have negative consequences. It is, however, possible that conflicts are the cause of a crisis.

Conflicts

2.1.4 Classification of crises

Typologies of crises found in literature are extensive and thorough, for which reason only those important for the further contemplation of this book will be examined.

It has already been shown that crises go through a development process. This leads to a phased subdivision of the crisis process becoming practice. As a rule, it is possible to differentiate between two to four phases of a crisis. The presently predominant three-phase crisis process is used as a basis in this book. Using time pressure as a characteristic, this divides the phases of a crisis into potential, latent and acute crises.

Potential crises are characterizing a phase in which the crisis is only an imaginary construct. They are, as such, neither ascertainable nor existent, for which reason this situation is described by Krystek (1987) as the 'quasi normal condition of the company' in which it constantly finds itself.

Potential crises

Latent crises describe the phase in which the crisis has already broken out but is not yet identifiable with the normal quantitative instruments available to the company. Countermeasures in this phase are not yet subject to noticeable restrictions.

Latent crises

The phase of an acute crisis is the period of time in which the destructive effect of the crisis is perceived and the company strives to cope. The symptoms apparent in the acute crisis phase – which should not, however, be confused with the causes – are, as a rule, recognized as an indication of crisis within a company. The perception of a crisis situation is revealed by means of company reporting.

Acute crises

The differentiation between natural and human-induced crises is particularly significant in tourism. Crises triggered by negative events in nature, for example, natural catastrophes (tropical cyclones, storm tides, floods, avalanches and earthquakes) differ considerably in their effect from human-induced crises; that is, events triggered by humans. As a rule, negative events attributed to humans as a trigger

Natural and human-induced crises

lead to a much longer loss of faith and, therefore, to more negative consequences than natural crises that can be traced back to inevitable causes. This could be observed, for example, in the consequences of the events in Los Angeles and San Francisco in 1992. Racial unrest in Los Angeles had an effect not only in terms of immediacy but also in long-term tourism losses, more than for the earthquake in San Francisco. There, arrivals actually increased in the 12 months following the earthquake.

Onset speeds

If the temporal distance between the onset of a negative event and the perception of the critical situation is considered, it is possible to distinguish between crises with fast and slow onset speeds. Crises with fast onset speeds are due to the sudden change detected quicker than is the case with slower onset speeds.

2.2 What are negative events in tourism?

2.2.1 The term

The occurrence of crises can be traced back to the onset of certain negative events. This is voiced by Steger and Antes (1991), who use the term interference potential in this context and define it as follows: 'interference potential – that is to say events which lead to the plans of the company going unfulfilled and negative effects occurring instead ...'. This shows that it is principally an event, which can also be an accumulation of individual phenomena that causes a stable situation to become critical. The use of the term 'interference potential' can be disadvantageous, however, due to people misinterpreting it as meaning an endangered area.

The use of the term 'event' is in fact more appropriate since it is generally defined as a particular, extraordinary occurrence. If this particular, extraordinary occurrence causes negative consequences, this could be termed as a negative event.

An analysis of events that would not cause lasting damage falls under the area of normal management and is covered by risk management.

> **Definition: Negative event**
> Negative events will be defined as all incidents pertaining to the organization's environment, which can cause lasting damage from the perspective of the concerned organization. This means that they can threaten, weaken or destroy competitive advantages or important goals of the organization. Thus, it is preferable to aim at a wide point of view, which considers negative events not only as security problems.

Diagram 8: Basic forms of negative events which triggered crises in tourism

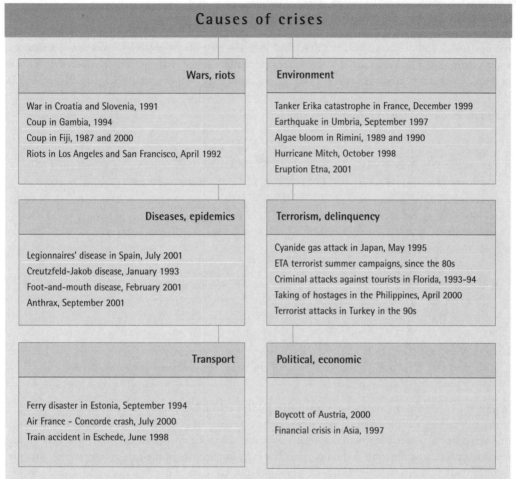

Causes of crises

Wars, riots

War in Croatia and Slovenia, 1991
Coup in Gambia, 1994
Coup in Fiji, 1987 and 2000
Riots in Los Angeles and San Francisco, April 1992

Environment

Tanker Erika catastrophe in France, December 1999
Earthquake in Umbria, September 1997
Algae bloom in Rimini, 1989 and 1990
Hurricane Mitch, October 1998
Eruption Etna, 2001

Diseases, epidemics

Legionnaires' disease in Spain, July 2001
Creutzfeld-Jakob disease, January 1993
Foot-and-mouth disease, February 2001
Anthrax, September 2001

Terrorism, delinquency

Cyanide gas attack in Japan, May 1995
ETA terrorist summer campaigns, since the 80s
Criminal attacks against tourists in Florida, 1993-94
Taking of hostages in the Philippines, April 2000
Terrorist attacks in Turkey in the 90s

Transport

Ferry disaster in Estonia, September 1994
Air France - Concorde crash, July 2000
Train accident in Eschede, June 1998

Political, economic

Boycott of Austria, 2000
Financial crisis in Asia, 1997

This selection of crises in tourism was aimed at highlighting those particular events, which have been forgotten outside the region. They show that many of the events which make us concerned, afraid or shocked have already happened in the past. Often, negative events appear only in slightly changed formats or in different circumstances. However, they tend to repeat in their basic form.

2.2.2 Noticing negative events

Negative events must be realized and in order to cause an effect they must be experienced directly or at least communicated in terms of primary and secondary experience. Experience shows that direct perception is of minor importance. Thus, the analysis of the communication of negative events is given particular importance here as well as to those participating in the communication process.

Regarding forms of communication, it is normally possible to distinguish direct communication, which takes place between people on a personal level, and mass communication, the central characteristic feature of which is the involvement of technical media. The latter occupies a central position for bridging the gap between the wider environment and the recipient of news. The recipient's family, friends and acquaintances are described as being part of the closer environment whereas the wider environment is characterized by groups, organizations, social stratum, etc., to which the recipient belongs. Today, mass media is used, on average, for more than 5 hours a day (Berg and Kiefer, 1992).

Diagram 9: Importance of information sources

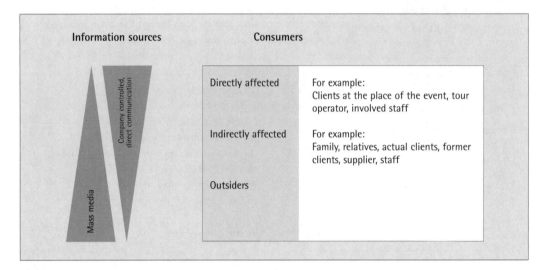

Within the communication process, mass media fulfils two fundamentally different functions: The first is the conveyance of information, the second, the changing of attitudes – an attitude is commonly understood as a person's learned and relatively stable readiness to behave more or less consistently towards an object or situation – and opinion. The high importance of the role as information provider is confirmed by empirical investigations. For example, 95 per cent of the American population get their information about the wider environment from the mass media (Kroeber-Riel, 1992). Contrary to the supposition that often prevails, it is, above all, the print media that determines the information status of the recipient. Television, to which this function is frequently attributed, actually performs rather an initiating function especially for events of emotional importance.

2.2.3 Dissemination influence variables

News factors

Various factors exert influence over the dissemination of an event by the media. Galtung and Ruge (1965) drew up a catalogue of news factors as selection guidelines that have since repeatedly been empirically investigated. In the first place it is important that the news communicates something new. It must, therefore, be topical. Besides, it must deal with an event of value. As a result, newsworthiness could be spoken of and implies, therefore, that the event must be of interest from the point of view of the recipient. It is indeed clear to see that the interests of the recipients are of an extremely differing nature; nevertheless, some similarities can be identified:

- The consequence, which the event has for the recipient of the information, that is to say one's own concernment, counts as well as the extent of the event, that means the scope of those primarily affected, as news value. Both can be summarised to describe the significance of the event. Due to this significance, it is possible to differentiate between hard and soft news. Whilst hard news places the aspect of the information at the fore, soft news fulfils the recipient's entertainment needs.

- The proximity of the event to the recipient is also an important criterion when assessing the value of news. Proximity stands, on the one hand, for the location of the event, on the other, for the importance of the information for the recipient. This applies both for hard and soft news. Skriver (1990) examined the significance of geographical proximity: he found that, for a report of not less than 10 cm in local newspapers, 39 dead are required for an event which took place 10 000 km away, 7 for an event 1000 km away and only 1 death is required for an event which took place 100 km away.

- Another characteristic is cultural proximity. According to an investigation by Adams (1986), U.S. news coverage of non-American natural disasters fluctuates depending on the cultural proximity of the dead to the American cultural circle. Accordingly, the extent of news coverage for a dead West European corresponded with that of three East Europeans or nine Latin Americans compared with that of eleven inhabitants of the Middle East or twelve Asians.

- Psychological proximity is another influential factor. This is understood as the event's relationship to the recipient's realm of experience. It is this factor, which has particularly significant consequences for tourism. Whilst, in the context of cultural proximity the number of dead is responsible for 3 per cent of news coverage, the tourism popularity of a country accounts for 33 per cent of this coverage. Moreover, this is intensified by tourists being the declared focus of attacks as Tscharnke (1995) proved on the basis of German Press Agency coverage.

- Even the human emotional aspect determines the value of news. Some examples of a number of factors which determine the value of an event are: drama, tension, romance, love and sex, humour and fun, adventure and risk, sympathy, tragedy, prominence, age, curiosity, struggle and conflict. For soft news in particular, it is the triggering of emotions, which determines interest in the news.

- Furthermore, the terms of reference, which are developing over a longer period of time, contribute to the selection of events (Mathes, Gärtner and Czaplicki, 1991). Journalists and other groups from the social environment see current events, which can be the object of news coverage, in the context of a cognitive scheme made up of previously collected knowledge and existing attitudes. This corresponds to the findings of behavioural science according to which Man's ability to understand relationships and the essential characteristics of a situation determine the selection of environmental signals.

The terms of reference, which influence the journalists' perception and assessment, develop, as a rule, over a long period of time. Many topics, classified as sudden and unexpected, can with the knowledge of those terms of reference, be put into perspective regarding their degree of surprise. Luhmann (1993) also confirms this, saying '...that risk assessment and the readiness for risk acceptance is not only a physiological but mainly a social problem. We behave as it is expected by the relevant reference groups or as we – whether in accordance with or against the general opinion – are socialised'.

If the various individual values and factors are aggregated, they form a total news value that determines the selection. Consumer interests are clearly at the fore in the definitive value assessment as they determine with their consumption, respectively, their purchase of the news, and the economic success of the news supplier. Nevertheless, other factors of news selection must also be considered such as the specific interests of the publishing houses, editors and journalists, the relevant statutes and press legislation and social, political and democratic interests. It is these last-named factors that often lead us to see the media apart from its infrastructure function, that is, the dissemination of news, as an independent factor that is forming the public opinion, and an organisation that is able to change attitudes and opinions.

2.2.4 The role of the mass media

The effect of information and assessments disseminated by the mass media on public opinion were examined in mass communications research. Within the various explanatory attempts, it is possible to distinguish the approaches of strengthening, conviction and agenda-setting (Kroeber-Riel, 1992).

Conviction assessment assumes that mass media is in a position to influence the recipient's attitudes and opinions contrary to his own views and in a direction desired by the media. Nowadays, this approach tends to be mostly rejected. Exceptionally, this effect tends to be attributed to themes that indirectly affect the recipient, in other words, which are of a more general social relevance and influence. However, this effect is only superficial or temporally limited (Dunwoody and Peters, 1993).

According to the strengthening hypothesis, the mass media confirms and strengthens existing attitudes and opinions by means of conveyed information. Because the recipient extensively avoids contradictions, he or she not only selectively takes on the numerous pieces of existing information but also assesses them just as selectively. Thus, news presented through the media has an effect on attitudes especially if information is sought for opinion-forming or opinions are formed for the first time.

A continuation of the strengthening effect approach is the agenda-setting approach, which is dominant in media research. Accordingly, by making certain events a subject of discussion, the media decides whether there is a place for them in public discussion. This is awarded a selection function, which applies, above all, if it concerns topics outside of the recipient's personal sphere of experience. Once this selection takes place, the media structures the themes that are subjects of the discussion by assigning them preferences.

Consequently, the mass media generates awareness and has a certain influence on the selection of topics for public debate. How far they bring about concrete changes in attitudes and opinions depends on a number of factors. What is important is that they trigger a process of information search, especially when dealing with topics of personal relevance. Therefore, the recipient uses a number of information sources and, as explained by the multi-stage communication process, uses both the means of personal and media communication.

The deviation from daily routine is responsible for negative events having an increased communication probability and a quicker dissemination process. Therefore, the significance of a negative event should be rated higher than that of a normal event. The globalization of communication services is ultimately responsible for events that once selected, have a quasi-unlimited audience. In addition, globalization means that another phenomenon can be observed that is of significance for tourism. An increased possibility to communicate a negative event worldwide causes the probability of incidents to increase where publicity is sought. This applies for terrorist attacks, which stand a good chance of being staged spectacularly if they are aimed at tourists.

On the other hand, localization of news reporting contributes to the detection of events to which no attention was previously paid to. Above all, when there is a news vacuum, these can spread in a kind of snowball effect until larger media picks them up. It should, therefore, be assumed that, once negative events occur, they are difficult to hide, which makes it necessary for every responsible entrepreneur to understand their functions and how to deal with them.

2.3 What is crisis management?

2.3.1 The term

The term management usually describes the leadership of an organizational unit. It is possible to differentiate between an institutional and a functional way of thinking. With regard to the former, management is a description of those groups of people who carry out management tasks, their activities and functions. As far as functional thinking is concerned, management is a term for all tasks and processes connected with the running of a working organization. In particular, these are planning, organization, implementation and control. The functional perspective of management can be extended to include a person-or material-related consideration.

Management

The first use of the term crisis management is normally attributed to the political sphere. Accordingly, it is said that U.S. President J.F. Kennedy used the expression during the Cuban Crisis of 1962 to describe the handling of a serious, extraordinary situation. The term crisis management must be disassociated from risk management. The latter is focussing also on those events, which for the organization or destination are not causing serious or lasting damage. However, after risk management was originally limited to risks which were insurable, a steady tendency can be observed which intends to cover with risk management all different kinds of risks. However, this extension of the conceptional framework is not recommendable. It leads to an equalization of risk management and management as risks are immanent and by definition part of the decision and management processes. But also the limitation to only insurable risks is no longer timely, as in this area financial innovation, as weather derivatives water the definitional borders permanently.

Crisis management

Often the reason why the activities started but also the areas for which they apply determine which activities can be classified as being part of risk or already of crisis management. These transitional areas cannot be avoided. But they are also of no major importance. Nevertheless, it must be noted that from a practical point of view, the occupation with risks – i.e. also the fact that they are insurable – in destinations is often only then undertaken systematically, when preparations of crisis management are undertaken. The same can be found in tourism companies, although here the occupation with crisis management is found often in its early stage of application. After the activities were carried out here at the beginning only as a secondary function, they are now taken on more often exclusively and are directly linked with the highest management level. Decisive is finally that only crisis management is concentrating in its broad span on negative events which have the potential to cause crises. For doing so, it is also using the opportunities of risk management in the area of crisis prevention.

As in management, there is also a differentiation between crisis management as a function and as an institution. Crisis management as an institution refers to groups of persons who are responsible for crisis management activities. They are the dominant bearer of the functional crisis management. Middle- and lower-level employees and external forces join with members of upper management levels as actors in a crisis.

Crisis management as a function refers to changes of tasks and processes when a crisis occurs. Different types of crisis management and corresponding activities are distinguished with regard to the process character of the crisis and the differentiation between its various phases.

> **Definition: Crisis management**
> Crisis management is understood as the strategies, processes and measures which are planned and put into force to prevent and cope with crisis.

In literature, the division of an active from a reactive form of crisis management predominates (Höhn, 1974; Krystek, 1979; Oelsnitz, 1993; Glaesser and Pechlaner, 2004). For the following analysis this division should be kept. In addition, four crisis activities can be distinguished. Assuming an ideal type of development, Diagram 10 portrays the activities over time.

Diagram 10: Phases of crisis management

Risk management		Crisis prevention				Crisis coping	
Risk management		Crisis precautions			Crisis avoidance	Limitation of consequences	Recovery
Analysis	Evaluation/ Planning	Protection/ Implementation	Training	Early warning	Adjustment	Employment of instruments	

Crisis prevention

Crisis prevention stands for the proactive anticipation of negative events, both mentally and in terms of preparation. In contrast to crisis coping, crisis prevention is characterized by continual occupation with the subject. It is comprised of the two areas, crisis precautions and crisis avoidance, in which both parts should not be necessarily viewed as temporally succeeding. They are rather independent parts, which, in practice and from a time perspective, can find themselves used one after the other or at the same time.

Crisis precautions

Crisis avoidance

Crisis precautions describe planned precautionary activities and measures for more effective crisis coping, which are carried out with the aim of lowering the extent of damage. This area is consequentially of a strategic nature and includes risk policy, but also prepares operative crisis plans. The object of crisis avoidance is to take measures that hinder the development of crisis out of identified crisis potentials. This is primarily the task of early warning, which deals with scanning and evaluation. The aim of early warning is to detect events in time and estimate their seriousness in order to quickly undertake countermeasures. The fundamental assumption, by which the sensibleness of avoidance crisis management is justified, is the possibility to advance the use of instruments. This is confirmed by observations of crises where, with the ex post contemplation, a cause or causes can be identified as the crisis trigger.

At least theoretically, an ideal point in time for early warning can be determined. On the one hand, it is known that the destructive effect of a negative event increases with time and on the other, the number of possible countermeasures decreases until the affected organization is no longer in control of the situation. At the same time, the cost of early warning cannot be viewed as a fixed cost but as an additional expenditure that is mainly connected to the realization in good time. This expenditure decreases over the course of time because the assessment of developments becomes simpler and, therefore, cheaper. By the time a crisis is detected using conventional instruments, the cost is zero. It becomes clear, therefore, that it is not the realization 'at the earliest stage' but 'early enough' in the sense of giving sufficient time for reactions that must be the objective of early warning systems to avoid crises. This 'early enough' varies depending on the endangered area and the possible negative event.

Apart from early warning, crisis avoidance deals with the adjustment of the organization to the situation in that it increases the reaction speed. Because this adjustment can be triggered by a negative event, the lines between preventive and coping activities become blurred.

Crisis coping has a defeating character. It is suddenly initiated and portrays an active and intended exertion of influence over the situation that can be carried out by the affected organization or others. It starts with the identification of a crisis situation.

Crisis coping

While dealing with the causes of crisis and while stopping them, all management instruments need to be employed to limit the consequences and to bring the crisis situation to an end. During the following phase of the recovery, all activities aim at overcoming the momentary negative consequences of the crisis. That includes the part of the 'lessons learned' through which the organization aims at avoiding future crises by learning from the present situation.

Limit the consequences

Recovery

Considering the process of crisis management as a whole, a fluid transition from prevention to actually coping with the crisis is revealed. Previously seen limitations of crisis management to coping activities in the sense of a coping crisis management do not make much sense. Rather the particular challenges are lying in the preventive area of crisis management. This corresponds to the way the praxis is dealing with negative events, where all management areas within a company become involved. Therefore, the activities of both prevention and coping should be subsumed to crisis management just as crisis management should be understood as an extensive management problem. This form of crisis management is dependent on the crisis phases, both part of regular corporate planning and also independent from it. The former is the case if it concerns preventive crisis management. The latter is the case if it concerns coping crisis management that is not only independent from regular corporate planning but can also change or replace its results.

2.3.2 The challenges for crisis management in the tourism industry

As a general discussion about crisis and crisis management were brought to the fore in the preceding remarks, a general concept for crisis management in tourism should be developed in the following. For this purpose, the tourism system is presented, the classification and description of units participating in tourism is looked into and the types and effects of negative events in tourism are investigated.

2.3.2.1 The tourism system

Tourism is a phenomenon of the modern era and describes, in general terms, everything connected with travel. Generally, there are three constitutive characteristics: change of location, temporary stay and the existence of a motive. According to the definition of the World Tourism Organization and the United Nations, tourism should be understood as 'the activities of persons travelling to and staying in places outside of their usual environment for not more than one consecutive year for leisure, business or other purposes'.

Diagram 11: The tourism system

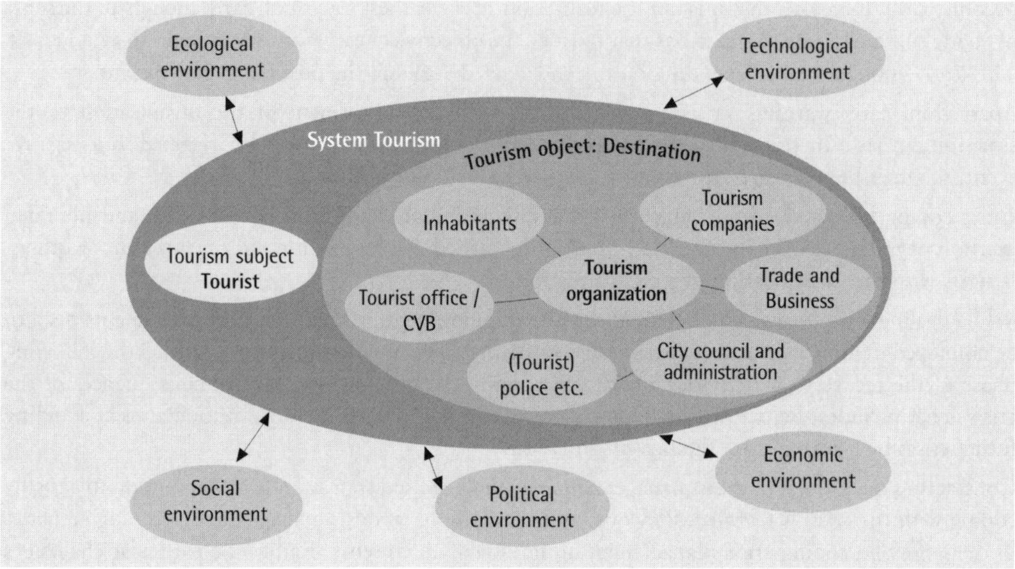

System-theoretic

Reverting to system-theoretic knowledge offers the most extensive portrayal of tourism possible, which is characterized, in particular, by interpersonal contact and numerous relations with the environment. Thus, the company is defined as a productive social system that maintains relations with its environment as an open structure. The different sections of the system are so much linked with one another 'that no section is independent of the other sections and the behaviour of the whole is influenced by the combined effect of all sections' (Ulrich and Probst, 1995). All elements outside of the company's system belong to the environment, which can be subdivided into dimensions and institutions. Taking a dimensional view on the environment, it is possible to differentiate between ecological, technological, economic and social spheres. If need be, this can also be extended to the political-legal sphere.

Taking an institutional view on the environment, it is possible to separate institutions or groups from individuals, such as the state, customers, competitors, capital investors, suppliers and employees. As a subsystem of tourism, the tourism subject – the tourist – can be distinguished from the institutional subsystems 'destination', 'tourism company' and 'tourism organization' (see Diagram 11).

2.3.2.2 The tourism product

The tourism product is varied and complex and is often constructed with the cooperation of a number of people and organizations. In tourism, even if those units that participate in service construction produce their own tourism products, according to predominant opinion, only the marketable service bundle is understood as being the actual tourism product because the respective service parts are bare-ly saleable on their own (Kaspar, 1991; Doswell, 1998; Bieger, 2002).

Because, as with other service products, the tourism product is predominantly immaterial, this makes the service that is to be provided difficult to assess. This uncertainty increases due to the distance bet-ween the location of purchase and where the service is provided. Expressed in information-economic terms, the tourism product is a belief or trust product that demands that the supplier is able to reduce uncertainty and risk, above all, in relations with potential customers.

The tourism product on offer is often divided into an original and derived offer (Kaspar, 1991, Müller, Kramer and Krippendorf, 1991; Freyer, 1995). Whilst natural factors, general infrastructure and social- cultural relationships, which characteristically have no direct relation to tourism, count towards the original offer, the derived offer incorporates factors that were knowingly created for the satisfaction of tourists' needs, for example, the tourism infra- and superstructure.

Recently, it was urged that the tourism product and the consumer goods product are treated the same way as well as the product components, 'original' and 'derived offer', were extended by the 'software' part of the offer (WTO, 1994a; Bieger, 2002). Where original and derived offer refer to the hardware characteristics of the product, software describes the so-called soft characteristics such as experience.

> **Assessing Quality**
>
> Because quality can be checked, three kinds of goods can be distinguished:
>
> - Search goods: product quality can be easily checked before purchase;
>
> - Experience goods: checking is only possible on demand;
>
> - Trust goods: impossible to acquire information due to prohibitive or high costs.
>
> Source: Haedrich (1998a), Kaas (1990)

From the demand perspective, the product can be characterized, generally, as a number of features that are combined and allow one or more of a prospective client's needs to be satisfied. By satisfying these needs, the product provides the consumer with a benefit. Building on the benefit gauge developed by Vershofen, which differentiates between basic benefits, that is, the material-technical side of a product, and additional benefits, that is, the emotional-spiritual side, Kotler (1984) developed three levels of the term 'product'. He describes the first level as the core product that is the actual core service of the product, therefore, that 'which the customer actually purchases'. The second level is the actual product that is identified by a unit understood by the customer as an object and that includes five characteristic features: quality standard, features, styling, brand name and packaging. Other services and advantages that accompany the product form a third level and describe the augmented product.

Basic benefits

This system was transferred to services – service describes, amongst other things, a combination of factors such as living things, material goods and nominal goods – by Bruhn and Meffert (1995) and the material and immaterial components of the product were also divided into three levels. In its first level, the model describes the core product as a fundamental service or mandatory component called for by customers. In the next level, the quality product incorporates those elements that stand for services expected by the customer as fundamentally desired components. Both services together refer to the so-called basic benefit, which can, therefore, also contain immaterial components and can be further understood in terms used by Vershofen. Separated from this is the additional benefit that forms the final level and describes discretionary services. Whereas those services provided as basic benefits

Additional benefits

correspond to customer expectations, activities that create additional benefits are useful in product differentiation and, eventually, for the creation of competitive advantage.

Diagram 12: Basic and additional benefits of a flight service

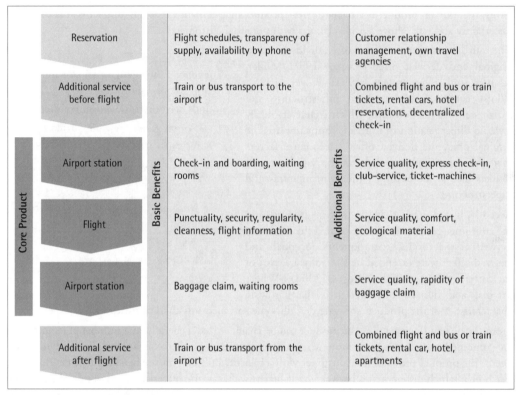

If this system is applied to basic tourism services, the core product describes, for example, overnight stay and catering services with regard to accommodation companies (the constitutive element is only the accommodation service itself that incorporates the granting of accommodation) or transport services as far as transport companies are concerned. Destinations can incorporate many types of core services of which swimming and golf are examples for activity-oriented holidays and cultural buildings or history are examples of core services for regional holidays.

In general, the majority of products on offer are so well developed that objective differences in quality are scarcely perceived by the customer. This dematerialization of consumption can also be observed in tourism. Even here a change towards a buyer's market took place and the fulfilment of the 'fundamental physical need to travel' is already seen as a foregone conclusion (Kroeber-Riel, 1986; Haedrich, 1993; Opaschowski, 1995; Kreilkamp, 1998). The objective functional quality of a product is a necessary, but by no means sufficient, prerequisite for market success. On the contrary, a product's competitiveness is determined by its ability to impart consumption or holiday experience.

The experience value becomes, therefore, the focus of considerations. Defined by Weinberg and Konert (1985) as '...subjectively experienced through the product, the service, ...the contribution made to the consumer's quality of life ...', it conveys experiences that are embodied in the world of feeling and experience. Schulze (1996) uses the differentiation between interior-and exterior-oriented consumption to make the function of experience in today's society clear. 'If glasses are bought in order to see better, a car for transportation, flour as food, etc., this is exterior-oriented behaviour.' Consequently, the quality of the product is not seen to be dependent on consumers because it concerns the product's objective features. This is different, however, for interior orientation. 'The interior-oriented consumer looks for glasses for which he already feels something, a car that fascinates him, a type of flour with which he can experience something: experience flour.' Finally, he concludes that, nowadays, holiday travel is 'called for exclusively due to interior-oriented motivation'.

Schrattenecker (1984) also addresses the issue of the strong influence that emotional criteria have on the selection process. Regarding the choice of destination, for example, she said: 'It should be assumed that the formation of a preference or a choice between target countries does not take place on an exclusively *rational* basis, but, in fact, an *emotional analysis* of the countries, which is predominantly based on the complexity of the assessable object, also takes place: there is, therefore, both rational and emotional content. For example, emotional criteria such as 'international flair' and rational criteria such as 'the existence of the opportunity to undertake water sports such as sailing, surfing and water skiing' could be a decisive factor when choosing a target country. These criteria are not mutually exclusive but complement one another: both the one – emotional – and the other – objective offer – are looked for.'

This is expressed in more concrete terms by Fesenmeier and MacKay (1996) who refer to the considerable significance of this experience value in the initial phase of travel decision: 'As such, destination decisions may be based on the symbolic elements of the destination (as conveyed in visual imagery) rather than the actual features.'

This quote makes it clear that the creation of competitive advantage within the sphere of core benefits is scarcely possible for the tourism product if the products are no longer unique and, as a result, their objective functional features are no longer discernible. If the two basic types of competitive advantage are used as a basis, the missing opportunity for material differentiation means that the choice remains between a cost leadership or immaterial differentiation strategy, which is also known as an experience value strategy. Bieger (2002) also confirms this: he regards only the possibility of software differentiation, under which he understands culture, systems, experiences, ambience and lifestyle, as useful for a destination with interchangeable resource getup, under which he subsumes capital, infrastructure and nature. Seen in the medium to long term, the emotional consumer experience provides a larger contribution to consumer quality of life in many markets, including the tourism market, than the basic actual and functional features of the product that are regarded as trivial. Therefore, it is the task of strategic and operative marketing to generate, impart and maintain these additional benefits that decide the purchase decision. These new aspects are, at the same time, the particular challenge of the strategic crisis management.

Experience value

27

Questions for review and discussion

- What are the differences between crises and catastrophes?
- Explain how the tourism product has changed and what impact this has for crisis management.
- Name the basic forms of negative events.
- How is the mass media affecting consumers?
- Explain the aim of early warning in relation to the terms 'at the earliest stage' and 'early enough'.

Suggestions for further reading

Adams, W. (1986), 'Whose lives count?: TV coverage of natural disasters', *Journal of Communication*, 36(2), pp. 113-122.

Kaspar, C. (1989), 'Systems approach in tourism: the Saint Gall Management Model', in *Tourism Marketing and Management Handbook* (S.F. Witt and L. Moutinho (eds.)), Prentice-Hall International, Hemel Hempstead, pp. 443-446.

Luhmann, N. (2005), *Risk: A Sociological Theory*, Aldine Transaction, New Brunswick, N.J.

McQuail, D. (2005), *McQuail's Mass Communication Theory*, 5th edn., Sage Publications, London.

Starn, R. (1971), 'Historians and Crisis', *Past and Present*, 52, pp. 3-22.

3   Crises' spheres of activity

How do negative events function, once they have been experienced or communicated? This is the core question that the assessment of preventive and coping management techniques is faced with. Initially, the question of primary interest is which areas of consideration should be meaningfully distinguished in order to carry out a precise effect analysis with particular reference to the affected organization. The following two investigations should be described as examples that deal with negative events in tourism.

Hultkrantz and Olsson (1995) examined the effect of the nuclear fall-out at Chernobyl on Swedish tourism. A result of their analysis was the determination that this negative event had various effects on tourism. Whilst inbound tourism was noticeably affected by the event, no changes to domestic tourism could be observed.

The WTO (1991a) examined the consequences of the Gulf War on tourism. In addition, it undertook a sectional and regional separation of the observed areas. As a result of its analysis, various significant developments were defined within regional considerations. These varied, not only in their intensity, but also in their direction. They incorporated not only downward trends but also stagnation and increases in international arrivals and journeys. Furthermore, sectional considerations observed that various market segments also reacted very differently to the same event. Whilst airlines, in general, suffered from the effects of the war, differences could be noted with long-haul jour-

Diagram 13: The various spheres of activity

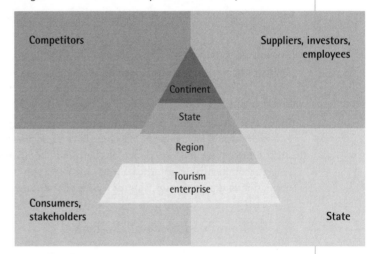

neys, which, in comparison, underwent a more intense reaction. This was the same for certain types of travel and hotel categories, which displayed more sensitive behaviour, and smaller businesses, which were more affected than larger ones.

Both investigations confirm that a different effect on the same event is possible. The foundation for a successful form of crisis management lies in this observation. It not only opens the opportunity to concentrate on and plan coping measures, but also indicates that the negative after-effects of a negative event can be diminished by strategic preparations.

Using system theory as a basis, the following spheres of activity are distinguished: consumers, tourism entities, competitors, state and supplier, investors and employees.

3.1 The consumer as a sphere of activity

Objectives

- To understand important factors and variables of the purchase decision process in tourism
- Learn to identify and analyze the factors influencing risk perception and risk assessment
- Differentiate forms of terrorist and criminal acts of importance to tourism
- Identify the legal limitations for tourist behaviour
- To realize the differing value of crisis management in time

Key terms and concepts

- Stakeholders
- Types of consumer behaviour
- Risk and involvement
- Cultural circle membership
- Crime and terrorism
- Package holiday maker and individual holiday maker

The tourism product takes the presence of tourists for granted. The potential or participating consumer 'tourist' can, without doubt, be identified as the most important part of this consideration. It is the tourist's perception of and reaction to negative events that dominates the activities of crisis management.

In the past, according to the rule of thumb tourists forgot about a negative event after a year or two. Normality would have in principle come back to an affected destination or organization after this time span. Drawing on the experience of the recent negative events, this passive attitude is however no longer recommendable. On the contrary, an active approach based on a thorough understanding of the perception and purchase decision processes of consumers is more than necessary.

3.1.1 The influence of stakeholders

Traditional marketing concentrates on a company's current customers and target groups that are viewed as potential customers. In this case, the aim is the creation of sales markets for the products on offer. The disadvantage of such behaviour is that other social groups within the environment of an organization, which are not considered as customers or potential customers, are neglected.

Stakeholders prove to be a particularly important influential factor for the company in a complex and rapidly changing environment. They announce their interests to a company as concrete expectations and claims. They aim furthermore to influence corporate goals, their implementation and the corporate behaviour. Haedrich (1998a) proved that, in 1991, only 40.6 per cent of the companies interviewed were in a position to implement their planned competitive strategies unhindered by social demands. The onset of a negative event will increase this number even further.

Example 1: Boycotts in the Tourism Industry

The role of stakeholders has become very important for the tourism industry. Their activities, especially their callings for boycotts, are not only often widely echoed in the media, but they are also targeting a sector in which the word-of-mouth propaganda has a very strong influence on consumers and their purchase decision process. These are some examples of recent boycotts in tourism:

1. General call for boycott against travel to Zimbabwe because of general political accusations (political causes)

2. Call for boycott in Germany against travel to Italy following the publication of a statement by the Italian Secretary of State responsible for tourism which caricatures German tourists (political causes)

3. General call for boycott against travel to Indonesia because of an alleged deforestation policy (environmental causes)

4. Call for boycott against travel to Thailand because of an alleged failure of dealing with Child sex prostitution (social causes)

5. Call for boycott in the United States of America against France and Germany after their governments rejected the Iraq war (political causes)

Boycotts are normally acts of social pressure groups that aim at changing a situation or drawing awareness on specific issues. They seldom are official acts of governments nor endorsed by them. However, the number of boycotts and their impact on destinations and tourism enterprises has increased significantly in the recent past. The economic impact of boycotts against countries is, however, very difficult to assess, as the consequences might be only realized on a long-term perspective.

The significance of stakeholders within the context of negative events is subject to some peculiarities that depend on the distance from the product and the type of product. For example, massive breakdowns at a former chemical plant of Hoechst plc in Frankfurt am Main (Germany) in 1993 mainly led to reactions within the stakeholder sphere and less on the part of customers (Schönefeld, 1994). In spite of waves of protest amongst residents and company stakeholders, the company's trade results showed a higher profit at the end of the financial year than in previous years. On the one hand, this is explained by the nature of the company's products that can scarcely be perceived by sanctioning end users. Therefore, Hoechst plc, for example, is scarcely recognized as a manufacturer of artificial fertilizers and insecticides in the case of the end product. On the other hand, buyers of insecticides or artificial fertilizers are not overly interested in the manufacturer's social reputation as long as it does not affect their own product sales.

The events surrounding the attempt to sink Shell's Brent Spar oil loading platform in 1995 can be cited as a further example from the production branch of industry. For weeks on end, the company was the focus of public interest and suffered immensely from the pressure of end users who boycotted Shell products – in this way, sales loss averaged at 20 per cent, in individual cases at more than 50 per cent.

At the same time, however, the company had no problems at all with aviation fuel and lubricant oil sales.

This makes it clear that the significance of stakeholders is greater, the closer the end consumer feels to the product and the clearer the ascent of concessions in the interests of the end product. This applies, in particular, for tourism. On the one hand, product components, although generally paid little attention, can easily be detected for the individual. As a rule, a negative event that occurs here can be identified and sanctioned without too many difficulties. On the other hand, tourism services can scarcely be used otherwise and, furthermore, cannot be stored for later use. Consequentially, the social tourism environment is especially sensitive for destinations and businesses. Immediate effects at the onset of a negative event should also be assumed.

3.1.2 The purchase decision process

Purchase decisions are complex processes that are influenced by a number of variables. Basically, there is a variety of individual knowledge to explain purchase decisions. This is translated into total and partial models of purchase decision. Total models, which attempt to draw all determinants together, have not, until now, been in a position to unequivocally copy the purchase decision process. Therefore, the majority of considerations are based on partial models that consider only a few necessary influence variables.

This also applies for the tourism decision process. Moreover, because this spans over a long period of time, the use of total models is made more difficult. Despite the peculiarities of tourism services, which underlie particularly complex information behaviour, knowledge transfer of consumer goods marketing is seen as something positive.

According to the experiences of modern consumer research, consumer behaviour is influenced by psychological as well as social determinants. In accordance with the number of those participating in the decision, it is possible to differentiate consumer and family decisions for the non-organizational sphere. The latter are not analysed in the following in order to reduce the complexity of the considerations and because it can be supposed that negative events will principally function in the same way. If psychological processes are considered, it can be seen that emotions, motivations and attitudes, known collectively as activating processes, have an effect on consumer decisions. They describe processes that are linked to the internal excitement and tension of the consumer and form the driving force behind their actions.

Motives form a hypothetical working model made up of fundamental driving forces, emotions, impulses and cognitive processes structured to determine objectives. Motives, through which the 'why' question of a journey should be explained, are significant in explaining visitor behaviour (Schratten-ecker, 1984; Frömbling, 1993). Frömbling (1993) points to the suitability of differentiating the quality of motives into higher and lower motivations according to their type of driving force. Nowadays, this separation, which can be traced back to motivation research according to which lower needs are satisfied before higher ones, are used to explain experience-oriented consumption. From this point of view, motives play an important role within the context of negative events.

Values are, on the one hand, seen in close relationship to motives, and on the other, equated with attitudes. They stand for fundamental moral concepts independent of short-term influences, which, moreover, are characterized by the social environment. Previously, values were not used in tourism research. Segmenting exclusively on their basis did not prove to be successful because visitors could not

Purchase decisions

Determinants

be significantly differentiated from non-visitors. The high temporal stability of values leads to them being of little significance as far as negative events are concerned.

Attitudes are differentiated from motives by their additional object assessments, for which reason they are seen to be relatively stable and consistent regarding their reaction to stimuli in the environment. If a destination is used as the reference point, attitude describes the subjectively perceived suitability of a destination for satisfying a motivation. Specific and unspecific attitudes are distinguished. With the help of unspecific attitudes that convey the general attitude towards holiday travelling, such as travel forms, no great explanation effect can be proved for visitor behaviour in a region. It is only with the help of specific attitudes which refer to the marked forms of a region that visitor behaviour can be analysed.

Using the A–B hypothesis, attitude is of relevance in the prediction of consumer behaviour. Frömbling (1993) also comes to this conclusion regarding travel behaviour: she points to the significance of the attitude towards the natural offer. Situative and personal factors along with economic restrictions put this into perspective in that we speak less of purchase behaviour indicators than purchase probability indicators. That no general validity applies becomes clear by means of the converse B–A hypothesis whereupon attitude towards the object is a result of the use or purchase and, consequently, is a result of this behaviour.

The mechanisms of mental information processing form the second part of the psychological process in connection with the decision process. The reception, perception and learning of information count towards these activities described as cognitive processes. In addition, the consumer is influenced by social determinants: the family and reference groups, which have an effect on the consumer in the closer environment, and the membership of cultural circles, which determines the wider environment.

With the help of various amounts of cognitive and emotional participation in selection behaviour, five different types of consumer behaviour are distinguished by Kroeber-Riel (1992). They are simple models of purchase behaviour that make the fundamental mechanisms clear – processes with little cognitive control are described as behaviour and not as decisions in the narrower sense. In comparison to comprehensive structural models, they have the advantage of only containing those variables necessary to explain behaviour. Their general usefulness in tourism is confirmed by Mühlbacher and Botschen (1990) and Frömbling (1993).

Types of consumer behaviour

Characteristic of habitual behaviour is either the upholding of decisions, which lead to repetition, or the adoption of certain behavioural patterns. These quasi-automatic processes require little need for information, the consequence of which is quick information processing. In the tourism sphere, this behaviour can be found, for example, in loyalty to the destination.

Impulsive behaviour is driven by affective reactions: this almost automatic behaviour can be traced back to situative and personal factors. This behaviour can be neglected in the tourism decision process because it is barely significant.

Simplified and extensive decisions are distinguished by high cognitive participation and are described as the only real decisions. Both types of behaviour dominate travel decision. Extensive decision is characterized by extensive intellectual control, which triggers a need for information. The consumer uses this in an attempt to recognize his alternative scope and assess the various possibilities. A consequence of this is a lengthy decision duration. Typically, this behaviour is only useful in tourism if the tourist has no experience of the product at all. But even decisions with high risk, for example, of a financial kind as well as products that have already suffered from negative events lead to extensive decisions. This shows that comprehensive and detailed information, provided either in written form or by means of recommendations, should be made available to tourists when making extensive purchase decisions.

Example 2: Old Patterns Changed so Fast

For many years consumers did not care too much about the different service providers within the package tour they bought. The airplanes, which were actually used, were paid little attention to when it came to purchasing more economic tour packages.

This changed in 1996 when a charter airline flight from the Dominican Republic crashed a few minutes after its take-off leaving all passengers dead. The flight was supposed to have been carried out by an Alas Nacionales Boeing 767. However, as the originally earmarked plane was not ready to use, it was replaced with a Boeing 757 from the Turkish airline Birgenair.

The immediate reaction of many travellers who were planning to take holidays was to look carefully and extensively into the different components of their package tour. They especially evaluated the part concerning the charter airline on which they requested detailed information including the aircraft model finally used. Such a habit had been until then very unusual. Even the detailed information, which was available to the general public in the U.S. on accidents and incidents of the different airlines and their aircrafts had not been used in the past by most tourists. Following the accident, this information also started to be consulted intensively.

The Birgenair accident demonstrated clearly how a simplified decision process can turn into an extensive decision process.

A detailed database on aviation accidents can be found at http://www.ntsb.gov/ntsb/query.asp

---

As far as simplified decisions are concerned, the consumer has experience of the alternatives at his disposal. Cognitive, emotional and social restrictions ensure that the consumer concentrates on the alternatives already known to him, that is, the 'evoked set'. The evoked set incorporates the amount of products that the consumer neither negatively assesses nor relates a particular risk with them. They are principally classed as suitable for satisfying the need. The consequentially restricted efforts to obtain information are more related to brand than product: this is the same in tourism (Kleinert, 1993). In this context, expressive key information such as test results or product recommendations by opinion leaders, which incorporate a number of individual pieces of information, are of great significance. Negative events could lead to a change in the important assessment criteria of simplified purchase decision if schematized spheres were previously of little significance in times of crisis.

3.1.3 The involvement aspect

Falling back on the involvement construct offers an extensive analysis of the consequences of negative events on the decision process. The involvement describes the internal commitment a consumer devotes to an object or activity. It is possible to differentiate, according to cause, between personal, object-specific and situative involvement.

Personal involvement is the extent of a person's concern for a circumstance. It is based on personal motives, attitudes, experience and knowledge. Over the course of time, this circumstance becomes

34

relatively stable and independent of the situation. In tourism, this form of involvement can be observed frequently, especially in the case of younger consumers. It is normally related to the activity, like skiing or diving, that a tourist is practising. This means that information about negative events, even if the level of diffusion is generally low, will be received with high attention, in segments where they affect, for example, enthusiastically practised activities. As a result, a quick diffusion of news amongst similarly interested groups of people is to be reckoned with. At the same time, negative events are constantly noticed and remembered for a long time by those involved at a personal level. This is independent of the decision situation.

The concrete effect of an event is dependent on the extent to which important product characteristics are affected. Subjective user assessment on the part of the tourist is decisive here. A tourist involved at a personal level assesses the circumstances in view of his experiences and knowledge more objectively.

Example 3: A Different Assessment

Personal involvement plays a very important role in tourism market segments which are more specialized.

Following the tragic attack on tourists in Luxor in 1997, Egypt's tourism sector suffered enormous losses. However, those interested in diving in the Red Sea did not react as normal sun and beach tourists. Most tour operators specialized in diving reported that after only a short phase of some 3 months of cancellations and absence, divers returned to Egypt much faster and in higher proportions than the normal tourist. In fact, since then, the arrivals of divers to Egypt increased annually in the higher two-digit range.

The same was observed in the case of the worldwide recognized and famous marathon event in New York City, which took place less than two months after the September 11 terrorist attacks in 2001. Although travel at that particular moment was reduced to the absolute minimum, and that planes were especially avoided, highly involved participants, both national and international, did not stay away from the event regardless of their feelings about security.

The same happened after the attack in Bali (Indonesia) in October 2002. In this case surfers were the first tourists to return to the destination. T-shirts with the slogan 'Osama don't surf' were very popular among the surfers and gave expression to their assessment of the situation.

In the case of the ship accident of the tanker Jessica in early 2001, its 600 000 litres of diesel fuel and 300 000 litres of heating oil, threatened the natural reserve of the Galapagos Islands (Ecuador). Although the unique natural reserves and wildlife were affected by this accident and that worldwide news reported the incident, tourist arrivals at the end of 2001 remained unchanged at 70 000 people. Since most of the visitors in this case also had a high personal involvement because of their scientific and ecological interest, the effects of this accident were judged differently to most other cases.

Object-specific involvement stands for the interest shown towards a product or service by the consumer. Functional-technical and social risk count towards its influential factors in the same way as frequency of use and the product's emotional appeal. Depending on the perceived differences in travel products of a particular category, the tourist feels a different functional-technical risk. If these differences are great, a high functional-technical risk exists, which gives rise to high object-specific involvement because the tourist endeavours to weigh advantages and disadvantages up against one

Object-specific involvement

another in order to avoid negative consequences in the future (Jeck-Schlottmann, 1987). If a high degree of object-specific involvement exists, it can be assumed that a negative event will have a more disadvantageous effect due to the greater load and a strong discrimination effect in comparison to positive stimuli (Romeo, 1991).

Object-specific involvement varies depending on the frequency with which the consumer uses the product. This can be related to a destination as well as to an activity. In this context, it becomes clear that tourists, who already have experience with the destination or type of holiday at their disposal, perceive the same event differently to inexperienced tourists.

Tourism products also assume social risk because they are of symbolic value. On the one hand, this symbolic value can be located in the membership of a particular reference group. On the other hand, 'going on vacation' is a status symbol that implies a higher standard of living. This aspect is of great significance and is subject to the particular danger of its value being put into perspective by a negative event.

In addition, the travel product has an internally defined emotional value that brings feelings of pleasure to the tourist. Adapting this experience value to travel ensures that the tourist – assuming little cognitive control – wants to have the product in order to enjoy the product experience. Interference in this experience or its destruction would ensure that this product is paid fairly little attention.

Situative involvement

Situative involvement is understood as a temporal component. This means that the tourist, depending on the decision situation in which he finds himself, analyses information related to his travel decision differently. The nearer the time for decision, the higher the related activation through which he is encouraged to intellectually or emotionally assess the variables related with his decision.

Continuous involvement

Total involvement

Personal and object-specific involvement are more stable in the long term and independent of situative events, like negative events. Thus, both are described as continuous involvement. The degree of attention paid by the consumer to a certain amount of travel products due to object-specific or personal determinants is, therefore, stable. Situative involvement, however, proved to be the most influential factor on the total involvement, dominating the object-specific and personal involvement.

This is also of considerable significance from the point of view of negative events. Depending on the point in time at which a negative event occurs, the tourist boasts a varying degree of involvement. As a result, various consequences must be reckoned with. This must be considered when analysing effects, developing strategies, implementing instruments and also with regard to timing. Also the media and message involvement exert influence over tourists as it has already been indicated (see Section 2.2.4).

3.1.4 The risk perception and assessment

Risk-theoretic investigations within the framework of consumer behaviour concentrate on the risk of false purchase decision with regard to economic and social risk. By doing so, however, only some of the risks and their consequences are considered. In particular, the important area of the consequences of a negative event, which does not require a purchase decision, is not taken into consideration.

For this purpose, the obvious thing would be to consider and fall back on research knowledge within the area of risk technologies. In the past, technologies particularly fraught with risk, such as nuclear power, caused the necessity to analyse the mechanisms of risk, unfavourable developments and the risk perception in greater depth. The continuous aim of these investigations was to find a risk acceptance threshold and develop strategies and instruments, in order to increase the acceptance of these risks.

Initially, the studies were the basis of a rather abstract relationship field, in which it was possible to differentiate between service providers and normative institutions, which therefore, required a monopolistic offer structure. It was only later that investigations entered into the differentiated social environment of the organisation already described (see Section 3.1.1).

Example 4: Driving is Safe but Flying so Risky!

Many mistakes made while coping with crises are the result of a lack of understanding of risk perceptions. The crisis following the attacks of 11 September 2001, clearly demonstrated that this deficit still exists. The attempts by many airline officials and politicians to convince the general public to board airplanes by simply arguing that 'Flying is safe' failed and were even seen as untrustworthy.

Understanding risk perception is the first step towards an effective crisis management. Airline professionals, as in this case, tend to use objective ways to assess risks. They are using odds such as the ones on the following table, which show how the chances of dying from a car accident in 1998 in the United States were much higher (1 in 6 212) than dying from an airplane accident, which were much lower (1 in 390 532). In the framework of this information therefore, officials were right in arguing: 'Flying is safe'.

Odds in the United States

Type of accident	Deaths, 1998	One-year odds
Motor vehicle	43 501	6 212
Air and space transport	692	390 532
Water transport	692	390 532
Railway	515	524 753
Fall on or from stairs or steps	1 389	194 563
Fall on same level from slipping, tripping or stumbling	740	365 200
Struck by falling object	723	373 787
During sport or recreation	685	394 523
Electric current	548	493 153

Source: Based on U.S. National Safety Council data for the year 1998 for the American population

Even the results which are achieved by looking at the number of passenger deaths per passenger mile of travel underline their argumentation as in 1999, the passenger death rate in the United States of America in automobiles was 0.83 per 100 million passenger-miles. In other words much higher than the rates for buses, trains and airlines which were 0.07, 0.10, and 0.003, respectively.

But why do these argumentation techniques fail? Consumers do not accept them, particularly for situations following a negative event. Consumers assess risks in ways which are best described by subjective risk perception. However, when an airplane accident occurs, they consider a flight far more dangerous than a ride with a car. An effective crisis management needs to have a thorough understanding of the mechanisms of these perceptions and must take them into account. Otherwise the efforts have to be multiplied to be, if so, successful.

In the majority of uses of the term risk, two fundamental points of view can be distinguished (an overview of the various risk concepts can be found in, e.g. Kupsch, 1973; Fasse, 1995; Jungermann, 1991). Using a risk expectation model, it was attempted to describe, free of any value, judgement courses of events based on rationality axioms. According to this approach, found mostly in insurance mathematics, risk is defined as 'expected damage'. It is a product of magnitude of damage and probability of occurrence.

The consideration of personal factors, which influence consumer risk perception, leads to a subjective risk assessment and to descriptive models being used as a basis. Particular attention is given to this knowledge that goes beyond the implied objective determinability of probabilities and consequences.

> **Definition: Risk**
>
> According to the objective risk assessment, risk is the product of magnitude of damage and probability of occurrence. The subjective risk assessment, which is of greater importance for the crisis management in tourism, also takes the personal factors of consumers into consideration.

For the further analysis of risk perception and risk assessment the following elements will be looked at: quantitative risk factors, qualitative characteristics of risk sources, individual consumer determinants as well as particular risk factors such as criminal or terrorist threat.

> **Example 5: Sharks and Coconuts**
>
>
>
> When it comes to sharks, at first most people remember the attacks of swimmers and surfers in Australia. Even for the Olympic Games in Sydney, the organizers were forced to take special measures to protect the swimmers, surfers and sailors from possible attacks from sharks and to communicate these actions to a sensitive worldwide audience.
>
> Coconuts and coconut palm trees on the other hand are perceived as the symbol for beach and sun holidays. Every child knows how coconuts taste, coconuts are available in every supermarket - people don't fear coconuts, while at home, nor while on holiday.
>
> However, the perceived risk is contrary to reality. Every year around 150 people die due to falling coconuts while the number of shark attacks in 2000 was exactly 79, which was slightly higher than the average from previous years. The number of those finally dying from shark attacks was in fact even lower. In 2000 it reached ten people and normally varies between 10-20 people per year. Of the 10 fatalities in 2000, only three were from Australia (from a total of seven attacks), two from Tanzania, and single fatalities from Fiji, Japan, New Caledonia, Papua New Guinea and the USA.
>
> Based on this information Club Direct, a UK based travel insurance provider, launched a special press campaign in 2002 warning tourists not to stay or camp under coconut trees. At the same time it was also pointed out that their travel insurance would cover not only the risk to be exposed to coconut falls, but also to shark attacks.

3.1.4.1 Quantitative risk factors

Both damage probability and magnitude of damage count as quantitative risk factors. Both components are subject to a distorted perception that is dependent on various influences. The use of mental heuristics on the part of the consumer is, above all, responsible for the distortion of damage probability, which is oriented towards the susceptibility and availability of the event. In part, the aforementioned supposition confirms that, within the sphere of preventive crisis management, concentration on the type of event enables a considerable contribution to the prompt identification of threatening situations.

All heuristics prevent the paralysis of the decision process and help to reduce search costs. Moreover, they are close to reality because they align themselves to experiences, but are also stable, which enables outside observers, with their knowledge, to hypothesize on possible behaviour. Among the important heuristics are the representativeness, availability and, anchoring and adjustment heuristics.

Representativeness heuristics describe the judgement of risk due to a perceived affiliation of an object or activity to a certain risk category or type. In doing so, a conclusion for the risk is drawn from well-known cases. The units or groups subject to this generalization know no boundaries (Holzmüller and Schuh, 1988). They can concern branches as well as destinations or holiday categories amongst others. In this generalization phenomenon, an important approach can be seen to explain why negative events have such different consequences.

According to availability heuristics, the probability of occurrence of an event increases depending on how easily it is remembered or can be imagined. 'If an airplane has recently crashed, then we concentrate on the event and disregard all successfully run flights when it comes to deciding whether or not to fly somewhere' (Perrow, 1992). This heuristic, which, in principle, leads to thoroughly appropriate and justifiable behaviour, is above all, subject to the particular influence of the media. On the one hand, this points to the possibility of being able, under consideration of the terms of reference, to promptly assess the event with regard to its possible development. On the other hand, this finding also implies danger. This comes from the fact that extreme and unlikely improbabilities are judged with an unequally high probability by just pointing to their risk. As an example Jungermann and Slovic (1993a) cite a doctor's obligation to explain even in extremely rare cases so that the patient's freedom of choice is ensured. This condition must, above all, be taken into account with regard to preventive risk communication, the fundamental sensibleness of which is confirmed in tourism.

According to anchoring and adjustment heuristics, orientation entities, the so-called perception anchors, are used to determine the probability of total system failure from the failure of a single entity. These heuristics become useful if related complex events are to be assessed.

Diagram 14: Memory

The influence of the temporal component is underlined through the following poll. The question: 'Do the terror attacks in the USA with their possible consequences have any impact on your travel behaviour for your next holidays?' was answered by the interviewed already within 3 months with a clear decreasing tendency.

	November 2001	January 2002
No, they don't have any influence	65%	69%
Yes	29%	14%
I still don't know	6%	17%

Source: FUR (2002)

Damage probability

Heuristics

Subjective assessment of damage

Above all, two areas influence the subjective assessment of damage: the potential for catastrophe and personal dismay. The potential for catastrophe of an event increases with the consequences that the event has. The likelihood of the event is of minor importance. The frequent death of smokers shocks, therefore, less than one airplane crash in which many die. It can be assumed that this assessment is deeply embodied in the consumer and can only be changed by a long-term change of values, if at all.

Personal dismay has, like the potential for catastrophe, already been looked at. They are both essential features for the mass media when selecting news. Geographic, cultural and psychological proximity determine how strongly the consumer feels the damage. This is to be expanded by a temporal component that expresses proximity to the actual decision and exerts considerable influence over dismay.

3.1.4.2 Qualitative characteristics of a risk source

The assessment of risk is, moreover, influenced by a number of qualitative characteristics. Among them is the fact that a voluntarily undertaken risk is classified and accepted as less tragic than imposed dangers. This aspect is important for two main reasons: on the one hand, the tourist must be given the opportunity to voluntarily take on risk. Daring and contrived publicity messages that conceal known risks not only have dissatisfaction as a consequence due to the deviation of the actual from the desired image, these also do not give the tourist the opportunity of deciding to take on that risk himself. Even if this opportunity is given, it does not necessarily mean that it is perceived. As a rule, consumers tend to avoid making risky decisions. Nowadays, this fundamental behavioural characteristic of avoiding risky decisions known as 'omission bias' is helped by a number of legal norms. Activities not carried out and through which damage could have been avoided are valued less than activities that finally lead to damage (Jungermann and Slovic, 1993a). Therefore, it must be made absolutely certain that the obligation to take a decision is enforced as frequently as possible for the tourist so as to keep the consequences of a negative event as low as possible.

Examples of negative events from the natural environment:	
Avalanches	Earthquakes
Bushfires	Forest fires
Floods	Landslides
Windstorms	Volcanic eruptions
Examples of human-induced negative events:	
Riots	Civil war
Kidnappings	Terrorism
Environmental pollution	Transportation accidents (aircraft, bus, railway etc.)

Responsibility

A further element close to the voluntary aspect is responsibility. Whereas the deciding criterion in taking risk on voluntarily is that it concerns the consumer's own decision, this is now about another area which we are exposed to, namely natural events. In order to make this point of view clear, Luhmann (1993) always speaks of risk, if decision is the basis, and of danger, if the responsibility is attributed to the environment, that is to say one is exposed to the event. Considerable importance

---

Natural vs. civilian risks

Whilst natural risks are classed as involuntary, uncontrollable, not attributable to society and, therefore, as more or less unavoidable – and obviously not as bad – civilian risks are seen as voluntary, controllable, attributable and avoidable – and, therefore, obviously worse.

Source: Jungermann and Slovic (1993a)

---

is attached to this division when assessing negative events. In general, human-induced negative events are perceived more threatening and tragic than events belonging to the natural environment.

In addition, it is also important to observe that there is a fundamental tendency to look for the culprits of a negative event. This fact, which can be traced back to psychological attribution research, illustrates a reason why people attempt to view more and more dangers as risks and to look for those responsible for them. If this is extended to the aspect that risky decisions are sought to be avoided, it is possible to understand why tourists, often only with hindsight, have a particular interest in, for example, the duty of the organizer to provide explanations, whereby they retroactively have the opportunity to avoid responsibility.

Events that can be controlled by the individual are also subject to a fundamentally more favourable assessment, which stands outside of that particular sphere of influence. An example of this is an airplane crash that, with the same damage probability, is seen to be more tragic than a car crash because the latter is subject to the control of the driver. It was after the September 11 attack that attempts were made to strengthen cockpit doors, to tighten the security control or to give, for example, the simple and practical advice to throw books and shoes at hijackers before trying to overpower them. Besides their objective value, travellers perceived these measures valuable, logical and sensed having an influence on the risk. In other words, these measures reduced the subjectively perceived risk.

Negative events, which are well-known and the frequent onset of which people are used to, are more likely to be accepted than new risks. Essentially, this can be traced back to the fact that no one has experience of an unknown risk, so the effect is hard to estimate and less easy to calculate. It is the consequence of this incalculability that everything possible is undertaken in order to place the event into an explanation pattern with the aim of understanding it.

A not inconsiderable potential for crisis is established for the affected organization here. It no longer only concerns the organization's plausible and serious efforts to explain the background of the concrete incident. Rather, the 'signal potential' of the event must be assessed, by which the potential danger that this event gives notice of is meant. Only by this way can we estimate how strong public interest will be.

If the explanation is not successful and, apart from the fact that it is the first time such an event has occurred, a bad assessment of the companies' behaviour is reached, this incident can easily become a negative example and will, in the future, be used as a comparison – well-known examples of this are the oil loading platform Brent Spar and the tanker Exxon Valdez.

3.1.4.3 Individual risk factors

Risk perception and assessment are influenced by a number of personal determinants. On the one hand, they vary depending on demographic variables such as age, sex and education. Therefore, a higher risk perception on the part of female tourists in comparison to men is ascertained just as a lower risk perception in young tourists aged 18-24 in comparison to older tourists is reported (the investigation that forms the basis of this referred to the United States and the United Kingdom; WTO, 1994b).

On the other hand, expert or lay status is also of considerable significance regarding risk assessment. Where experts rely on quantitative characteristics in order to assess risk, laymen prefer qualitative features. In addition, experts tend to overrate probable but momentous events. Laymen, on the other hand, tend to rate improbable but momentous events higher from a risk point of view.

(margin notes:) **Control of the event**

Frequent onset

Personal determinants

A further factor can be seen in cultural circle membership which contributes to people perceiving and assessing events in a different way. This can be traced back to various social, behavioural and development forms. This is confirmed by the events of the mid-1980s in Europe at which time the number of U.S. arrivals decreased considerably due to terrorist attacks whereas, at the same time, internal European arrivals increased (Ryan, 1993; Hurley, 1988). A similarly sensitive attitude towards negative events was reported for the Japanese as a consequence of news coverage about sex tourism in Hong Kong and the Philippines as well as for Europeans as a reaction to the nuclear fallout at Chernobyl (Gee and Gain, 1986). This particular risk aversion has even stronger consequences in comparison to other cultures since, after the consequential absence from the destination, a recuperation process only occurs very slowly. Also the custom to contract travel insurances which cover against the many risks of travelling is an indicator of culturally-based forms of different risk assessment. While on the one hand some 80 per cent of tourists from Scandinavian countries decide to contract such insurances, only 20 per cent of the tourists from Spain consider them necessary.

Example 6: Cultural Circle Membership

The brutal massacre of 58 foreign tourists and four Egyptians in Luxor by Islamic extremists in November 1997 destabilized Egypt by greatly damaging its tourism industry, the mainstay of Egypt's economy. Before the November massacre, with some 4.2 million visitors, the tourism industry was set to generate in 1997 nearly US$ 4 billion in revenue for Egypt, making tourism the country's most important source of foreign exchange.

The Luxor attack triggered an immediate cancellation reaction and a sustainable downturn of bookings to Egypt as a holiday destination in 1998. The overall development of international tourists' arrivals in Egypt dropped by 12.8 per cent. Tourist executives estimate the Luxor incident cost Egyptian tourism about 50 per cent of its annual revenues. 'By any account, it was a catastrophe. I myself lost something like 85 per cent of my business,' said Ilhamy el-Zayyat, head of Egypt's Chamber of Tourism and owner of a major travel agency.

While most of the important European source markets had similar forms of decline after the attacks, Switzerland and Japan have to be examined more closely. In both cases, the dismay of the respective national group played a part because 35 Swiss and 10 Japanese were victims in the attack. However, the unusually abrupt and long-term slump has to be traced back to culturally-caused risk adversity. This was repeatedly confirmed for the Japanese.

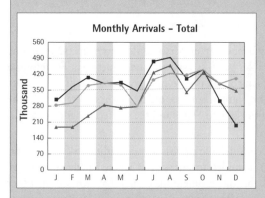

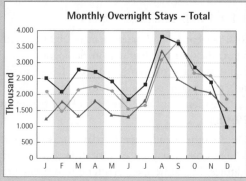

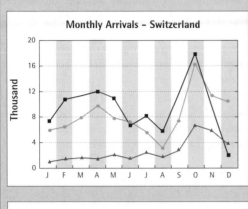

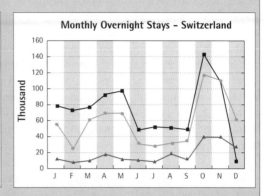

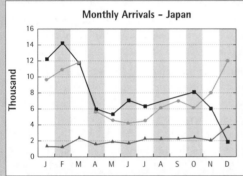

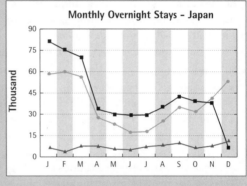

Source: Based on unpublished data from the WTO

●— 1996 ■— 1997 ▲— 1998

The observation of the development of the Russian source market is particularly interesting. Due to a cultural circle membership which makes them perceive these events less important and risky, tourist arrivals and overnight stays to Egypt have increased tenfold since 1991. As the following diagrams of monthly arrivals and nights from 1996 to 1998 show, this growth trend continued even after the Luxor attack.

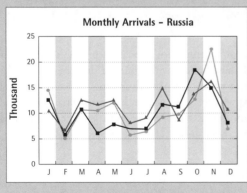

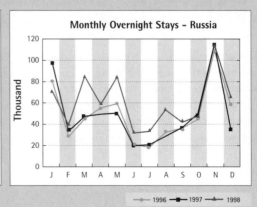

Source: Based on unpublished data from the WTO

●— 1996 ■— 1997 ▲— 1998

Dismay of a national group

In addition, the dismay of a national group is of great significance for tourism. Miami, for example, was long known for having an above average rate of violent crimes, but it was the murder of a German tourist in April 1993, which caused a sharp decline in the number of German visitors. It indicates that, for tourists, there is a differentiation between general threat and becoming victims themselves. The former is perceived and accepted in the sense of a backdrop but does not have any further consequences. A perceivable reaction only takes place if a person from the national group to which he belongs is threatened. It is not a question of threat aimed at citizens from a particular country but seen from the point of the cause, it is a rather coincidental fact. Whilst the former is explained by the fact that criminal or terrorist activities are carried out against tourists because of their nationality, here it concerns a general threat that is only seen to be more tragic because a representative of the tourist's own group is affected.

Example 7: It Happens Only to Others, Until... – The Thing with the Nationals

At the beginning of the 1990s Florida gained an inevitable reputation of being home for serious crimes committed against residents and tourists, who seemed to be lucrative targets for petty criminals. In 1992, in Dade County alone, over 12 000 crimes against visitors were reported. Despite this, tourism grew as foreign tourists did not feel affected or concerned by this violence.

However, things started to change when the first tourists from important foreign source markets became subjects of these attacks. In 1993, the number of attacks against tourists peaked as more than ten tourists from Canada, Great Britain, Germany and Venezuela were killed. These attacks, some of them quite brutal, received heavy national and international media coverage. Emotions ran high and the British Sunday Times even titled the Sunshine State as the 'State of Terror'. The European tourists' acceptance of crime changed rapidly from this moment on. Once they learned what had happened to their countrymen, they suddenly felt related and endangered to become the next possible victims of murderers and serious robberies. As a result, Florida's image as a sunshine and holiday destination became the place of occurring tourist nightmares. Tourist arrivals declined heavily. In particular, the number of German visits to Florida dropped by one-third from 608 000 in 1993 to 411 000 in 1994. This meant a severe economic loss for its tourism industry, which amounted in 1993 to US$ 28 billion and was the most important source of revenue for the state's economy.

Following these incidents, numerous federal and local initiatives aimed at improving the security for tourists were established. They not only reduced the crime rate to its lowest level in 25 years but also helped the number of tourism arrivals to grow once again.

The different individual risk factors discussed give an overview of the most probable and most important influence variables. In practice, several of these factors will influence the situation at the same time. For example, the peculiarity that conflicts in which U.S. Americans are involved is causing a general decline in international trips of U.S. tourists which always occurs due to national group and cultural circle membership factors. However, the circumstance that negative events cannot be classified due to a lack of geographical knowledge and, therefore, have greater effects also plays a role.

3.1.4.4 Particular risk factors – criminal or terrorist threat

The security aspect as a subsection of negative events occupies a special place. Security is generally defined as the fear of becoming a possible victim of violent crime, flight safety, terrorist acts, etc. (WTO, 1994b; Smith, 1998).

Criminal activities are indeed a continuous component of daily life but, in the context of tourism, they increase in significance. First, tourism activities – discovery of new areas and activities, taking risks – make tourists especially vulnerable targets. Second, tourists are especially during this recreation phase, confronted with situations they originally intended to escape from. In this sense, it is not so much the material loss that the tourist suffers which is important but rather the immaterial damages caused to him such as the demonstration of his vulnerability or the loss of positive impressions of his holidays.

Criminal activities

> **Security**
>
> The great significance of security during the travel decision process is confirmed by the Longwood's study which places the security of a destination in second or third place when selecting a destination.
>
> Source: Kemmer (1995)

In light of their relationship to tourism, criminal activities can be classified as shown in Diagram 15.

Diagram 15: Classification of criminal activities

Type 1	Tourists are incidental victims of criminal activity that is independent of the nature of the tourist destination
Type 2	A venue that is used by criminals because of the nature of the tourist location, but the victims are not specifically tourists
Type 3	A location that attracts criminal activity because tourists are easy victims
Type 4	Criminal activity becomes organized to meet certain types of tourist demand
Type 5	Organized criminal and terrorist groups commit specific violent actions against tourists and tourists facilities

Source: After information from Ryan (1993)

Provided that it concerns a general criminal act, the victims of which are tourists, no effect on general tourism development must be reckoned within the short term. This must, however, be put into perspective inasmuch as that it can cause a complete change of attitude in the long term. This leads, if not to a change of destination in the sense of another country, to a re-orientation when choosing a region and resort. In addition, these activities are only accepted to a certain extent: as soon as they bring serious injury or the death of a person in their wake, tourist behaviour suddenly changes. Despite a continuing attractive image, a destination is then classed as dangerous.

It follows that a systematic encounter with criminal acts cannot be avoided; it must be a permanent component of product policy for the destination manager. On the one hand, the remedying of causes by which it is clear that criminal activity can scarcely be completely prevented belongs to this class and on the other, the enlightenment of tourists. It is important for the tourist to know the dangers that exist in a destination in order to adjust their behaviour and, secondly, to set these in relation to the usual danger at the location. That way, the tourist is in a position to undertake his contribution towards preventing a dangerous situation.

Terrorism

Terrorism occupies a special position within the sphere of negative events. Seen from a general point of view, terrorist activity causes only a slight decline in tourist arrivals provided that tourists are not explicitly defined as the target. This situation changes suddenly, however, if tourists are expressly declared as the object of attack and systematic aggression leads to injury and death. Here, two different situations can be distinguished in which the tourist is understood either as a symbol of the sending state or as a part of the economic system of the destination. Whilst, in the first situation, the group of endangered people can be clearly defined, this is more difficult in the second case. Here, almost every tourist can be the target of an attack.

> **Definition: Terrorism**
>
> Terrorism is defined as criminal, violent acts or threats aimed at persons, institutions or objects to intimidate or demoralize a government or the population or, for achieving political or social aims.

In the first case, threat probability for tourists grows in direct relation to how politically exposed the country of origin is, that is, its activity and siding in international conflicts and crises. The aim of the attack is to communicate something to the sending state, which is disregarded under normal circumstances. This exterior-oriented activity has a greater effect, the more serious it is, the more exposed the place in which it takes place is with regard to tourism and the greater the related potential for catastrophe is. The latter explains attacks on airplanes that make use of the potential for catastrophe and, therefore, the deterrent effect. They also make use of the circumstance that approximately one-third of international tourists use the airplane as a mode of transport.

In the second case, tourists are used against the recipient state, region or destination, that is, interior oriented. The importance of tourism as an economic sphere and source of foreign currency for the recipient state contributes to this. Also, this sphere is made interesting by its extraordinary sensitivity.

The Basque terrorist organisation ETA, which has made tourism objects the target of its attacks since the 1980s, is referred to as the founder of such activities. It is not the tourist but the state of the target country, in this case Spain, which should be affected. In contrast to their usual tactics, advance warning of the tourist attacks were given and times were chosen when only few tourists would be present. This solution, which was the only one accepted by the supporters of the terrorist organisation, was also the reason why tourism was scarcely affected. ETA's behaviour has since frequently been copied, for example, by Sendero Luminoso which has, since 1989, defined the tourism sector in Peru as a target and the PKK, which has also attacked tourism targets in Turkey since 1991 (Smith, 1998).

As well as this purely interior-or exterior-oriented direction of terrorist activity, a mixture of the two can also occur. This is the case, for example, with the IRA's bombings that have persisted since the mid-1980s and have targeted both the economic system of the United Kingdom and British tourists in Northern Ireland.

Diagram 16: International tourist arrivals and arrivals by air

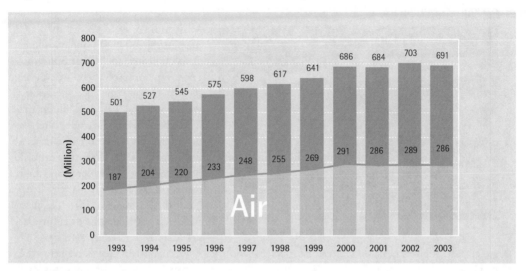

Source: Based on WTO data, 2005

3.1.4.5 Risk acceptance

Despite the influences described, it should not be overlooked that the tourist is prepared to accept a certain amount of risk. The effort to avoid risk actively applies to the exceeding of a particular tolerance threshold. Apart from the aforementioned influence factors, the level of this individual threshold value is determined by, the credibility of the affected organization, the speed of its actions and the repetition of the events.

Tolerance threshold

By dealing with issues of public concern, it has become known that the sensitivity threshold, therefore the willingness to accept a certain event, is reduced if the event is repeated. This is the same when products are recalled. Events otherwise perceived over the course of time as unrelated are felt, due to repeated call-backs, to be related and as such more attributable to the responsibility of the affected company. It should also be considered that events perceived at a stage of high involvement need much less repetition to be remembered than those with low involvement. Thus, it can be seen that the repetition of an event has a negative effect on the tourist's tolerance threshold.

Seen as a whole, negative events scarcely have an effect on consumer behaviour as long as they remain within the relevant individual tolerance threshold (Schrattenecker, 1984; Gu and Martin, 1992). The intention to visit or purchase a tourism product only starts to decrease once this threshold has been exceeded.

Example 8: Mountains – A Dream Without Limits

The Mont Blanc Massif, Picture: PGHM

Most tourists go to the Mont Blanc massif to spend their holidays hiking and climbing in the mountains. However, some of them will never return. Despite the fact that every year more than 70 hikers die in the Mont Blanc massif (Europe), there is no impact on those to come. It is a well-known fact that this massif produces a lot of incidents and that some hikers have lost their lives. Nevertheless, most of them see it as their greatest challenge to climb the legendary Mont Blanc, with its 4807 meters, the highest peak of Western Europe. Even if they return injured, they don't leave the mountain with bad memories, as it was and is the dream for which they are prepared to forget everything they are normally concerned about and for which they are prepared to accept the highest risk you can run: Your life!

The more than 900 rescue missions of the specialized mountain rescue service 'Peloton de Gendarmerie de Haute-Montagne' (PGHM) in the past years proved the risks but also showed, that they do not have an impact on the enormous attraction this massif continuous to play for many hikers.

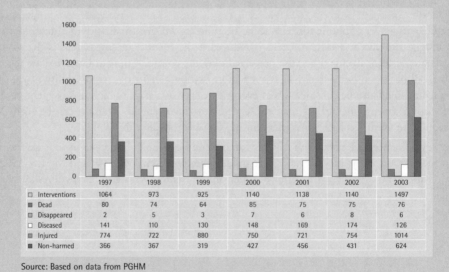

	1997	1998	1999	2000	2001	2002	2003
Interventions	1064	973	925	1140	1138	1140	1497
Dead	80	74	64	85	75	75	76
Disappeared	2	5	3	7	6	8	6
Diseased	141	110	130	148	169	174	126
Injured	774	722	880	750	721	754	1014
Non-harmed	366	367	319	427	456	431	624

Source: Based on data from PGHM

3.1.5 The legal aspect – behavioural restrictions

In order to assess the reaction of tourists to negative events, it is also necessary to consider the legal implications of these events on the tourist. The following evaluations will use the German legislation as an example because it is considered to be one of the strictest of its kind in the world. The respective legal sources will vary from legal system to legal system. However, they all form an additional framework that has to be considered when analysing the consumers' sphere.

With reference to legal consequences, considerable differences exist in German law between individual tourists and package holiday tourists.

3.1.5.1 Possibilities for the individual tourist

Individual tourists can terminate various types of contract directly with the service provider. According to German law, these are, for example, accommodation contracts (§§ 535 ff CC; CC stands for German Civil Code), hospitality contracts (§§ 651, 433 ff CC) or transportation contracts (§§ 631 ff CC). These types of contract are of considerable significance for domestic tourism.

However, the individual tourist has no particular opportunity to terminate a contract on the grounds of a negative event. In exceptional cases, the right for an extraordinary notice of cancellation may exist. The prerequisites shall not be discussed here. If the contracts are agreed abroad, it is possible that the individual tourist will have to validate his claims in front of a foreign court. This entails considerable expense and various judicial difficulties.

3.1.5.2 Possibilities for the package holiday tourist

The situation for package holiday tourists is different. They conclude a contract directly with the tour operator that includes various services (a detailed appreciation of contractual relations applicable to tourists is given by WTO, 1985). According to the German law for package holidays (§§ 651 a to l CC), German law and German jurisdiction apply for this legal relationship as long as the holiday was booked with a German tour operator.

Various legal opportunities are open to the package holiday tourist. They are explained in brief here:

- Before the start of the holiday, package holiday tourists have the right to withdraw without cause (§ 651 i CC). In this case, the tour operator can claim appropriate compensation (the cancellation fee for a package holiday with flight can be 4 per cent of the holiday price 30 days before the start of the holiday and up to 50 per cent, 6 days before). Based on their General Travel Conditions, tour operators also allow the tourist to change his or her booking given that the tourist has to cover the cost of that change. From the legal point of view, the originally concluded travel contract is still in force. This serves, in particular, the interests of the tour operator.
- If the holiday has already begun, warranty claims due to deficiencies (§ 651 c CC) and the right to withdraw due to considerable deficiencies (§ 651 e CC) or as a result of acts of God (§ 651 j CC) are valid. The deficiencies of the contractually agreed service package with the tour operator can be of a varied nature. Every year, this list is extended by judicial decisions. Generally, the tour operator has to guarantee, regardless of negligence and fault, the success of a holiday and they bear the risk of failure. The tour operator is not liable if the interference lies outside of his area

of influence; that is, it does not concern a risk that could have been managed by the tour operator.

3.1.5.3 The term 'act of God'

The term 'act of God' is not defined either in § 651 j CC or in any other similar regulation. An exemplary listing of relevant causes of interference, as was included in a previous governmental draft of a law about tour operator contracts, is also lacking (Bundestag, 1977). Within the framework of the right to withdraw, the term 'act of God', according to personal liability law, is understood as an '... event coming from the outside, showing no operational relation and not averted even by the most extraordinary diligence' (BGHZ 100, 185).

> **§ 651 j CC Termination due to acts of God**
>
> (1) If the journey is materially hampered, endangered or negatively affected due to acts of God which could not be foreseen, when the contract was signed, both the tour operator and the traveller shall be entitled to terminate the contract in accordance with this provision.

Acts of God do not belong to the area of risks of either the tourist or the tour operator. Just based on the occurrence of such an event, it cannot be concluded, however, that there was an act of God in the sense of § 651 j CC. Rather, it must always be examined whether, in the case assessed, the conceptual characteristics of an act of God are given.

> **Definition: Act of God**
>
> An act of God is defined as an event coming from the outside of the affected organization, showing no operational relation and not averted even by the most extraordinary diligence.

Interfere considerably

The event must interfere considerably with the holiday, questioning the contractual benefits of the trip as a whole but not necessarily the holiday's feasibility. According to legal practice, problems with the provision of holiday service (e.g. destruction or damage to accommodation), impairment by environmental pollution within the destination (beach pollution due to an oil spill) or personal threat (war, terrorist attacks, radioactive contamination) are examples that belong here. According to the decision of the Federal Supreme Court (Bundesgerichtshof) this kind of interference is assumed, if, for the concrete case such development can be assumed with considerable likelihood. In the concrete case of a hurricane this likelihood of occurrence was 25 per cent.

As a rule, courts draw upon the respective assessments of the Foreign Office (FO) when deciding what is an act of God. The FO gives, for example, a general travel warning for a particular region or declares a destination to be an area of crisis. In this case, the existence of an act of God can be assumed. Being aware of the economic significance of its assessment, the German Foreign Office, for example, emphasizes the information character and rejects all legal consequences.

Unforeseeable events

What is important in the classification of certain incidents as acts of God is that it concerns unforeseeable events. That means that at the time of booking they did not exist. For this reason, political unrest and general political crises in a destination – like, for example, Sri Lanka, China, Turkey and Egypt – were not viewed as acts of God. Decisive in the assessment of predictability is whether the tour operator could reasonably be informed about the conditions at the destination when the contract was concluded and whether there is a 'concrete probability' and not just a conceivable possibility. This has to be done by using all modern means of communication available to the tour operator. The tour operator's duty to enquire and to inform exists until the start of the holiday. If this obligation is not carried out, there is a deficiency that the tour operator is responsible for and entitles the customer to claim for indemnification.

From the point of view of crisis management, this duty to enquire and to inform may conceal an explosive situation: a tour operator

> **Indisputable examples of acts of God**
> - War or the threat of war due to civil war conditions;
> - If tourists are systematically attacked as a named target;
> - Impairment by environmental pollutions of a catastrophic nature which are serious and out of the ordinary (e.g. epidemics, natural disasters, radiation danger from Chernobyl).

undertaking particular efforts, using preventive measures, to remove the possible crisis character from negative events is constantly faced with the decision as to what information should be made available to the tourist. At the same time, warning cannot be given of every unlikely event. As has already been illustrated, as risk perception increases, the more improbable the event is. Nevertheless, the danger exists that important information is not relayed to the customer. Therefore, a compromise should be found, which must be accompanied by a good understanding of the various effects and their context.

The legal consequence of acts of God is the mutual and extraordinary right to withdraw from the contract. By this, the tour operator will be relieved of the consequences of extraordinary and incalculable events. After an effective withdrawal, the tour operator must refund the holiday price already paid after the cost of services provided has been deducted. In addition, the tour operator is obliged to return the tourist home although the tourist must cover half of any additional costs. In contrast, the individual tourist in the same type of crisis situation must undertake a return journey at his or her own risk and expense.

3.1.5.4 No 'act of God' with regard to general life risk

Disturbances that are assigned to the tourist's general life risk or impairment of the environment in the destination are not subsumed under the heading acts of God. Areas that concern normal, natural risk to the tourist and are not travel specific, e.g. muggings, thefts, etc. are not understood as general life risks. The legal practice also neglected isolated threats or acts of terror to be acts of God, which are not linked to extensive disturbances or are the cause of them. However, as soon as this risk becomes a specific risk for the tourist, the tour operator is obliged to inform the tourist (Führich, 1995a; Niehuus, 2001).

Also in the case of the impairment of the environment, the tourist must take on the risk for himself or herself. It is assumed that the tourist can gain a picture of the conditions by consulting generally accessible information sources. However, if the tour operator makes concrete promises concerning the environment, he or she has to accept liability. Moreover, all risks that have a negative effect on the particular purpose of the holiday must be observed by the tour operator and conveyed to the tourist. If this does not happen, the reason for liability comes, not from the risk itself, but from the fact that this information was not given to the tourist. It becomes clear that, when negative events occur, the package holiday tourist is entitled to considerable reaction opportunities even after the start of the trip.

3.1.6 The temporal aspect – phases of travel decision

The majority of travel decisions are not made at short notice but take place over a longer period of time. As a consequence, negative events may affect consumers at different phases of their travel decision. This influences the effect that the onset of the event has on the consumer and makes the introduction of a time component necessary.

Example 9: Rimini and the Algae Effect

Since the establishment of the first bathing resorts by the mid-1800s, the Romagna Coast in Italy profited from growth of tourist arrivals and tourism-related infrastructure. The tourism development was traditionally based solely on the resources of sea and beaches. Domestic tourists as much as foreigners, among these predominantly Germans, found it an ideal destination for relaxation and family holidays.

The effect of a temporal aspect can be illustrated by two increases in algae build-up which happened at different times of the year in Rimini (Italy) and were each followed by different consequences.

In June 1989, the excessive growth of algae in the Adriatic Sea and the appearance of large patches of mucilage caused a serious crisis for tourism. The first patches of the new algae were reported exactly on 28 June, shortly before the high point of the bathing season and the start of holidays in Germany, which has the biggest share of foreign tourists to the coast. The phenomenon continued throughout the month of July and it was not until 6 August that the algae started to disappear. The press covered the situation intensively and amplified the negative image of the destination. Hoteliers put immediately made every effort to avoid the loss of the season. Various actions such as mobile swimming pools on the beaches, floating barriers against the mucilage and price discounts tried to alleviate the crisis. In view of the situation, foreign tourists in particular preferred not to book their summer vacations in the Romagna Coast and cancelled their reservations in order to spend their summer vacation at other destinations that could guarantee them sea, beaches and sun without pollution. After all the crisis passed, a chain reaction followed: the negative image of the destination was not only tied to the pollution of the sea but also to the negative aspects that had been latently present before, such as chaos, crowds, noise, criminality, etc. Furthermore, the negative image was extended even to those areas that originally had not been affected at all by the incident.

As a result, the total number of tourist arrivals decreased by more than 25 per cent with respect to the previous year. In particular, the sector of intermediate and large-scale tourism with the highest quality standards and greatest attraction to foreign tourists suffered a loss of 50-60 per cent more than any other sector. In fact, the smaller and more familiar residences and boarding houses could rely on their loyal clients and repeat customers, because of their personal relationships and more domestic guests. Also, there were hardly any changes concerning the second-home system, while the number of rented accommodations went down by 40-50 per cent.

It is interesting to note that an earlier growth of algae in the Adriatic Sea had appeared a year before, exactly on 15 August 1988. But at that time tourism was not affected much as the late

---

season had already begun and most visitors had already completed their holidays at the seaside. The media had also paid little attention to it.

Source: Becheri (1991)

3.1.6.1 Orientation and decision phase

In the orientation phase, the tourist can be described as being absolutely free in his or her decision choice. Fundamentally, he or she knows neither personal, social nor legal restrictions of the concrete travel decision. Information about holiday activities and destinations is constantly absorbed, assessed, rejected and learnt (Datzer, 1983b; Kroeber-Riel, 1992; Frömbling, 1993). Expressed in general terms, impressions that are gathered in this phase form the tourism image of the product. (A destination's tourism image is a refinement of the general image of a destination. The latter is established over a long period of time and does not necessarily include tourism information; see also Section 3.2.2).

Orientation phase

Unlike other products, the consumer pays greater attention to the tourism product in this phase. Two influences, in particular, are responsible for this: on the one hand, travel is strongly influenced by the tourist's desire for adventure and curiosity, the consequence of which is frequent changes not only of destination but also of activities. On the other hand, travelling must be classed as a fundamental need, which encourages the tourist to constantly search for information. Besides this fundamental interest, the development of various involvement components becomes important. Situative involvement is the least developed in this phase. The actual determining influence on the current overall involvement level comes from the consumer's personal involvement. This means that events that affect objects of personal interest to the tourist will be disseminated quicker and paid more attention. In addition, it can be assumed that in this sub-phase, mass media coverage is of comparably little consequence. This applies, above all, if it concerns well-known events. Nevertheless, extraordinary events with a high potential for catastrophe and a crisis management that is carried out badly can contribute to these incidents being remembered in later travel decisions, especially if they are discussed for a long time.

Within the orientation phase, there comes after this time span, one point from which the normally passive position of the consumer to search for information becomes active. At this point, the decision process, which is actually difficult to define, begins and can last from one to several months. Situative involvement increases to its highest value and dominates total involvement from then on. Generally, prominent characteristics of this active and targeted search for information are that they are practised more by younger tourists than older ones, in the same way as first-time visitors ask for and lay claim to more information on the social environment than people returning to a destination (Sönmez and Graefe, 1998a). This can be explained by the high purchase risk that the tourist experiences in this situation (Kroeber-Riel, 1992). In this way, it becomes clear that young people and first-time travellers, who are extremely dependent on reference groups, are especially dependent on the public attention that is paid to a negative event. It can also be concluded that negative events, the consequence of which is unfavourable public attention, particularly influence these groups and the tourism products dependent on them in this phase.

Decision process

In addition, it generally applies that information searches are dependent on the educational level: a tourist with a higher school education takes stock of more neutral information sources and processes the information more cognitively. Regarding negative events, active information search can, however, be identified by the threshold value of personal risk acceptance. This is confirmed, on the one hand, by the generally high interest of tourists to be informed about the probability and extent of negative events (Sönmez and Graefe, 1998a). On the other hand, by the fact that this information is not always actively sought, 65 per cent of the interviewed people of the German 'Reiseanalyse', a well-known regular survey, claimed not to consider information about negative events or only in simple circumstances. The answers to the question on whether they had considered reports of unrest, natural disasters or crises when making travel decisions, are shown in Diagram 17.

Diagram 17: Consideration of crisis reports

Answers	Respondents in %
No, I don't take any notice	24.2
Yes, I think about them and consider them but don't put too much effort into it	41.0
Yes, I take such reports very seriously and consider them when travelling	28.8
No answer	5.9

Source: Based on Braun and Lohmann (1989)

Critical phase

Generally, this phase is particularly critical. Because a far greater amount of alternatives is available to the tourist, smaller well-known events ensure that the products become excluded from further considerations. The danger of this early exclusion from the evoked set lies in the fact that this takes place at a point in time when, as a rule, no travel agency has been visited yet (WTO, 1994b; for the importance of destination selection in the decision process, see Braun and Lohmann, 1989). Moreover, the consumer has not yet articulated a desire and potentially explanatory information cannot yet be given in a targeted manner. Experience has shown that this critical period of time for planning summer holidays lies somewhere between the beginning of December of the previous year and the end of March and, for winter holidays, sometime in September/October. However, this is moving more and more to the point of travel due to a tendency towards travel decisions at short notice. Besides the need to take particular precautions for these sensitive times, it remains to emphasise that, from the customer's point of view, the value of crisis management fluctuates over the course of the year. It is important to recognise this temporarily changing value of crisis management and take it into account when reacting.

3.1.6.2 Post-decision phase

This period of time begins once the travel decision has been made. This phase can also be subdivided into a period of time which begins when the inner decision is made and a time span which begins with the contractually agreed travel decision. It cannot be determined exactly when this inner decision has been made unless it is documented. Fundamentally, however, its existence is confirmed. After it has been made, the sought after and perceived information is basically used to confirm the choice that has already been made. This behaviour, as explained by the dissonance theory, is confirmed for decisions based on great efforts, as it is the case for the travel decision, which is normally an extensive or limited decision. A consequence of this is the unequally favourable evaluation of the choice made in comparison to the rejected alternatives (Raffée, Sauter and Silberer, 1973).

Braun and Lohmann (1989) also point to this circumstance of edging out alternatives. They found that 86.6 per cent of the tourists questioned within the survey, claimed after the realisation of their holiday that no other destination had come into question as an alternative. This high value irritates and was even classed by the authors as 'very improbable' because, under such circumstances, it could not have anything to do with a decision any longer. They reported similar doubts with regard to the results of the survey because only 3.7 per cent of the tourists questioned claimed that they had changed their travel plans once decided. On the other hand, these numbers illustrate that, after a travel decision is inwardly made, a higher acceptance threshold for negative events exists. It is also of interest in the circumstances at hand that this threshold value is influenced by the cognitive overlap of alternative products (Mazanec, 1989). If selection possibilities lie closer to one another, reorientation is easier for the tourist and his decision process is hardly lengthened at all. This insight, which will be dealt with further under the destination sphere of activity, already suggests the disadvantage of a similar perception of products which makes reorientation considerably easier for the consumer.

The signing of his contract means that the tourist's actions are – as already illustrated in the legal discussions – restricted in various ways. If it is not related to the right of the package holiday tourist to withdraw due to considerable deficiencies or as a result of acts of God, then the tourist is subject to the peculiarities of the right to terminate a contract. The latter, however, incorporates cancellation costs. At the same time, however, the company is also very interested in satisfied customers who they also wish to serve in the future. The probability of a long-term customer relationship and the extent of economic loss determine the company's reactions.

3.1.6.3 The holiday phase

In this phase, the tourist has already started his holiday. Confronted with a negative event at this point, the tourist is a direct participant and will react depending on the personal threat to him or herself. In this phase, the individual tourist can make no further claims provided that they are not in direct connection with the service provider or are covered by specific risk insurance. The package holiday tourist, on the other hand, can refer to the circumstance that the tour operator must, regardless of negligence or fault, take responsibility for the success of a holiday and the danger of failure and, in addition, he has the right to withdraw if an act of God takes place.

In both cases, it can be assumed that holidays cannot be repeated. Holidays once applied for and approved cannot be credited back. An exception arises if the employee becomes ill on holiday and the sick days are therefore not calculated as holiday. Moreover, compensation guidelines as stated in § 651f CC which can form the basis for compensation due to untaken holiday are useful to the package holiday tourist. As a result, the only alternatives for those affected, apart from remaining at the destination, are a return home or an improbable and costly redirection to a new destination. The latter is accordingly connected with considerable additional financial effort.

Important in this phase, also towards the customer, is the credibility of actions the organisation carries out. Their significance increases the more long-term the service provider's interest is and the more intense the multiplying effect the tourist can exert.

3.1.6.4 The post-holiday phase

The post-holiday phase is different from the orientation phase in that a close reference to the holiday exists and the tourist still has a very clear picture of the holiday in his mind. His attitude towards the destination and the service provider is based on direct experience and is more stable in contrast to attitudes based on experience indirectly made. The consequence of this is a higher behavioural relevance. How much this applies also to travel behaviour depends, above all, on the tourist's basic motivations. Trips undertaken with the aim to discover something seldom lead to a repetition, whereas other motivations more often will.

However, this phase also increases in significance where experience values are used to sell the tourism product. For the tourists, it is as important as for other consumers, to reflect on the experiences made and to be able to share this with other people (Boltz, 1994). If this reflection and stabilisation is not successful, dissatisfaction can set in. This can no longer affect the trip undertaken but can affect the person's future travel decisions. In all cases, the tourist, as the observer of the negative event or as the qualified assessor who knows the destination or has carried out the activity, is asked for his opinion. As a result, he essentially influences the future value of the product (for the significance of this type of information in travel decision see Braun and Lohmann, 1989).

Diagram 18: Phases of travel decision

Aspects \ Phases	Orientation phase	Post-decision phase	Holiday phase	Post-holiday phase
Situative involvement	low high			
Legal limitations • Right to withdraw • Extraordinary right to withdraw • Deficiencies		Package holiday tourist Package holiday tourist	Package holiday tourist Individual tourist	
Expected consequences from visitors and consumers	Strong decline to be expected	Depending on contractual terms	Low, depending on the long-term interest the service provider has	Not existing, if not regular guest

As shown above, two variables dominate the effect that a negative event has in the consumer sphere of activity: situative involvement and legal restrictions. But, the assessment of consequences is also dependent on a number of individual aspects as was previously indicated. Even if the majority of tourists visit destinations in seasonal peak periods, it should be observed that not all tourists are in the same phase of travel decision when a negative event occurs. The consequently different situations and the differing reactions of tourists should be taken into account for later use and mix of the instruments.

Questions for review and discussion

- What is the importance of stakeholders?
- What types of consumer behaviour are important for tourism?
- What is the meaning of the term 'subjective risk assessment'?
- Which are the factors influencing risk assessment and risk perception?
- What are heuristics?
- What causes a different perception of natural and human-induced negative events?
- Which basic forms of terrorism can be distinguished?
- What are the consequences of criminal activities on tourism?
- Describe the legal differences between a package holiday and an individual tourist.
- What is understood by the fluctuating value of crisis management over time?

Suggestions for further reading

Council of the European Communities (1990), *Council Directive 90/314/EEC of 13 June 1990 on package travel, package holidays and package tours,* EEC, Brussels.

Führich, E. (2002), *Reiserecht,* 4th edn., C.F. Müller, Heidelberg.

Hoffman, B. (1998), *Inside Terrorism,* Victor Gollancz, London.

Kroeber-Riel, W. (1992), *Konsumentenverhalten,* Verlag Vahlen, München.

Luhmann, N. (2005), *Risk: A Sociological Theory,* Aldine Transaction, New Brunswick, N.J.

Poustie, M., Ross, J., Geddes, N. and Stewart, W. (1999), *Hospitality and Tourism Law,* International Thomson Business Press, London.

Rubio-Ayache, D. (2004), *Droit du tourisme,* Éditions BPi, Clichy.

Tversky, A. and Kahneman, D. (1974), 'Judgement under uncertainty: Heuristics and biases', *Science,* 185, pp. 1124-1131.

Useful websites

www.dgfr.de
www.ntsb.gov/ntsb/query.asp

3.2 The tourism product as a sphere of activity

Objectives

- To name the influential factors which determine a destination
- To explain the different forms of competitive advantage of destinations
- To understand the importance of the different forms of competitive advantage with regard to negative events
- To understand the importance of the image for a destination
- To explain the consequences that a negative event can cause on the image
- To explain the problem of responsibility and its importance in times of crisis

Key terms and concepts

- Destinations
- Distance hypothesis
- Competitive advantage
- Basic and additional benefit
- Scenery effect
- Image
- Tourism organizations

The following discussion is focussing mainly on tourism destinations. They can be described as the most essential tourism product and were in the past frequently affected by negative events. Nevertheless, the following discussions, findings and conclusions are useful for tour operators as well as for other service providers whether from the tourism industry or not.

Destinations

Destinations can be rated differently: Continents and states are described as destinations. The WTO's Silk Route project, which incorporates countries along the 12 000 km long Silk Route in the Euro-Asiatic area, or the Slave Route, which supposedly unites 15 states on the African continent, are examples of this. But individual states, regions or even individual hotels are also considered to be destinations (WTO, 1993; Doswell, 1998; Haedrich, 1998b; Bieger, 2002; Kotler, Haider and Rein, 1993) make less of a differentiation and speak about towns, regions and nations). Regarding the size of the geographical area, no fundamental upper or lower limits exist at all. However, this list should not give the impression that it has to do with a hierarchical overlap-free gradation of levels, between which there is a clean dividing line. Rather, it is only a form of today's product understanding in line with market requirements. It replaces the traditional order of tourism responsibility which is oriented towards political areas of influence. Only the consumer's perception decides what is understood as a destination and how big this is. With

Destinations

When considering what a destination is, the same criteria are of use in the selection as those which are used for market segmenting. This means that, as well as efficiency, the temporal stability of the concept is also important in the same way as decisions should come to a potentially heterogenous distinguishing which, however, should be as homogenous as possible.

this understanding of the tourism product, it becomes clear that a geographical area can be a component of more than one destination. For example, it can also be an integral part of the smaller destination of a beach vacationer just as it is at the same time, an element of Europe as a destination for an American tourist on a round trip.

That which determines a destination is predominantly influenced by tourist motives and distance. Motives are the focal point of the considerations. An activity holiday ensures that 'activity' is the core of the offer around which further services are grouped. They determine at the same time the activity radius of the destination for the tourist, that is to say its geographic dimension. The riding holiday maker understands destination as a larger area than a beach holiday maker, the pilgrim as a larger area than a business traveller.

Motives as influential factors in determining a destination are complemented by the distances, which lie between the traveller's departure location and his destination. Depending on the distance, a destination is described as a greater geographical unit if they lie further away from the hometown of the tourist. This effect is known as the distance hypothesis, according to which the image of a destination is more facetted the closer it is. This assertion corresponds furthermore with findings made that, with increased distance, the media pursues the event with simultaneously decreasing attention. The following has an effect for a negative event: news value decreases with increasing distance, which means that the less probable incident receives public attention. In addition, image is defined by few factors by which the number of events that have a direct relationship with these factors decreases.

Increasing distance can, however, also be disadvantageous. If negative events can no longer be precisely assigned to a geographical area, neighbouring regions can also suffer the effects of the events although they probably weren't affected by them at all. Nevertheless, changes happen over years, which make a temporal dimension necessary when assessing destinations.

Distance hypothesis

Example 10: Appalling Africa

Africa is one of the world's regions most affected by undifferentiated judgements, as the former Secretary-General of the World Tourism Organization Enriquez Savignac pointed out. Although the continent is composed to date of 54 different countries, Africa is often perceived as one region when it comes to negative effects.

Many tourists classify the whole of Africa as a risky location. European travellers first visit destinations in the Americas, then Asia and finally South America. Only those who have already seen most of the world start considering Africa as a destination. Carter (1988) analysed why so many tourists desist from visiting Africa. He found that the image of Africa that holds sway in the major source markets of tourism is dominated by the belief that African des-

---

tinations are risky because of a perceived lack of social stability within the region. Tourists could rarely explain this perceived disorder in causal or historical terms. They rather express it as an inherent characteristic of the region as a whole as if it were part of the geography.

Carter also found that most of the tourists classified destinations in Africa as risky because they were all seen as locations of illnesses and particularly infection diseases. Tourists generally associate news reports on HIV/AIDS (which reached in some countries infection rates of more than 20 per cent of the adult population), the cholera or the Ebola virus, with the whole region of

Africa rather than to the dangerous area. Africa is viewed as a marginal region that is alien and, by and large, this feeling of alienation is a source of fear and evasion for these travellers. Many of these defined Africa as a single undifferentiated territory that was dangerous. Even in the estimations of different countries the same equivalence was drawn between the political instability of the rest of Africa and danger.

The common perception of Africa as a continent wracked by conflict, famine and HIV/AIDS, are key obstacles to the wider success of its tourism industry. Neither is the continent a land of unrelenting disaster nor is Africa a single country, as the media often portrays it. These perceptions need to be dispelled. Discerning tourists would never consider cancelling their holidays to France or the United Kingdom over conflict in the Balkans, but would likely abandon holiday plans in an African country over the outbreak of a conflict in another country thousands of miles away.

Source: Carter (1998)

3.2.1 The competitive advantage

Like other products, destinations rival each other. They must develop special advantages that are as unique as possible in order to be competitive. To assess these advantages and, therefore, be able to better estimate the consequence of negative events, the destination's services must be closely viewed.

3.2.1.1 Determination of relevant competitive factors

Tschiderer's (1980) approach is already classical. He defines the holiday location products as a bundle of market services. In his opinion, these are made up of a constant core part and a derived variable offer. He describes the natural offer as a core service of the service bundle, 'which, with few exceptions, is the core of holiday tourism and, therefore, the deciding element of the service'. It is this focus on the natural offer which functions in a restricting manner and is no longer appropriate. Frömbling (1993) holds a purchase-oriented perspective to define the service characteristics of the tourism product and uses the previously discussed terms, basic and additional benefits. To define competitive advantage, she divides the motivations of tourists into primary and secondary needs. Whilst she sees the primary motive for travel as being the need for a holiday, she believes the following, amongst others, to be secondary needs: active health aspirations as a need for security, socialising and social contact as a social need, prestige and status as a need for recognition, experience and spontaneity as a need for self-realisation. As a result, Frömbling (1993) uses Maslow's motivation hierarchy to which she remarks: 'The Maslow model makes it clear that, in tourism, there are obviously certain basic needs which must be satisfied to a certain extent for everyone'.

> After deciding to go ahead with a holiday or journey, a tourist is confronted with many tourist areas and holiday offers. These are especially similar in their basic benefit characteristics and, inasmuch can be described as homogeneous. (...) The satisfaction of holiday requirements which go beyond the basic benefits can, therefore, following the general benefit theory, be defined as additional benefits which are strived for when holidaying or travelling. Only these secondary requirements (the need for experience) lead to a differentiated perception of the (...) offers supplied by tourist regions.
>
> Source: Frömbling (1993)

Here it should be established that, when using the Maslow needs hierarchy, it should be observed that – apart from the lowest level, the basic needs – the sequence is different for most people (see also further criticism in Kroeber-Riel (1992); Ahmed (1996) also points to the geographical aspect which exerts influence over motivations and the satisfaction felt). This is explained, for example, by people for whom prestige is more important than love. Further – and this is where the essential criticism of Frömbling's behaviour is declared – it can be assumed that there is no doubt that a holiday provides recreation for holiday makers. Moreover, the general classification of relaxation as a primary need is not helpful. The important question is rather what the individual understands by recreation. A person from a large and crowded city perhaps sees this as being a beach holiday whilst someone from the country relates this to a city break. A manager who spends hours in meetings sees recreation in the seclusion of a cruise whilst an assembly-line worker might be attracted by the nightlife of Majorca. The more clichés that are hidden in these examples, the more, however, they bring the fundamentally different understanding of recreation to the fore.

The knowledge that what tourists understand by recreation can be completely different, is reflected again in the approach of Gutiérrez and Bordas (1993) who speak of the tourist's basic needs in this context. In Diagram 19, they assign a few chosen basic needs to the corresponding type of tourism.

Diagram 19: Examples of tourist's basic needs and the corresponding tourism offers

Basic Need	Type of Tourism
Resting under the sun	Practising sports
Sun & Beach Tourism	Sports Tourism
Discovering other cultures	Facing nature
Cultural Tourism	Adventure Tourism

Source: Adapted from Gutiérrez and Bordas (1993)

Essentially different to the usual definitions of holiday motivations is the fact that it attempts to define primary needs. These help to identify the basic services of a product. It is only then discernible who should be considered as a competitor at all as the following example shows: 'Rio de Janeiro, for instance, competes in the markets of 'sun and beach' and 'conventions'. In each of these markets, it has different competitors. It probably competes with Cancun in the market of 'sun and beach' but not on the one of 'meetings' where it maybe has Mexico, D.F. as a competitor, among many others' (Gutiérrez and Bordas 1993).

Basic and additional benefits

If we follow this approach further, there opens a possibility to define the basic and additional benefits of the tourism product. If we consider, for example, a golf player, his primary need in a holiday is golf. The destination that interests him as a golfer must, consequentially, consider all other golfing destinations as competitors. Golf forms, therefore, the basic benefit of the holiday, the additional offer of the destination represents the additional benefits. This is different for a study trip. In this case, the aim of the holiday is probably the broadening of knowledge about a particular country or an analysis of the culture. The required basic service can, therefore, only be provided in this country.

For an in-depth analysis, these basic and additional benefits are combined with competitive advantage. According to Porter (1998a), it is possible to distinguish two basic types of competitive advantage: cost leadership and differentiation. From the customer's point of view this means that the customer is offered either a higher value – material or immaterial – in comparison to the competing suppliers or a comparable service for less money.

3.2.1.2 Differentiation advantage in basic benefits

Attaining competitive advantage over the basic benefits of holiday travel is becoming increasingly difficult. An essential reason for this is the progressive globalization of tourism, which extends the tourism offer and demands the fundamental interchangeability of services. (Keller and Smeral (1998) give a detailed list of the most important factors of supply and demand that influence globalization and increase competitive pressure in the sense of interchangeability). On the one hand, it can be seen that the number of destinations that offer interchangeable basic services such as the beach holiday has increased. It is also clear, on the other hand, that some services are unique and cannot be imitated.

The pyramids of Egypt are an example. A tourist, who, motivated to undertake a cultural holiday, wishes to analyse these testaments to contemporary history, has no opportunity to substitute them. Pyramids or the cultural dimension of Upper Egypt are, therefore, a competitive advantage in the basic benefits of the destination that cannot be imitated.

Destinations with competitive advantage in the basic benefits are in principle more crisis resistant and have a faster recovery.

This is similar for pilgrims whose destination, a holy site, can be substituted by other holy sites but only to a certain extent because each of these locations is characterized by a unique cultural object. Every year, this is spectacularly repeated in the eyes of the world public when Mecca is the aim of innumerable pilgrims although the risks due to the massive crush take on considerable dimensions and the results, time after time, are death and injury.

Examples of competitive advantage within the immaterial area of basic benefits are *emotional tourism* when war veterans, for example, return to war locations and *military tourism* by which soldiers formerly stationed abroad return to those locations (Smith 1998).

After seeing these examples, it is easy to understand that some destinations, seen from the primary need, cannot be substituted. This does not mean, however, that destinations with competitive advantage in their basic benefits are immune to every type of negative event. Rather, this points to a generally higher acceptance threshold as far as negative events are concerned.

At the same time, this type of competitive advantage allows us to conclude that holidays in these destinations can certainly suffer from negative events, which means that the number of tourists who tour the destination will decrease. However, this effect will only last for a short time. The latter can be explained by the fact that potential tourist's needs have not been satisfied. It is in this case not so much the general desire to take a trip which inspires the tourist but the much more concrete travel motives. Therefore, travel to this destination is not suspended as soon as it is affected by a negative event but only postponed until the conditions are more favourable. For this reason, it can be concluded that greater crisis resistance and a quicker opportunity for recuperation can be obtained through competitive advantage in the basic benefits of the destination.

3.2.1.3 Differentiation advantage in additional benefits

The situation changes enormously if this advantage of non-interchangeability of the core service does not exist. In this case, it can be attempted to achieve a differentiation in the additional benefits of the product, that is, to attain a unique position in the consumer's realm of experience.

This type of competitive advantage is reached through the establishment of additional and sustained emotional benefits. This includes the fact that these must be hard to imitate. Only then one can speak of competitive advantage through experience profiling. It is finally the higher social or psychological importance of the product that determines why it is preferred to other functionally similar products. At the same time, it must not be forgotten that the existence of basic benefits is still a necessary prerequisite for market success. A beach destination such as Rimini can have its differentiation advantage in the area of the additional benefits but must also ensure that the basic benefit of a beach destination is still intact. If this is not the case, the destination suffers regardless of the competitive advantage that exists in the additional benefits (see also Example 9).

Because of the fundamental interchangeability of many destinations as regards basic benefits, this type of competitive advantage is of increasing significance. The efforts to attain a differentiation within the area of additional benefits can be observed, for example, in Spain – the traditional destination for beach holidays – where emotional dimensions are constantly emphasized within the strategic marketing measures. But even various African destinations try to connect emotional aspects to their beach holidays in order to make them more competitive. Excursions to slavery documentation centres are one of many measures within the framework of the WTO's Slave Route project, which should establish competitive advantage in this product area (WTO, 1995).

A particular quirk of this competitive advantage is its imaginary emotional basis. This makes it especially susceptible to negative events because spoiled realms of experience cannot be reproduced by objective arguments. Moreover, the fundamentally long-term formation of these competitive advantages demands considerable temporal and financial resources. Both make it clear that the possibility of a negative event must be considered very promptly, that is, in the planning process of additional emotional benefits (see also Sections 4.1.5 and 5.1).

Diagram 20: The significance of basic and additional benefits

	Basic benefits	Additional benefits
Differentiation advantage in basic benefits	Competitive advantage	Don't exist or are not decisive regarding competitiveness
Differentiation advantage in additional benefits	Essential prerequisite	Competitive advantage

The basic and additional benefits have a different significance depending on the competitive advantages.

3.2.1.4 Cost advantage

Cost advantage describes, besides the differentiation advantage, the second fundamental form of competitive advantage. With a cost leadership strategy, the organization offers a comparable standard product at a lower price than its competitors. It is important that the product attributes are perceived by the tourists to be identical or equivalent to that of the competition. Interchangeable beach destinations that develop in regions with favourable infrastructure and wage costs are an example of this type of competitive advantage.

Destinations using the cost advantage are exposed particularly to risks from the point of view of negative events. Their perceived interchangeability and concentration on price, on the other hand, means that only the price can be used as an instrument. Price, indeed, proves to be an appropriate instrument for reducing increased risk perception but this behaviour leads to a fundamental problem with regard to cost advantage: it comes from the fact that, as a rule, the reserves to cut the price are lower than for a company with differentiation advantages. Whilst this will be dealt with later in the section on strategic crisis management (see Section 5.1.1), the signal effect due to price cuts should first be mentioned as it makes the range for price cuts known and will lead, in the future, to changed expectations.

3.2.1.5 The time dimension

On initial consideration, the temporal aspect is of significance within the context of the onset of a negative event and travel phases (see Section 3.1.6). Depending on the travel phase in which the customer is, a negative event has different consequences. The customer's situative involvement, which varies over the course of time, was fixed as the essential determinant for this difference. The temporal aspect has further significance in the area of offer where it can be used to define competitors.

In this sense, destinations are not static but dynamic products. Mainly the influence that natural factors have on the tourism product causes the competitors of a destination to change.

Time dimension

This influence is illustrated, for example, in the competitive assessment of the Canary Islands. There, those responsible for tourism assumed, for a long time, that Morocco, Tunisia and Madeira are year-round competitors for the European source market. Only later was it discovered that summer competitors are not the same as winter ones. Whilst the Greek Islands and Majorca should be seen as competitors in the summer, this changes to the Caribbean Islands in the winter.

Source: Gutiérrez and Bordas (1993)

The circle of competitors can, therefore, differ depending on regular and recurring temporal intervals. In extreme cases, this can mean that there is, temporarily, no substitute destination due to the temporal factor.

Altogether, it remains to be recorded that knowledge of this temporal dimension should not be underestimated because it helps, in case of a negative event, to assess not only the effect on the destination but also on the competitor.

3.2.2 The image

The fact that the image a consumer has of a destination is dependent on factors that are of both the tourist and non-tourist sphere of influence, makes the most comprehensive approach possible seem advisable in order to be able to assess the effect of negative events on the product. Images are always useful when thus describe pictures or visual constructs that function comprehensively, demonstrate a high degree of complexity and, although stable and inflexible, can still be influenced (Mayerhofer, 1995).

> **Definition: Image**
> Image describes the abstract mental copy that a person has of an object, in this case a destination.

Images are the result of a continuous process of opinion-forming, which takes place independently of concrete decision situations. They are composed of objective and subjective, right and sometimes also wrong ideas, attitudes and experiences. The term image should be distinguished from the stereotype related to people that is marked by value assessments. Furthermore, it should be distinguished from prejudice, which is taken from the external social environment and is, as such, less open to influence.

Trommsdorff (1990) describes image as 'a multi-dimensional construct made up of denotative and connotative product characteristics ..., which simultaneously reflect the structure of a one-dimensional attitude phenomenon'. If the attitude towards characteristics was illustrated on a good-bad continuum, 'the image has characteristics on several dimensions, namely the subjective impressions of the product's individual (non-material) characteristics'. The number of attempts to define the terms attitude and image are ample and can be explained by the fact that they describe hypothetical unobservable appearances which means that there can be no correct or incorrect definition.

Scientific analysis spent a long time on the question of whether image should only incorporate connotative, that is non-objective items, or also denotative, that is objective, criteria. The practical use has proved that a division is in fact inadvisable, especially because of the great significance of emotional values in tourism. Progress was also made in the area of image measurement. With the introduction of non-verbal image measurement (NVIM), emotional mood factors can be better grasped through pictorial images and it becomes easier to understand them. Problems that previously arose due to linguistic formulation by the interviewees of visual stimuli and their subsequent retranslation into pictures through market researchers were omitted. This also applies to the problem of translating word stimuli in international image elevation; nevertheless, the various meanings that pictures can have in different cultural circles should also be taken into account.

> **Definition: Realm of experience**
>
> The realm of experience is the total of all ideas and perceptions which a person or group of people connect to a particular object. It is based on cognitively recorded, learnt and examinable facts and the connection with subjective, emotionally loaded interpretations of certain characteristics of the object in question.
>
> Source: Fuchs (1993)

A further consequence was the introduction of the term 'realm of experience' as a description of a widely fanned-out image. This then agrees with the idea that subjective and objective assessments almost always flow together in product assessment and cannot be considered without one another.

Furthermore, realms of experience concern a construct that should be more widely understood than image. Where the former only incorporates denotative and connotative word stimuli in its measurements, non-verbal stimuli are also included, which allow the pictures to be understood. The consumer's realm of ideas is described as the most comprehensive even if the pictures can, in the widest sense, be seen to be smell, taste, hearing or other stimuli (Kroeber-Riel, 1993a; Mayerhofer, 1995). The construct realm of experience can be used, therefore, to record more extensively how a consumer or tourist experiences an 'object, brand name, company or county, town or region' (Mayerhofer, 1995).

In the rest of this book, the terms image and realm of experience will be used synonymously; however, it is expressly indicated that the term image is meant in its wider form to include connotative and denotative characteristics.

3.2.2.1 Country image

A general image of a country is built automatically and independently of whether the country comes into question as a holiday destination. Of interest in the following is the external image of a destination. Self-image, that is, the way the inhabitants of a destination view that destination, is of no significance for tourism itself. The country image is a result of general information that the consumer constantly takes in. It is the constant news stream of political, economic and social events as well as the impressions that have been gained about the country's products. The result is a non-tourism specific country image. The term country image used in the following can be synonymous with destination image. As a rule,

Skiing in Madrid

Skiing in Madrid. This picture shows how much the dominating image of Spain and especially of Madrid is influenced by general impressions. Madrid has two ski resorts within immediate reach (30 km) and another one only some 100 km away. However, Spain or Madrid are seldom associated with skiing.

however, this image is closely related to political or geographical borders with which the country's characteristic details are particularly emphasized (Meyer, 1981; Fakeye and Crompton, 1991).

According to Mayerhofer (1995) the country image is particularly influenced by the following:

- Population characteristics (also when meeting them as tourists in one's own country);
- Countryside;
- Cultural and religious aspects;
- Landmarks;
- Food and beverages;
- Famous personalities;
- The country's competence as product and service manufacturer (made-in-image);
- Representative products, movies, events, literature and music of the country.

This influence is not one-sided. As the country's image is influenced by these factors, it also reflects back on these. There is also a constant relationship of change between country image and its influential factors.

Brandenburg Gate

The Brandenburg gate is an extraordinary example of how fast a landmark becomes a national and touristic symbol. Becoming the focus of attention following the German reunification, this landmark attracted, only for the New Year's Eve celebration of 2003/2004, more than one million people, 250 000 more than for the traditional party at Times Square in New York.

Example 11: Swissair: The End of a National Symbol

The example of Swissair demonstrates the correlation between the country's image and the factors influencing it and shows the importance of a negative image transfer.

Up to now it was thought that mainly products and companies could use the positive sides of the country-of-origin image. Airlines are a prominent case for those who use and stress the image of a country.

The bankruptcy of Swissair shows how a positive image transfer can easily fall back negatively on a country's image. As many airlines do, Swissair used and promoted the country's traditions on board, painted on the aircrafts the national colours and used the national flag on the tailfin. It was widely perceived as an ambassador for such Swiss values as reliability, quality, solidity, security and openness to the world.

The white cross on the tailfin was a symbol of Swiss values carried around the globe.

> But its highly ambitious expansion plans in an increasingly complex and competitive environment finally led to the closing of the company in 2001. What was once useful turned to be a handicap of enormous consequences for the country as a whole, for its tourism and for other sectors that profited from the classical Swiss values.
>
> An editorial in the newspaper Le Temps concluded: 'The white cross on red on the planes carried our reputation around the globe: it stood for quality and discipline. Since yesterday that's history. Worthless!' The broadsheet Neue Zürcher Zeitung (NZZ) pointed it out even clearer: 'The pictures screened around the world of confiscated planes and planes grounded due to lack of fuel; the reports of stranded passengers... will not only inflict massive damage on Swissair's image but on the whole of Switzerland.'
>
> Sources: Le Temps and NZZ, 3 October 2001. Picture: Unique (Airport Zurich)

Country image is also formed dependent on the respective political system and the relationship with other nations. In that sense, a national component of the consumers has to be taken into account for the country's image assessment, similar to the cultural differences of risk assessment previously discussed. For example, American tourists class Iraq, Somalia, Libya, Lebanon and Syria as risky destinations due to lasting political tension. They prefer products from 'free' countries to those from 'unfree' countries and judge products from more developed countries to be of higher quality (Sönmez and Graefe, 1998a; Lebrenz, 1996).

The non-tourism specific image has a considerable influence on whether a destination comes into question for holidays or not (Meyer, 1981; Kotler, Haider and Rein, 1993; Schweiger, 1992; Gutiérrez and Bordas, 1993). This is in accordance with the fact that the decision as to whether a destination is one of the considered alternatives is taken very early and mostly without aid of from, for example, travel agents.

3.2.2.2 Regional image

From the point of view of negative events, the regional image is of great significance in the sense of an area which covers several states. It can be consciously constructed and used in order to market a region as a tourism destination. This approach is often used if the individual image is not perceived by the market. The WTO's Silk Route and Slave Route projects are examples of this. But even an unconsciously constructed, potentially undesired regional image can emerge and has no specific tourism background. Such an image of a region is based on information which is constantly taken in – above all, by news coverage. Examples of regional images are offered by Uzbekistan and Kazakhstan whose country images are normally not individually experienced by consumers. This is different, on the other hand, for countries such as the USA or Japan which are attributed an independent country image by European tourists.

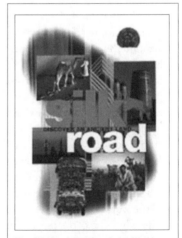

The Silk Road Project of the World Tourism Organization.

Diagram 21: Relative change in international arrivals in the Middle East 1967-2001 (in percentage)

Event	Country			
	Israel	Egypt	Jordan	Syria
The six day war, 1967	-7.0	-45.0	-52.0	-17.4
The Yom Kippur war, 1973	-14.8	-1.1	+5.3	-31.6
The Lebanon war, 1982	-13.0	+3.4	+29.5	-24.1
International terror, 1986	-17.0	-13.6	+2.6	+5.0
Intifada, 1988	-15.0	+3.8	+26.0	+4.6
Iraqi threats, 1990	-5.0	+3.8	+16.2	+5.8
2nd. Gulf war, 1991	-17.0	-15.0	-15.4	+8.8
Al Asqa Intifada, 2000	-54.4	-45.6	+16.3	+12.4

Source: WTO and Mansfeld (1995)

Within these areas, which are perceived to be regionally connected, negative events have an effect on all countries independent of whether they have actually been affected. This case has already been observed many times. For example, India and the Maldives suffered from the terrorist events in Sri Lanka and the putsch in Uganda affected East African tourism as a whole (Mansfeld, 1995; Buckley and Klemm, 1993; Hall, 1994). Mansfeld (1995) submits a more extensive analysis: he believes that the negative regional image of the Middle East can be traced back to the continuous Arabic-Israeli conflict. A result of his analyses of the most important conflicts from 1967 to 1992 was the proof that these respective negative events caused a general negative trend in the region. At the same time, it was possible to observe different effects on the countries analysed, which correlated with the extent of their involvement in the conflict. If we speak of the degree of actual involvement, it should be noted that it depends on the degree of involvement perceived or understood by the tourist. For most events, this is strongly influenced by news reports in the consumer's country and in line with predominant public opinion. It was also observed that Turkey, Greece and Cyprus, which also belong to the region, were only affected by the events when these became international crises and caused general problems such as an increase in transport costs. Otherwise, these countries have been spared by the effects. Sometimes they even profited by being substitutes. This development is explained by the relatively well-developed country images of Turkey, Greece and Cyprus, which made the countries immune to the spillover effects.

In brief, it can be concluded that countries or regions, which incorporate several states, can be doubly affected by negative events:

- First, in that the country is directly affected by the negative event. This refers both to involvement in the conflict as well as to the location of the event.

- Second, because the country is affected by spillover effects of the negative event.

In the second case, the surprise effect is unequally greater. This can frequently be traced back to the fact that those responsible in tourism were not aware that their country was perceived by tourists in the same image sphere as the affected destination. The effect that self-image may differ from the external image can be observed when the analysis of tourists' image is carried out unsatisfactorily or from the perspective of the destination's manager.

3.2.2.3 Destination image

The image of a destination is vital for the customer's product choice. The customer decides what is understood as a destination, that is to say whether it is a resort or even a region. This means, in addition to the finding made already that a geographic area can host several destinations, that a geographical area can have several different competitive advantages at its disposal. This also shows that, even under normal circumstances, a differentiated analysis of important customer segments should be aimed at. Provided that overlapping and contact points exist due to the 'scenery effect', the most consistent strategy possible should be targeted. This aspect is also of significance within the context of negative events because the different customer segments related to these destinations normally react differently. This reaction is influenced by the strength of the respective competitive advantage as well as by the different acceptance thresholds.

> **Scenery effect**
>
> The scenery effect describes the circumstance that other target groups in the same geographical location considerably influence destination perception and product assessment. This effect will later be considered in more detail.
>
> See also Section 7.3.1.

This already indicates that there are strategic possibilities to manage a crisis. This will be examined in greater depth later on (see also Chapter 5). It is important however to first examine three essential variables which influence the imagination, assessment and effect of negative events of the destination image.

3.2.2.3.1 The experience dimension

The tourist's experience of a destination has – as has already been illustrated – influence on the purchase risks associated with product choice (see also Section 3.1.2). This diminishes if the destination is repeatedly chosen. However, experience also influences the susceptibility of the destination image towards negative events. The increasingly more important emotional product differentiation must first be learned by the consumer in order to be effective. This can occur in the form of symbolic experience or direct learning. If the product differentiation is learned by direct experience, that is to say by having been on holiday, it is clear and free of contradiction to the actual experience of the product. The customer is in this case aware of the emotional product advantages and can better assess whether the negative event had an effect on such components.

However, if the product differentiation is a result of symbolic experience, that is to say learned through advertising and other influential components, it can come to differences between the attraction and

> **Different reactions**
>
> The different reactions of the customer segments could be, for example, seen in Israel:
>
> Violent and terrorist acts over the course of 1996 caused a decline in international tourist arrivals. The effects were more extreme in the area of normal package holidays than in the segments of round tours, pilgrimages and cultural trips where there were hardly any cancellations. Competitive advantages embodied in basic benefits, as with cultural trips or pilgrimages, prove to be more resistant when the security situation worsens. Other areas such as beach holidays where Israel has no recognisable competitive advantage react more delicately to the same events.
>
> Source: Priel and Peymani (1996)

experienced image (Ahmed, 1996; Fakeye and Crompton, 1991). Handling and correcting these differences must be the constant aim of destination marketing since under normal circumstances differences can also lead to dissatisfaction. Especially for the case of symbolic experience it can be expected that potential tourists reject a destination more quickly due to a lack of understanding of the effect on the realm of experience, which remains still unknown. This assumption is in accordance with attitude research according to which only attitudes gained by direct experience are relevant for tourist behavioural prognosis (Kroeber-Riel, 1992; Frömbling, 1993).

Example 12: Terrorism as a Tourism Mood Killer?

The Basque separatist group ETA, has been targeting Spain's lucrative tourism industry since 1979. But rather than killing tourists, ETA has aimed at hurting as much as possible the Spanish economy with a dependency of some 12 per cent of its GDP on tourism. Their activities were mainly committed along the Costa Dorada around the places of Cambrills and Salou and in southern Spain. No tourists were killed in any of those attacks. The most serious tourist-related attack was in 1996 when an ETA bomb exploded at Reus airport in Tarragona, injuring 35 holidaymakers.

Following a 14 months truce since September 1998, ETA reinitiated its terrorist campaign in 1999 and warned foreign tourists in March 2001 explicitly not to spend their holidays in Spain, as there could be 'unexpected consequences' during their stay. Since then, several bombs in typical Spanish tourism destinations caused injury and death and underlined the seriousness of this warning.

Despite ETA's terrorist activities, travel warnings issued for the first time against travel to Spain and the devastating attacks of 11 March 2004 in Madrid, those events have neither affected the arrivals of foreign tourists to Spain nor have tourists expressed increased interest in cancelling their holidays after such attacks. This can be mainly explained through the direct experience that most visitors already have of Spain, a classical destination with a high number of repeat customers.

The same observation can be made in the case of Turkey, also a destination which has a strong interest in international tourism but which struggled against several terrorist attacks by the Kurdish PKK. In this regard investigations of the German market research institute 'Studienkreis für Tourismus und Entwicklung' have shown that only 24 per cent of the German population feel subjectively secure following domestic conflicts in Turkey, whereas on the contrary 79 per cent of those who actually had been in Turkey the previous year expressed they wouldn't feel affected at all.

3.2.2.3.2 The geographical dimension

The consumer's background also has an influence on destination image. Depending on which regional sphere the tourist comes from, they link other experience dimensions with a destination. In contrast to the previously discussed influence of cultural and national components on risk assessment, the geographical dimension has a much more concrete product reference.

This means that regionally differing destination assessments are not influenced in the same way by negative events. This opens a further opportunity for crisis management. People from regional areas whose perceived images are less affected by a negative event could be preferred as a target group.

Example 13: Geographical Roots Influence Tourists' Perceptions

The image of a tourist destination consists of the sum of individual and subjective ideas, impressions, beliefs and expectations that a potential tourist has accumulated over a specific period of time. Each of these segments has been shaped by various factors such as the media, press, friends' and relatives' experiences, literature, etc. It is evident that each visitor has developed its very own image of one specific destination. However, it is possible to attach specific groups to specific types of images. Groups could be classified by age, type of holiday, travel experience, life-style and actual position within the life-cycle.

Ahmed investigated the significance of a tourist's geographical origin in relation to its image of the U.S. state of Utah as a tourist destination. He could prove, based on more than 1900 questionnaires from residents of 6 different U.S. regions that the ideas of potential visitors to Utah were different depending on their respective geographical origin.

Analysing Utah's total image and its five major constituents (outdoor recreation resources, outdoor recreation activities, culture, night-life and liquor laws), he found significant differences in the perceived images: In respect to the total image as much as for the perception of culture, people from the 'Intermountain-West' (Arizona, Colorado, Idaho, Montana, Nevada and New Mexico) found Utah to be 'most impressive' whereas people from the Eastern states (Connecticut, Delaware, Washington D.C., Kentucky, Maine, Maryland, Massachusetts, New Hampshire, New Jersey, New York, Ohio, Pennsylvania, Vermont, West Virginia) were 'least impressed'. Concerning the image of outdoor recreation resources, people from California were 'most impressed' whereas people from Washington and Oregon were 'least impressed'. Residents from the Midwest (Illinois, Indiana, Iowa, Kansas, Michigan, Minnesota, Missouri, Nebraska, North Dakota, South Dakota and Wisconsin) made up the group, which was 'most impressed' by Utah's nightlife and 'most liberal' concerning the liquor laws.

Ahmed traced these different perceptions back to regionally differing moral concepts, tastes, behaviour and subcultures, amongst others. He emphasised that the mere identification of the total image of a tourist destination is not sufficient for promotional success, as the total images might be negative whereas constitutional segments might be perceived positive or even outstanding.

Source: Ahmed (1996)

3.2.2.3.3 The image effect of security events

Even the security issue is important within the context of destination image. Whilst, in its first form – which has already been considered – it is responsible for the general security situation being classed as dangerous, security events can also destroy experience values of the destination image. Buckley and Klemm (1993) describe, for example, the damage to experience values in Northern Ireland: 'A favourable image is an essential requirement of any tourist destination. The problem with any kind of civil unrest is that unfavourable images are beamed across the world so that even those who are not afraid of terrorism will be discouraged from taking holidays there. It is not so much that the area is dangerous; it is more that it does not look attractive. If such an influence applies for a long time, it can be assumed that the security event not only influences the image but actually dominates it. Lennon (1999) illustrates this in the case of Belfast, which is still classed as a war zone.

Gartner and Shen (1992) could empirically prove that security events bring about a change in image dimension. By comparing the image of China both before and after the tragic events on Tiananmen Square, the authors surprisingly ascertained that this incident mainly affected the perception of natural attractions that became significantly worse when influenced by the violent clashes. Gartner and Shen (1992) correctly assumed, therefore, that these previously unperceived elements are also important for the tourism image under normal circumstances.

These comments illustrate that the effect of security events must been seen in a wider sense as it was previously the norm. Whilst, as a rule, the aspect of the increased insecurity has an immediate and short-term effect, the parallel observable influence on image also comes to fruition in the long term. In the most extreme cases, security events dominate the image so much that they are seen as independent from the actual threat. A typical example of this is Vietnam. The destination's image is still marked by the Vietnam War regardless of the actual security situation. Instead of fighting against this image, the destination knowingly uses it as an attraction.

> **Kashmir, the Switzerland of India**
>
> Surprisingly as it may seem nowadays, tourism used to be the number one industry in Kashmir. It was an ideal destination where Indians used to travel in the summer to escape from the heat and in the winter for sports. It was in fact considered India's honeymoon Mecca and reservations had to be made long in advance in view of the high demand.
>
> Since the beginning of the Kashmir conflict however, in the late 1980s, the region received a prominent place in the media and appeared regularly in reports about the tensions. As a result, Kashmir with its extraordinary beautiful countryside did not only experience a total breakdown of the tourism demand but has also an image totally dominated by negative impressions.

3.2.3 Product responsibility

If, due to the legal framework of an organization, it is clear within a company where the limits lie and what the management's responsibilities are, we meet a more difficult situation in tourism.

Normally the tourism supply in classical destinations is characterised by the small and medium-sized business structure. Hardly any destination is set up only as a tourism product. Instead classical administrative districts are more or less influenced by the management of a tourism product 'the destination'. While in destinations such as Las Vegas or Majorca the importance of tourism is already obvious since it represents its main activity and consequently the tourism organization plays an important role, the majority of all destinations are not in such a privileged position. In the latter, tourism is considered just as one of the several economic activities and the tourism organization has a difficult stand due to the large number of stakeholders and their differing interests even during normal times.

Problems under normal circumstances are caused by restricted influence possibilities and the fact that decisions for something at the same time imply decisions against something, which, because of the larger number of participants, often leads to a compromise with the smallest common denominator. Thus, a responsibility problem arises. Therefore, Bieger (2002) cites the minimum requirement that tourism organizations must be non-profit organizations to help reduce conflicts of interest. The result is that there are a number of interest groups who are interested in having product responsibility but do not want to share this. Then, there is the problem of statement, the answer to the question what product, respectively, destination image, should be built up and maintained. Homogeneity of interests, the existence of centralized structures, the acceptance of leaders, etc., belong to those factors that exert influence over the problems.

Diagram 22: The concept system of the tourism organization

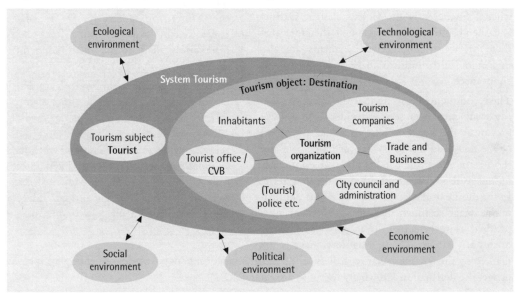

The tourism organization is the bearer of the services to be provided for the destination. It is responsible for the overall planning and marketing as well as the representation of interests, whether governed by public or private law. However, the tourist office is responsible for operative daily business.

Problem of responsibility

Even if it is implied that these problems are solved in times of a positive, market-creating marketing, particular difficulties arise in the case of negative events, which, in part, have their roots in the consequences of the decision and special responsibility. If the problem of responsibility in crisis management is analysed, it can be realized that the legal responsibility is not necessarily identical to the responsibility for the destination. Comparing companies and destinations reveals a further interesting facet. Normally, it can be assumed that the management of a company becomes active to ensure its continuing success or to lower the impacts and, in a worst-case scenario, it can be made legally responsible. Most destinations, on the other hand, only consider the problem of responsibility in times of crisis and disregard preventive possibilities. Whilst normally, there are a number of persons 'interested in power', under these circumstances, no one wants to take on the responsibility.

However, this is not sensible. Crisis management is a public good for a destination because the exclusivity principle cannot be used. Besides, the image, an important part of the confidence-building measures, for which normally the tourism organization is responsible, is strained. Therefore, in order to be prepared for negative events, the tourism organization must be aware of its responsibility and assign it from the beginning, particularly if it concerns a public-legal structure in which calm, careful and balancing actions dominate. This is even more important taking into account that correct and solving actions are seldom rewarded while actions that fail are almost always sanctioned. Consequentially, management responsibility is not as freely taken on in such situations especially if multiple responsibilities allow the decisions to be shifted to other institutions.

Moreover, there is also a statement problem in crisis management. The lack of understanding of marketing strategies even in normal circumstances, which applies for most destinations (Gutiérrez and Bordas, 1993), often leads to an ineffective cocktail of activities, which, normally, only has the aim of playing the events down. However, what is destroyed or impeded is exactly what is important in the long run: the organization's credibility.

It remains to be ascertained that the regulation of product responsibility is important for a destination. In a crisis situation, the destination image is placed under close scrutiny as the otherwise rather seldom observed statements and behaviours of the tourism organization are viably carried out directly in the public eye. This also can be seen as a chance for crisis management, which should be used with the right and proper preparation.

Statement problem

Example 14: The Century Floods in Saxony during August 2002

During August 2002, the east and southeast of Germany as well as parts of Eastern Europe were stricken by floods of historical proportions. The region of Saxony was particularly hit. After days of rainfall, the rivers of the Ore Mountains and the Elbe turned into turbulent waters which overflew their banks and flooded valleys and destroyed dams, houses, bridges and roads. Twenty people lost their lives in these floods. One hundred and ten were injured. Thousands had to leave their houses and in Dresden alone, 30 000 people had to be evacuated. This  natural disaster caused the biggest rescue operation of the last fifty years. At times, more than 40 000 fire-fighters, 25 300 soldiers, 10 000 servicemen of the German Federal Agency for Technical Relief (THW) and 25 000 volunteers were struggling to fight the effects of the floods. This catastrophe had far-reaching consequences for the flourishing tourism in Saxony. In some places of the region, the whole tourism infrastructure (hotels, restaurants, sights, etc.) was obliterated and the means of transportation were strongly affected. Following the first news on the catastrophe, a strong wave of cancellations took place.

Through the negative media reports and continuous calls for donations, a negative image of such dimensions was caused that potential tourists stayed away from the destination even when travel became possible once again. The number of guests in the regions most strongly hit by the floods fell in the month of August and September by 40 per cent in comparison to figures from the previous year. In total, the arrivals of tourists in Saxony decreased for the year 2002 by 362 000, more than 8 per cent. For the city of Dresden, the losses from the tourism industry were estimated at 164.3 million Euros.

The media immediately labelled the floods as 'the floods of the century', which indicated the enormous impact that this event had on everyone. Theuerkorn observed however that the crisis awareness among those responsible for tourism was very low. They generally considered crises in tourism in other regions of the world more likely and normal but they refused to accept that they

---

could take place within their own areas of responsibility. Consequently, there were no crisis management procedures in place. Theuerkorn also found the common view that crises could generally only be solved spontaneously and through improvisation but not with the help of prevention measures. This point of view has not even been revoked after the experiences of August 2002. For this reason, but also because of the limited financial and personal room of manoeuvre of the tourism organizations, their prevention measures are still limited rather to the legal obligations for their own organizations (e.g. fire protection and escape routes) while higher-level tourism crisis plans are still missing for the destination.

The Saxony floods showed the cross-section character of tourism and its dependence on the public sector. In this connection, due to the size of the area of the catastrophe, an overlapping of several administrative and territorial areas of competence was caused. Only in Saxony, more than 18 districts were affected by the floods and as a consequence, 18 local governments, tourism organizations, etc.

Theuerkorn found that the problem of responsibility was rather limited in this case. On one hand this catastrophe reached a stage that went far beyond the borders of destinations. On the other hand, because of the complex overall situation those legally in charge, i.e. the County District Commissioners, did not take care or only very little of important problems for tourism. In this vacuum, local and regional tourism organizations as well as representatives from the private sector took their place. Although tourism organizations had, due to the missing interest of the higher levels, a relatively wide room of manoeuvre at their disposal, they had to face financial and personal constraints and were limited because of the dismay of their own organization. Nevertheless, thanks to their own initiative, cooperation, creativity, financial reallocation and sponsoring, they were able to initiate different activities for the recovery. That way, tourism in Saxony reached, after a year, the level of tourist arrivals prior to the crisis.

Despite this success, many small and medium-sized tourism enterprises and organizations complained about the insufficient support they had received and the little consideration of their interests compared to those of large companies. They especially criticized the application and distribution of funds, how the indirect damages were reflected in their financial compensations and the concentration of promotional campaigns only in favour of the large destinations. These differences in the determination of goals of the  crisis management were especially of importance as tourism in Saxony is dominated by SMEs. These companies have more difficulties to compensate their losses and finance their recovery than larger ones. The case of the floods in Saxony underlines the need for an efficient crisis management to ensure effective crisis coping and in the long-term sustainable tourism development.

Source: Theuerkorn (2004)

Questions for review and discussion

- Are destinations always affected in the same way by negative events?
- How important is the form of the competitive advantage when it comes to negative events?
- What is understood by 'scenery effect'?
- Name examples for the basic and additional benefit of the tourism product.
- How important is the time dimension when it comes to determination of competitors?
- How can the image of a destination be best measured?
- What is understood by 'self-image' and 'external image' and what are the consequences of the non-consideration of the foreign image?
- Explain the consequences of negative events on products whose differentiation was directly learned in comparison to those learned through symbolic experience.
- Explain the practical consequences of the 'problem of responsibility' of destinations during times of crises.

Suggestions for further reading

Ahmed, Z. (1996), 'The need for the Identification of the Constituents of a Destination's Tourist Image: A Promotional Segmentation Perspective', *Tourism Review*, 51(2), pp. 44-57.

Buckley, P. and Klemm, M. (1993), 'The decline of tourism in Northern Ireland – the Causes', *Tourism Management*, 14(3), pp. 184-194.

Gartner, W. and Shen, J. (1992), 'The impact of Tiananmen Square on China's tourism image', *Journal of Travel Research*, 30(4), pp. 47-52.

Gutiérrez, C. and Bordas, E. (1993), 'La competitividad de los destinos turísticos en mercados lejanos', in *Competitiveness of Long Haul Tourist Destinations* (AIEST (ed.)), 35, AIEST, St. Gallen, pp. 103-211.

Lennon, G. (1999), 'Marketing Belfast as a tourism destination', *Tourism*, 47(1), pp. 74-77.

Mayerhofer, W. (1995), *Imagetransfer*, Service Fachverlag, Wien.

Porter, M. E. (1998), *Competitive Advantage*, Free Press, New York.

World Tourism Organization (2001), *Special Report No. 18, Tourism After 11 September 2001: Analysis, Remedial Actions and Prospects*, WTO, Madrid.

3.3 Competitors as spheres of activity

Objectives

- To realize the fundamental reactions of competitors
- To recognize the range of one's own reactions

Key terms and concepts

- Reaction of competitors
- Sanction possibilities

In the case of a negative event the competitors of a company or destination, can either become an alternative to the affected organization or also be affected. The aspect as to who should be considered a competitor has already been mentioned. It brings forward the question of the advantage that a competitor can gain from a situation of a negative event.

Viewed in general, the disadvantageous development of a destination is an advantage for competing destinations. This applies all the more if it concerns negative events that are limited to a local area and do not influence the volume of tourists as a whole.

In the first case, when only one company or a particular destination but not the competitors are affected by negative events, the following reaction possibilities exist for competitors:

- First, they can refrain from taking every form of advantage.
- Second, they can use the event to their advantage in that they emphasize the defects of the competing product within the framework of comparative advertising. This behaviour is clearly directed against the affected organization and contributes actively to the problem being publicized.

> The competitors of the Fijian Islands reacted for example to the political instability of 1987 with an advertisement comparing the safety of their own destination:
>
> Golden beaches, coconut palms and no coups!
>
> War in the Solomons ended 1945. Why risk Fiji?
>
> Source: Hall (1994)

- Third, competitors can confine themselves to indicating the non-existence of the defects in their own products. This type of reaction always comes into question if it is already well known that a negative event has occurred.

> During times of general uncertainty even just the announcement of a product modification is considered as a clear signal from competitors. After the attacks on a passenger plane with a surface-to-air missile in Kenya in 2002, British Airways announced the installation of antimissile systems on their aircrafts.

In the future, a more active form of reaction on the part of competitors will have to be reckoned with. Continuously growing pressure to compete as well as the legal expansion of advertising possibilities (comparative advertising), introduced in Europe by the EU in October 1997, are two essential influential factors. This applies, above all, to the third case in which the non-existence of the defect for the own product is indicated in a 'cautious manner' without directly mentioning the competitor.

The legal and economic sanction possibilities open to the affected organization determine their opportunities to stop this advantage-taking. They can be classed as low. Seen from a legal point of view, there is no way of stopping such behaviour on an international level. Even from an economic point of view, sanctions are of relatively little use due to the polypolitical market structure of destinations and businesses (this is different, e.g. for tour operators building an oligopoly in Europe).

Sanction possibilities

Independently of the possibilities that the affected organization has, it is finally the consumer who decides about the success of the attempted advantage-taking. Only if he approves the competitor's behaviour and, therefore, buys their product, do these actions make sense.

Example 15: Think Swiss – Fly Thai

The following example illustrates the growing competition between companies. In October 2001 the Swiss airline company 'Swissair' went bankrupt (see also Example 11). This bankruptcy was unexpected and was followed by a very emotional discussion of managerial and ethical values in Switzerland. The Star Alliance member 'Thai Airways' used this moment and launched in early 2002 a Swiss wide promotional campaign directed against the efforts to rebuild what became the successor airline 'Swiss'. The campaign, which included in its advertisements all the graphical elements previously used exclusively by 'Swissair', was widely recognised and accepted by the public. It also received mainly positive comments from the specialised travel press.

Picture: Thai Airways and New Identity

Fundamentally, it can be ascertained that the willingness of a customer to accept such rival behaviour rises with increased distance from the moment the negative event occurred. Behaviour initially interpreted as exploitive is then understood as informative and explanatory. The acceptance of active advantage-taking is also influenced by the customer's will to sanction. Because of the stronger growing tendency of sanctioning nowadays, some already speak of it as a fundamental need of our time. Moreover, the decision against a product is favoured by the interchangeability of products as a result of which the sanction of a product does not signify a fundamental abandonment. It remains to be assumed that this development will be more important for tourism in the future.

If in addition to the concerned organization, several or all competitors are affected by the negative event, this impact is caused either directly or indirectly. The generalization effect is responsible for the indirect effect by which an undifferentiated transfer of attitudes is applied to other similarly perceived objects. This occurs, for example, because products belong to the same categories, the same branches or to the existence of a 'meta attribute' such as the same nationality. In comparison to those directly affected, those indirectly affected will find out about this normally only at a later stage. In both cases, rival behaviour is fundamentally oriented to solve problems. From the point of view of the affected organization, it is advantageous that mutual efforts are undertaken to counter the event and its effects. Associations to which the affected organization belongs also have an important function. As representatives of common interests, they are in a position to be objectively active towards the political sphere and social pressure groups.

Example 16: WTO's Tourism Recovery Committee

Following the attacks of September 11 on the United States of America, a worldwide need for communication and coordination was advocated by WTO's 14th General Assembly and led to the establishment of a Crisis Committee which was later renamed 'Tourism Recovery Committee'. This Committee was the first of its kind to deal on an intergovernmental and worldwide level with the issue of crisis management in tourism. It is comprised of governmental representatives from different regions of the world (21), representatives of each of the different private sectors of the tourism industry (15) and leading experts on the subject.

The Committee met for the first time on 11 November 2001 in London on the occasion of the World Travel Market and discussed the initial report on the consequences of the September 11 attacks, which had been prepared by the WTO Secretariat. The members of the Committee presented the experience of their countries and companies in facing the actual crisis as well as their first plans, both strategic and operational, of how to handle this situation.

This first meeting of the Committee was followed by two regional meetings for the Mediterranean countries where tourism plays a very important role (in Madrid, Spain on 30 January 2002 and in Tunis, Tunisia on 1 March 2002). Two other full meetings followed (in Berlin on 15 March 2002 and in London on 12 November 2002), especially in view of increased terrorism actions against the tourism sector in that same year (Djerba, Tunisia; Bali, Indonesia and Mombassa, Kenya). A Recovery Committee Meeting was organized in

Members of the Tourism Recovery Committee at the Madrid meeting

Phuket, Thailand from 31 January to 1 February 2005 in reaction to the Tsunami in Asia in December 2004. In view of the wide and devastating consequences of this event this meeting was finally convened as an extraordinary session of the WTO's Executive Council.

All meetings were based on the common interest to recover as soon as possible from the initial crisis and to benefit from the mutual exchange of experience. The following especially important issues were addressed:

• Monitoring the evolving situation and its impact on tourism;

• Strengthening WTO's activities in the areas of security and tourism image building;

- Supporting WTO Members, providing them with regular information and recommendations on how to handle the situation;
- Ensuring the co-ordination and consistency of the messages communicated regarding the evolving state of the tourism industry.

In addition, the Committee used as much as possible, either through its Chairman or another representative, the chance of communicating the messages of all countries concerned in a single voice.

Questions for review and discussion

- Explain what role associations can play in the context of crisis management.
- What sanction possibilities are at the disposal of a tourism company against those competitors that take advantage of a crisis situation?
- What are the chances of stopping such behaviour on an international level?

Suggestions for further reading

World Tourism Organization (2002), *Special Report No. 19, Tourism Recovery Committee for the Mediterranean Region*, WTO, Madrid.

World Tourism Organization (2002), *Special Report No. 20, The Impact of the September 11th Attacks on Tourism: The Light at the End of the Tunnel*, WTO, Madrid.

World Tourism Organization (2002), *Special Report No. 21, Climbing Towards Recovery?*, WTO, Madrid.

3.4 The state as a sphere of activity

Objectives

- To understand the actions of the state during times of crisis

Key terms and concepts

- State
- Political process
- Foreign and domestic consequences of actions of the state

3.4.1 The inner view

Companies or organisations are limited in their freedom of action by the intervention of the state – state describes all horizontal administrative bodies, namely legislative, judicial and executive. Regarding its tasks and functions in most West European countries, this covers a development from liberal constitutional state to the welfare state of the present. The state perceives increased tasks whose common characteristic is providing a service for society, such as environmental protection, the promotion of specific economical areas and catastrophe precautions. This is accompanied by an increased interlocking of the public and private spheres which then leads to a restriction on private autonomy. Seen as a whole, legal regulations are influencing more and more the different areas of life.

Following the question of which factors lead to these cost-effective decisions or decisions that curb the freedom of action, phase models can be used to illustrate the political decision process. According to Dyllick's (1992) three-phase model, the first phase describes the articulation of the problem in which a great number of problems compete for the attention of political instances and public opinion. Regarding perception and assessment, the same criteria apply for political decision makers as were mentioned in the consumer sphere of activity. Moreover, it is confirmed that political representatives behave like rational vote maximizers (Bieger, 2002). As a result, their preferred interest applies to that which promises them more votes, leads to more fame or helps them to get increased support from important groups. Already today, it can be observed that, in this phase, influences take on unconventional forms and the significance of stakeholder and interest groups increases.

Restriction on private autonomy

Phase models

> **Example 17: The Aviation and Transportation Security Act**
>
> Since the terrorist attacks of 11 September 2001 on the United States, the issue of transport security – and in particular increased air transport security – has moved to the top of the agenda of the U.S. Government. The government recognized that in the current situation airlines and airport operators alone could not handle this critical issue anymore.
>
> How fast such a process of market articulation, policy formulation and implementation can be is illustrated by the Aviation and Transportation Security Act (ATSA) which President Bush

signed into law on 19 November 2001, just 10 weeks after the attacks. This showed the vulnerability and failing of the actual system. The ATSA established among other things a new Transportation Security Administration (TSA) within the Department of Transportation. The main objective of the Act was to enhance the national airport security services, which are now under federal management and control. In particular, the TSA and companies under contract with it now operate the screening of individuals and property. The new law requires additionally the qualification, training and testing of all employees as much as the presence of uniformed Federal law enforcement officers at all commercial airports. The Federal Government is now particularly in charge of the following:

- Supervision of the passenger and baggage security at 420 commercial passenger airports within the USA
- Performance of intensive background checks, training and testing of screeners and security personnel
- Purchasing and maintaining all screening equipment
- Oversee patrolling of secure areas and monitoring of the quality of the airport's access control
- Cooperating with other law enforcement authorities at the federal, state and local levels as well as being a key facilitator of coordination regarding homeland security.

In the phase of policy formulation, the concrete and already prioritized problems are combined with programmes and aims. Because it has already been indicated that experts and laymen scarcely agree on the ways and forms of assessing risks, it is significant which way risk assessment decision makers should follow. In this phase, an important role falls on the lobbies and pressure groups who are heard as experts and affected people and who, through self-obligation, can influence further legislative activities.

In the phase of policy implementation, programmes, respectively, laws, are issued, monitored and, if necessary, sanctioned as offences. It is only with this implementation that the actual effect of a political decision can be judged.

State regulations should not only, however, be viewed as cost-effective but also as a measure to ensure a sustainable tourism development. For environmental problems that are not necessarily caused by tourism, state intervention is sometimes the only opportunity to prevent negative events. The careless contact and misuse of resources in the form of water contamination or air pollution frequently appears as a causal area of tourism crises.

Sustainable tourism development

Example 18: Erika and Prestige

The legally complicated issue of international cargo transported by seaways illustrates that only the state or, like in the following cases, the international community is able to prevent effectively negative events of enormous consequences for both nature and tourism.

On Wednesday, 13 November 2002, in stormy weather conditions, a serious accident occurred with the oil tanker 'PRESTIGE', which was sailing off the West Coast of Galicia (Spain). It was reported that the ship, with 77 000 tonnes of heavy fuel on board, was in danger of sinking because of a large crack in the starboard side of the hull. Upon request of the owner and his insurer, the Dutch salvage company 'SMIT' took control of the vessel. The ship was towed to sea, and while the discussions were ongoing on where it could find a safe haven to transfer its cargo to another ship, the situation deteriorated on board.

On Tuesday morning, 19 November, the ship structure collapsed and the tanker broke in two some 100 miles off the Spanish and Portuguese coast. The dangerous cargo was spilled into the sea and caused enormous pollution off the Galicia coast, a very important fishing and tourism area.

A similar accident took place less than 3 years ago, when the oil tanker 'ERIKA', which carried 35 000 tonnes of this persistent and difficult to clean oil, polluted the coast of France. In both cases, the oil tankers were old single-hull tankers that offered little safety in the event of an accident.

Trails of the Prestige

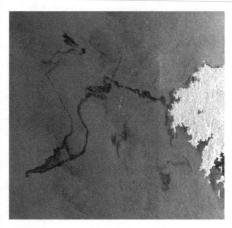

Picture: Taken on 17 November 2002 with a radar satellite of ESA's Earth Watching Project. The picture shows the spilling oil of the Prestige spread across an area of 100 km.

As measures by single countries are of no major impact when it concerns maritime safety, the European Union took the initiative and adopted a set of measures that will effectively ban these substandard ships from European waters in the future. These initiatives, which have no doubt financial implications for the companies affected, will benefit not only the environment but also the tourism sector, both of which were strongly affected by both events.

Compensates damages or losses caused

It is important to remember the other side of the welfare state that helps businesses affected by negative events. This side appears if the state compensates damages or losses caused by the incident in order to ensure, for example, the further existence of a company or the whole branch.

However, the state as a sphere of activity reacts more slowly than the other spheres. Whilst the latter forget negative events over the course of time and, therefore, do not have any effect, political decisions

Political norms

Quasi-everlasting effect

that lead to laws or other political norms have from then on a quasi-everlasting effect. This is cost-effective both for the organization directly affected and the rivals included in the legal decisions. Practice shows, however, that in every case it is possible to influence the reaction of the state and, therefore, the consequences through exemplary behaviour. This option is recommended not only for the case where the organization has a legal responsibility but also for the case where the organization is just attributed this responsibility.

One of the many typical examples is the compensation of the Spanish government after the attacks on commuter trains in Madrid on 11 March 2004. The government paid those affected some 25 million Euros for 'missed profits'.

3.4.2 The outer view

International tourism is part of the foreign trade of a state. If, for example, an American citizen travels outside of the U.S., from the point of view of the U.S. economy, an import of tourism services takes place. At the same time, an export of services takes place if it is looked at from the point of view of the receiving country.

While considering this for the aspects of crisis management, it has to be taken into account that foreign trade and especially the import of services and goods from other countries have always been the object of limitations and regulations. This happened in forms of tariffs i.e. customs, or non-tariff barriers i.e. all other remaining forms. The advice or the warning not to travel to a specific country is from this perspective a non-tariff barrier as it increases the barriers of importation of tourism services.

The travel advice is normally prepared and issued by the ministries of foreign affairs. They exist in the first place for the protection of their own citizens. Safety and security were two of the major reasons for which previously nomadic and individual human beings started to live together in cities and other settlements and later formed states. The modern state continues to provide this protection and maintains a great number of systems which, whenever necessary indicate potential risks and threats to all its citizens. This includes that in more and more states the services are established for the first time or existing procedures are improved which aim at those citizens travelling or living outside of their home country. Diplomatic and consular services, military forces but also evacuation and rescue services have been used in the recent past more and more often for citizens, who while being abroad found themselves in extreme and difficult situations. As evacuation and rescue services are limited, very costly and are to be used only in the extreme situations, travel advice has also from this point of view, an organizational and economic dimension for the issuing state. With its travel advice, the issuing foreign office aims at regularly informing its citizens on threats to their personal safety arising from political unrest, lawlessness, violence, natural disasters, epidemics etc. so that they can, in good time, take the necessary steps to leave the troubled area by their own means. The practical interference of the state, especially in forms of evacuation and rescue services needs to be limited to emergency situations.

> **Example 19: MedEvac, the Flying Hospital**
>
> Since the year 2000, a completely equipped airbus of the German Air Force is operational for the transportation of the wounded and ill in case of emergency. A second aircraft can be made available within three days. Each of these flying hospitals has six modern highly equipped intensive-care beds as well as thirty-six transportation facilities for recumbent patients. Each aircraft has a crew of thirty medical doctors and assistants. Besides the military use of this aircraft, the MedEvac has already been used several times to transport tourists from abroad back to Germany.
>
> On its first mission in the year 2000, the MedEvac brought fifty Palestinian children for medical treatment to Germany. In April 2002, twelve heavily burned German tourists, victims of the attacks in Djerba (Tunisia), were repatriated. In May of the same year, French citizens who were seriously wounded during the attacks in Karachi (Pakistan) were flown back to France.
>
> At the request of a German travel insurance company in March 2004, the MedEvac transported thirty-three seriously wounded tourists of a bus accident from Mexico back to Germany. This mission became its first commercial flight as the costs were fully covered by the insurance

company. At the turn of the year 2004, in a total of three rescue flights, a hundred and thirty severely injured German and other European tourists, victims of the Tsunami in Asia, were carried back from Phuket and Bangkok (Thailand) to Germany.

Prior to these flights there had been other rescue operations carried out by the German Air Force. A well-known mission took place in 1978 when two airplanes brought back to Germany tourists who had been severely injured in the gas explosion on the camping ground of 'Los Alfaques' (Spain). At that

Picture: German Airforce. Inside of the MedEvac.

time, the flights were still limited to the transportation of the victims. Only nowadays it is possible through the MedEvac to also provide medical treatment to severely wounded patients.

Travel advisories, which nowadays are issued within a few hours after a negative event has taken place, also have political and economic implications for the country concerned. Although travel advisories have in this sense always been subject to foreign political controversies (see Example 31), the intensity and quality of those disputes increased undoubtedly after the attacks of 11 September 2001 in the United States. While in the past those controversies were in most cases limited to the simple exchange of positions, the current strategies and techniques become clearly more sophisticated and professional. They increase on the one hand the escalation of the political controversy but contribute on the other hand to an improved opinion forming since the mechanism, schemes and details are discussed. (For a detailed discussion on travel advisories see also Section 4.2.1.3.4)

While travel advisories are fundamentally aimed at citizens travelling abroad, other measures can also be taken towards another direction and be aimed at inbound tourism. This happens often to improve the security in a country. In this case, the economic consequences are mainly limited to the issuing country and especially to its tourism industry. The political consequences, however, still exist as the following example illustrates.

Example 20: Tit for Tat

The attacks of 11 September 2001 on the United States changed the security environment dramatically. The government of the U.S. introduced measures so far unknown, both in quality and quantity. Among these was the introduction of new visa policies and new passports including biometrical data. Some countries were required to undergo more rigorous security controls than others. This differentiated treatment created problems.

As from 5 January 2004, Brazilians entering the U.S. were required to provide fingerprints and photos and had to accept a more thorough security check than the other travelers. This not only led to queuing and longer delays. Brazilians also saw how citizens from other countries were passing through the immigration lines without undergoing the same procedures. The political reaction did not take long.

In a tit-for-tat move Brazil decided, on account of human dignity and the right to reciprocity, to implement the same controls on U.S. visitors to Brazil: digital track check, photo, fingerprints, even the payment of a visa of US$ 100 (the same amount as the U.S. was charging Brazilians). At the same time, Brazil's Foreign Ministry officially addressed the U.S. government and requested that Brazil should be taken off the list of countries subject to the additional security measures.

This official incident was widely reported and made it a case of international interest. However, this retaliatory response was not unanimously shared in Brazil. In view of the negative impact of this new policy on tourism, the local authorities of Rio de Janeiro, Brazil's number one destination, together with its private sector, requested that these new measures be stopped. To lower the immediate impact, the city of Rio de Janeiro welcomed American tourists at the airport with flowers, a charm bracelet and a T-shirt saying 'Rio Loves You'.

Following talks, the situation normalized. However, the case of Brazil illustrates well how tourism, one of the world's biggest economic activities, is increasingly becoming a tool of foreign policy.

3.5 Investors, personnel and other spheres of activity

Objectives

- To learn about further spheres of activity

Key terms and concepts

- Capital funds
- Rating agencies
- Responsible management

Capital investors, rating agencies, employees and suppliers of the company or destination belong to the other elements of the institutional environment. Suppliers are only mentioned to complete the picture. They should not be considered as the observations made within the area of the tourism product as a sphere of activity can be also transferred onto the components of the service bundle.

Financial resources are of great importance above all in tourism infrastructure projects. Above all, hotels prove themselves to be particularly investment intensive. This is intensified by the high proportion of foreign investment. As long as the real estate which, as a rule, serves to secure liabilities, is not affected by the negative event, it is of interest for the capital investor if the effects can be controlled in other activity spheres and have no long-term consequences. This applies in the same sense for other business activities where it concerns relations with external capital investors. Furthermore, it is important that a growing part of investors is judging the management decisions with an ethical viewpoint. What has been observed previously in the wider social

Capital investors

> **Finance costs**
>
> Rating agencies such as Standard&Poor's or Moody's not only estimate the consequences of a negative event but also evaluate the quality of the actions taken by the concerned organization. Their analyses and reports have a considerable influence on the extent to which a negative event is also followed by further financial impacts. For a good borrower the degrading by one notch from 'A-' to 'BBB+' increases his cost of refinance by 0.6 per cent.
>
> Rating agencies act fast. In the case of Hurricane Katrina, for instance, only two days after the storm hit land they had already the first evaluations prepared on how the storm had affected the region and alerted for possible downgrading of different bond issuers.

environment of organizations, that social pressure groups intend to influence the companies, can be found nowadays also in the group of capital investors. Besides a small part of politically attuned stock funds in Europe, with an estimated US$ 40 billion under management, which is only invested in companies they consider socially responsible, there is also the far larger universe of mainstream institutional investors in both the U.S. and Europe who have started to look at corporate-behaviour after the case of Enron as part of their overall performance reviews. Thus, the handling of capital investors which is of an indirect nature, is becoming an increasingly important sphere of activity.

From the personnel point of view, it has to be considered that tourism companies have a strong interest in the temporary employment of personnel (for further personnel aspects, see also Section 7.2.3). This is because seasonal fluctuations in demand, which scarcely allow year-round employment, are responsible for this. Furthermore, the tourists' individual needs or national habits contribute to the employment of foreign personnel such as bakers, chefs and tour guides. On this temporary staff, especially if it is foreign, negative events will always have an effect if their personal safety is threatened. Otherwise the consequences will be minimal.

> **Responsible Management**
>
> Munich Re is not only the world's largest reinsurance company but also an important institutional investor. In this function, the company increasingly presses companies into which they invest to apply sustainable and environment-friendly practices. Following this principle, the company aims in the near future to have 80 per cent of their investments in corporations which are either listed in the Dow-Jones-Sustainability (DJSI) or in the British FTSE4Good-Index.

3.6 Ranking of activity spheres

An essential characteristic of crisis situations is the limitation on the resources available to the affected organization. At the same time, this means that the affected spheres have to be weighed and prioritized based on their importance. For most organizations, this importance is derived from the influence that the respective areas exert over business success. Seen from a general point of view, the consequence for the different spheres vary according to the respective branches. For production companies, for example, they will basically increase costs, as the effects will be primarily legal norms and less from the sales market.

In tourism, it should be assumed that the consumer, that is, the sales market, occupies first place in the activity spheres. In the majority of cases, the events unleash a sales rather than cost-sided effect. The consequence of the effect is essentially determined by the market constellation in which the affected unit or units are located. From this point of view, competitors are also important. The social environment of the affected organization, which can be more widely viewed than the amount of actual or potential customers, is also important in tourism. At present, interest groups and stakeholders are of little importance but the generally high interest that is shown towards tourism contributes to the fact that themes with negative events are quickly disseminated and paid great attention. Moreover, this influences the state sphere of activity that should be ranked after the social environment sphere. Its mobilization is essentially dependent on public opinion on which the affected organization should already have concentrated. The potential for catastrophe of the event has an accelerated effect on the inclusion of the state. If it is great, it can induce the state institutions taking on a leading role. In this case, the affected organization unexpectedly and very quickly takes on a defensive position.

Findings made within the various spheres of activity form, like knowledge of the general order – this can, of course, change due to events and other influences – the basis of preventive measures as well as helping to contribute to the overall optimization of the company's actions in coping with crises.

Questions for review and discussion

The state as a sphere of activity

- What are the consequences of the actions of the state?
- Does the state react only by applying sanctions and regulations?
- What are the services the state makes available for its citizens?

Investors, personnel and other spheres of activity

- How do capital investors react to negative events?
- What is to be understood by responsible management of a tourism company, from the viewpoint of a capital investor?

Suggestions for further reading

World Tourism Organization (2000), *Global Code of Ethics for Tourism,* WTO, Madrid.

World Tourism Organization (2003), *Tourism Recovery Series,* WTO, Madrid.

World Tourism Organization (2005), *Tsunami Relief for the Tourism Sector – Phuket Action Plan,* WTO, Madrid.

World Tourism Organization (2005), *Proposal to Channel Funds for the Economic and Operational Recovery of Small and Medium-Size Tourism Enterprises Affected by the Tsunami,* WTO, Madrid.

World Tourism Organization (2005), *Tsunami: One Year on – A summary of the implementation of the Phuket Action Plan,* WTO, Madrid

4 Methods of analysis and prognosis

Objectives

- To evaluate techniques of analysis and prognosis to determine their suitability in the identification of important areas and events
- To understand the consequences of a negative image transfer
- To describe the development stages of an early warning system
- To be able to evaluate the suitability of early warning systems based on indicators or weak signals

Key terms and concepts

- Techniques of analysis and prognosis
- Negative image transfer
- Similarity measurement
- Early warning systems
- Indicators
- Weak signals
- Travel advisories

As has already been illustrated, preventive and coping crisis management must be distinguished within crisis management. The aim of preventive crisis management is taking precautions and to avoid crises.

Firstly, areas of the organization must be identified that are especially threatened by negative events or are of such significance that they must not be exposed to threat at all. This interior-oriented identification and evaluation of possible problematic areas within crisis precautions is followed by strategic and operative measures with which the organization protects itself from the environment. Only then and on basis of these findings is the environment of the company to be looked at by early warning systems in order to indicate possible changes and allow a prompt reaction on the part of the organization (also, internal areas of the company can be the causes of crises but should not be considered further as they are subject of normal management).

The sequence of identification and early warning systems is not a hard rule as the results of early warning can lead to a complete change in the previously defined areas at threat. Nevertheless, the consideration in this sequence corresponds to practical actions.

4.1 Identification of important areas and events

Every business has a number of critical or important areas that are responsible for its success. In first place are the company's competitive advantages. There are also other areas that turn out to be important once the negative event has happened. Whilst the definition and maintenance of competitive advantage is already the task of normal management, competitively irrelevant areas must also be examined in the present identification process in order to promptly recognize their unknown influential effect on the organization in unfavourable circumstances. This examination should, as far as possible, include a future perspective.

If this perspective is extended to the fact that, from the point of view of negative events, a number of incidents are known through the occurrence of which crises in tourism were unleashed, the situation in Diagram 23 arises.

Diagram 23: Situation matrix

		Events	
		Known	Unknown
Areas	Known as important	1.	2.
	Unknown as important	3.	4.

1. The first quadrant describes the situation in which an already known negative event occurs and affects an area classed as important. Because both areas are known, a more comprehensive analysis is at this point unnecessary.

2. The second quadrant refers to the circumstance that an area classed as important is affected by a negative event previously unknown in its effect or appearance. The surprise is caused by the event or the form of the event.

> SARS is a typical example of a negative event previously unknown which caused enormous consequences for the tourism sector worldwide. The special challenge of SARS was its unknown origin rather than the challenge of a fast spreading epidemic.

3. The third situation is if the event is known in its threat potential, but it affects an area classed as unimportant, it is the third situation.

4. The fourth case describes the constellation classed as the most problematic for crisis management describes the fourth case. An unknown negative event affects an area, the importance of which is

unknown. Therefore, almost every piece of information is seen to be relevant because a differentiation according to its importance appears to be impossible.

> This case happened for example in Australia during the SARS crisis. Although Australia was only marginally affected by SARS, it was dependent on airport hubs in Asia, which was until then an area unknown as important. The latter affected Australia together with the up to that moment unknown negative event SARS.

Apart from the simultaneous increase of knowledge about the importance of certain areas, the ideal is to strive for the reduction of unknown events. The latter is, however, scarcely feasible due to the sheer number of negative events. For this reason, the identification of tourism product areas classed as important is the main practical aim of crisis precautions. It is only with this knowledge that effective preventive measures can be taken and, on the other hand, early warning can be made possible.

In the following, selected analysis and prognosis techniques should be evaluated on their ability to identify important areas and events for crisis management. The prognosis techniques already considered at that point serve under these circumstances to identify important areas if the event is known or, vice versa, the identification of important events if the area is known. At the same time, they are of use in the fourth case when especially the scenario analysis is used to identify weak signals (the consideration of the fourth case in which the importance of neither the area nor the event is known takes place in Section 4.2.2).

4.1.1 Cross-impact and vulnerability analysis

The cross-impact analysis is a quantitative method of analysis from which correlation between factors is determined and illustrated. The aim is to be able to assess the strength and succession of these correlations.

Among the number of forms that the cross-impact analysis has experienced over the course of time, it is at this point the ability of this analysis instrument to evaluate the effect of possible events on important areas within an organization or its strategies that are of interest. For this, possible environmental developments are placed on the rows of a matrix and the pursued or planned strategies of the important areas are placed in the columns. Subsequently, experts assess the effect of environmental developments on the areas or strategies in that they enter the assessment value of a given scale into the matrix. The positive assessment values of a scale describe opportunities arising from environmental developments, while the negative ones describe threats.

To finally evaluate the effects of events, positive and negative assessments are added up separately in each row. The value acquired by this process makes noticeable which of the various environmental events should be seen as a particular threat (high negative value) or opportunity (high positive value). The equally carried out additions across the columns allow the assessment of the important areas or their strategies across all general conditions.

Diagram 24: Cross-impact analysis

Environment	SBF 1	SBF 2	SBF 3	SBF 4	Effect +	Effect −
1. Economy as a whole						
Gross National Product	−3	−2	0	+1	+1	−5
Interest	−3	−3	−3	−2	0	−11
2. Political–legal environment						
Environmental protection	−1	+2	0	+1	+3	−1
Subsidies	0	+1	+1	0	+2	0
3. Technology						
New product technology	+2	+2	+3	−1	+7	−1
New process technology	−1	0	0	+1	+1	−1
4. Demography/culture						
Population development	−1	+1	0	0	+1	−1
Attitude towards consumption	+2	+2	−1	0	+4	−1
Effect +	+4	+8	+4	+3		
Effect −	−9	−5	−4	−3		

Legend: SBF = Strategic Business Field

The expected effects can be marked on a scale from −3 to +3.

Example: Environmental development ... depicts a threat/opportunity of SBF ... .

Threat   Opportunity

| −3 | −2 | −1 | 0 | +1 | +2 | +3 |

Source: Adapted from Köhler and Böhler (1984)

The results of cross-impact analysis can be improved by the vulnerability analysis that allows the information to be extended to the event's probability of occurrence. This value raised by questioning experts is applied to the relevant scenarios and their effects acquired by the use of cross-impact analysis. By illustrating the urgency of the reaction in this way, the necessity of adjustment is indicated and information is generated about the importance of the events to be observed.

Evaluation

⊕ The cross-impact analysis is generally a suitable instrument with which important areas of the organization, respectively, events, can be identified.

⊕ It is however, problematic that the events and areas for the evaluation have already been pre-selected.

⊖ It should be borne in mind that the use of this generated information is strongly determined by the corresponding qualification of the experts.

4.1.2 Interaction matrix

Similar to the cross-impact analysis, the interaction matrix relates the selected areas with one another in order to identify dominant and critical cycles. Therefore, it is valued how strongly the causes, which are entered in the rows, are influencing the effects, which are entered in the columns, using an assessment range of 0 (no) to 3 (strong influence).

Diagram 25: Interaction matrix

Active relationship — to — from	1.Motorized individual traffic	2. Pedestrians	3. Traffic infrastructure	4. Tourism attraction	5. Countryside	6. Air/noise	7. Trade/business	Active sum (AS)	Quotient (AS/PS)
1. Motorized individual traffic	–	3	2	3	1	3	2	14	1.4
2. Pedestrians	1	–	1	1	1	0	2	6	0.5
3. Traffic infrastructure	3	2	–	3	3	2	3	16	2.3
4. Tourism attraction	2	1	0	–	1	1	3	8	0.5
5. Countryside	1	3	2	3	–	1	1	11	1.2
6. Air/noise	1	3	0	3	2	–	1	10	1.1
7. Trade/business	2	1	2	2	1	2	–	10	0.8
Passive sum (PS)	10	13	7	15	9	9	12		
Product (AS*PS)	140	78	112	120	99	90	120		

Source: Adapted from Müller and Flügel (1999)

Active (AS) and passive sums (PS) arise from addition by row or column. Finally, the product P (AS*PS) and the quotient Q (AS/PS) are calculated and an active, passive, critical and inert value is defined.

These elements help to answer various questions. With the active value, the highest Q figure, the element is defined which influences other areas the most but is least influenced by other areas. Thus, this variable has the greatest leverage at its disposal. Vice versa, the lowest Q figure, which is exposed to the strongest influences of the other areas but itself has the weakest influence. The critical value, the highest P figure, indicates the area with the highest level of dependency. This exerts great influence over other areas but, at the same time, is most strongly influenced by these. Thus, chain reactions are a consequence of changes to this value. This is different for the inert element, which records little influence both on and from other areas.

Evaluation

➕ The interaction matrix is an instrument with which areas and events can be comprehensively and systematically examined with regard to their dependability.

➕ Particular strength lies in the complexity reduction and extensive analysis possibilities.

➖ The expert experience which is also necessary in this case, influences the value of results and is disadvantageous when the events and mechanisms are unknown.

4.1.3 The Delphi method

The Delphi method is a qualitative prognosis method, which aims at making relevant and uncertain events more precise. It is attempted by repeated expert surveys under step-by-step publication of the results of each round to acquire information and, in particular, to evaluate the value of extreme judgements. Anonymity amongst the participants should counteract the pressure to conform, which is otherwise expected. At the same time, however, this causes an increased risk of isolated individual prognoses. In order to avoid this, the participants are given after each round statistically prepared information on the results of the previous round.

Evaluation

➕ Suitable for the assessment of future important areas and events.

➕ The lack of pressure to conform is of advantage as is the possibility of allowing newly acquired information to be included in the survey.

➖ Required anonymity only allows an indirect learning process between participants.

➖ Only of limited use for complex processes.

➖ Obligation to justify extreme judgements also contributes to avoid these in view of a lack of will or ability to explain.

- Time involved, which can be up to 6 months and, thus, is not applicable for the assessment of many events.

- The quality of the respective moderators determines also the quality of the prognosis result.

4.1.4 Scenario analysis

With scenario analysis, a technology is available for the analysis of the environment as well as for the estimation of the consequences of certain strategies pursued by the organization (Kahn and Wiener, 1967). In contrast to most quantitative and qualitative prognosis methods, the scenario analysis is not based on the premise of time stability. That way, problems that have become visible through the use of traditional prognosis technologies and became especially clear in the context of the 1973 oil crisis can be mainly avoided (Kreikebaum, 1993). Global and firm-specific scenarios are distinguished according to the considered area. Whilst the former considers general environmental scenarios, the firm-specific scenarios, which are of special interest for our analysis, explore concrete business conditions.

In contrast to quantitative trend extrapolation techniques, several possible, plausible and consistent future pictures are developed but, at the same time, illustrate the development paths that lead to these events. Therefore, a number of other prognosis techniques such as creative technologies are used secondarily. This allows both quantitative and qualitative information to be processed. In order to reduce the efforts, the number of scenarios to be drawn up is normally restricted to two or three. They should include both the extreme future situations and, if necessary, continue to depict the current situation. Typically, the process has a seven to eight step approach and includes analysis techniques such as the cross-impact and vulnerability analysis.

Example 21: Preparing for the Avian Flu – Scenario Planning at Visit Scotland

After the first detection of SARS and the Avian Flu in 2003, the world was alerted to how fast infectious diseases could spread. As the World Health Organization alert was kept high, Visit Scotland, the national tourism organization for Scotland, started to look into the consequences of a possible spread of the Avian Flu on its local tourism industry.

The scenario technique was used to understand how future changes could impact on Scottish tourism. After reviewing existing literature, Visit Scotland staff and a research team followed an 8-step approach:

Step 1   A review of the existing scenario produced by the Scottish Executive Health Department was made, looking particularly at the assumptions and implications for the tourism sector.

Step 2   A brain storming session was held to discover issues and relations of concern. Two scenarios, the 'it's out there' and the 'it's here' were drawn up together with the key assumptions. Storylines for both scenarios were then written.

Step 3   The economic impact that the key assumptions in both scenarios would have on the tourism sector and the wider economy of Scotland and the UK, were generated using the

'Moffat Model' – a single country static computable general equilibrium model used in Visit Scotland.

Step 4   The results were presented to the Scottish Executive after having been reviewed by the scenario planning group. The feedback was incorporated into the storylines to improve realism further.

Step 5   Major stakeholders from the UK tourism industry were identified to examine the scenarios and invited for workshops.

Step 6   Stakeholders were divided into two groups for half-day workshops. Prior to the workshop participants received the scenarios together with key literature, as well as a medical briefing on the Avian Flu at the beginning of the meeting. Pre-set questions were used to stimulate the discussion. Both groups used the hexagon modelling as the facilitating device to structure their comments and ideas (see pictures below).

Step 7   The scenarios were then evaluated for reality and validity and the comments used to improve them further.

Step 8   Based on the improved scenarios which helped to understand the impact of the event and the consequences and interactions within the different spheres of activity (consumer, public sector, tourism industry), Visit Scotland identified the important issues for this type of crisis. Based on these, concrete priorities for actions and steps to best prepare Visit Scotland and the tourism sector for the Avian Flu were then formulated.

The Economic Impact of Scenario 2

Moffat Economic Impact Model for Scenario Two: "It's Here!"

Macro Results	£ million change	% change
GDP	-26,641	-38.0
Welfare	-24,727	-43.8
Employment (FTE jobs)	-272,340	-14.8
Balance of trade	0	0.0
Government revenue	-4,251	-16.5
Daytrips expenditure	-910	-40.0
Domestic Tourism expenditure	-763	-47.5
Rest of UK Tourism expenditure	-2,042	-59.5
International Tourism expenditure	-1,191	-78.6
Domestic plus Rest of UK Tourism expenditure	-2,805	-55.7
Overnight Tourism expenditure	-3,995	-61.0
Tourism plus Daytrips expenditure	-4,906	-55.6

Tourism Parameters	Percentage change in demand
Domestic Daytrips	-40.00%
Domestic Tourism (total)	+0.00%
Domestic Tourism (Business)	-50.00%
Domestic Tourism (VFR)	-30.00%
Domestic Tourism (Holidays 1-3 nights)	-50.00%
Domestic Tourism (Holidays 4-7 nights)	-50.00%
Domestic Tourism (Holidays 8+ nights)	-50.00%
Domestic Tourism (Other)	-50.00%
Domestic Tourism (Car)	+0.00%
Domestic Tourism (Train)	+0.00%
Domestic Tourism (Coach tour)	+0.00%
Domestic Tourism (Regular bus/coach)	+0.00%
Domestic Tourism (Boat/ship)	+0.00%
Domestic Tourism (Air)	+0.00%
Domestic Tourism (Other)	+0.00%
Domestic Tourism (Friends/ Relative's House)	+0.00%
Domestic Tourism (Hotel/ Motel and guest houses)	+0.00%
Domestic Tourism (Self catering/ rented	+0.00%
Domestic Tourism (Bed and breakfast)	+0.00%
Domestic Tourism (Touring caravan and camp)	+0.00%
Domestic Tourism (Static caravans)	+0.00%
Domestic Tourism (Other)	+0.00%
Rest of the UK Tourism (Total)	+0.00%
Rest of the UK Tourism (Business)	-60.00%
Rest of the UK Tourism (VFR)	-50.00%
Rest of the UK Tourism (Holidays 1-3 nights)	-60.00%
Rest of the UK Tourism (Holidays 4-7 nights)	-60.00%

Tourism Sector Parameters	Productivity
Large Hotels	-10%
Small Hotels	-10%
B&B Guest Hse	-10%
Self Catering	-10%
Caravan And Camping	-10%
Restaurants Etc	-10%
Railways	-10%
Other Land Transport	-10%
Sea and Air transport	-10%
Transport Services	-10%
Recreational Services	-10%
Retail Distribution	-10%

Other sector parameters	Productivity
LFA: Specialist sheep	-10%
LFA: Specialist beef	-10%
LFA: Cattle and sheep	-10%
Cereals	-10%
General Cropping	-10%
Dairy	-10%
Mixed	-10%
Forestry and Fishing	-10%
Coal Extraction	-10%
Quarrying	-10%
Meat Processing	-10%
Dairy Product	-10%

The 'It's out here' scenario simulated with the Moffat economic impact model.

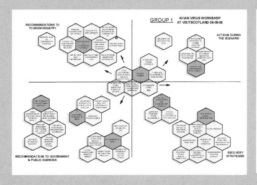

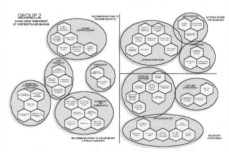

Source: Visit Scotland (2005)

Evaluation

➕ Suitable for the assessment of future important areas and events.

➕ The greatest advantage lies in the hypothetical description of future pictures which, although not exact, are, however, logical. Through this, possible interactions in the various situations with their consequences are made clear independent of the probability.

➖ Quality of the results produced by the scenario technique is influenced, to a great extent, by the qualification of experts who are responsible for the content.

➖ The same applies for the selection of the extreme and trend scenarios.

➖ Depending on the complexity and dynamics of the environmental situation, which is especially high in an international context, the problem is intensified by the non-consideration of influential factors.

4.1.5 Negative image transfer

The concept of image transfer, is based on the assumption that associations related to the brand or product influence consumer behaviour. Thus, it is normally attempted to transfer associations already connected to a brand or a product and, which influence the consumers' behaviour positively (positive image components) onto another product. This image transfer includes associations that must be perceived with the product but must not necessarily be marked by this.

Image transfers are also taking place when negative events occur. The predominant number of negative events, if they do not result in direct, lengthy and objective destruction of the product, are only so effective because similar to a positive image transfer, they construct certain negative values or destroy image dimensions positively connected with the tourism product. Both forms of image transfer are based on the same mechanism, the only difference is that reverse effects occur. Romeo (1991), who examined the retransfer of negative information to family brands, also confirms this. He found this to be aided by the same factors that otherwise influenced positive image transfer. The circumstances that favour or impede image transfer can be divided into four influential areas (Mayerhofer, 1995):

- Image concepts;
- Type of product and event;
- Businesses;
- Consumers.

In the discussion about the consumer and product spheres of activity, the last two circumstances have already been explored in depth. Therefore, image concepts and types of products and events are made the focal point of further considerations.

4.1.5.1 Image concepts

Functional, symbolic and usage situation-based brand concepts are distinguished to explain the influences of image concept. Whilst functional brand concepts are based on sharing the similar physical characteristics or performing similar functions, usage situation-based brand concepts are based on sharing the same usage context, for example, camping equipment. In both cases, the consumer's image is marked by certain individual product characteristics. On the other hand, symbolic brand concepts are characterized by an abstract and holistic image. The authors trace this back to different memory structures that are the basis of these concepts.

Park, Lawson and Milberg (1989) could ascertain that the products of functional and usage situation-based concepts are perceived as similar and matching even in the absence of a brand concept. This can be traced back to the same characteristics and situations of use which form their basis. On the other hand, similarity is not seen in products with symbolic concepts under the same circumstances. Here, only a present brand name increased the perception of the product as fitting. Their similarity assessment remains, however, unchanged.

This different transfer potential is also of interest from the point of view of negative events. They make public a fundamentally different endangered position of products with functional and usage situation-based image concepts in comparison with symbolic concepts. The initially attested low scope for image transfer for functional and usage situation-based image concepts also limits the amount of possible negative events. They can, above all, be found where a use or function reference to the product exists. At the same time, these findings make the essentially higher susceptibility to symbolic concepts clear.

4.1.5.2 Types of product and event

The second group of influential factors deal with the type of product and event and the relationship between the two. If the type of product is considered, the effect of image transfer is considerably influenced by the possibility to assess the product. Experience goods that are only examinable by utilization are far more suitable for image transfer than search goods with which a previous assessment is fundamentally feasible (for further influences such as age of the product, brand strengths, etc., see Chakravarti, MacInnis and Nakamoto, 1990; Smith and Park, 1992). Applied to crisis management in tourism, this means that the tourism product as an experience good is generally more susceptible to image transfer in the aftermath of a negative event.

> **Similarities**
>
> Experts perceive both superficial and more deep-seated similarities better than laymen but they assign them low significance if they are only superficial. This supports the previously mentioned supposition that a high personal and product-specific involvement on the part of tourists encourages a fundamentally more extensive and thorough assessment of the incident.
>
> Source: Muthukrishnan and Weitz (1991)

The event, on the other hand, is assessed differently depending on how well it is remembered. An easy to remember, typical event has a clear, limited effect. Knowledge of risk research also confirms this. On the other hand, it was ascertained that incidents that cannot easily be integrated into the explanation pattern have consequences that are more difficult to estimate and cause fundamentally greater uncertainty on the part of consumers.

The variable essential in explaining transfer possibilities, which is now an indication of transfer probability, forms the relationship or proximity of product and event. The constructs similarity and fit are used to better analyse this.

The similarity, relevant in this case only from the consumers' perception, refers in the case of a positive image transfer to how similar product attributes, the satisfaction of needs or the use are. This must be transferred to the situation of a negative event as it does not concern two products but a negative event that is similar to the product benefits, its satisfaction of needs or its use. It was fundamentally confirmed that the possibilities of image transfer are greater the more similar the product and the event are. (Boush and Loken, 1991; Muthukrishnan and Weitz, 1991; Smith and Park, 1992).

In practice, the construct similarity is of great significance for analysing the effects. If we take a look at use relationship, it explains why events have a different meaning in destinations than those that befall the tourist in his hometown. While tourists see a bus accident at a holiday location in connection with the tourism product, they consider a bus accident at their hometown and on their way to work related to work rather than related to their hometown. For this reason, strategies that ignore such circumstances can already be classed as unsuitable. Nevertheless, it is still quite common to compare the destination's low criminality rate in comparison with the home country of tourists, who have been victims.

The second construct, 'Fit', describes how far the product and event fit together and are perceived as matching by the consumer. Obvious matches, coming from basic benefits and competitive advantages, are distinguished from not so obvious matches. As obvious associations increase the image transfer possibility, negative events are more damaging if specific tourism associations accompany it or if the area affected by the incident is associated with tourism in general. In addition, the findings of Chakravarti, MacInnis and Nakamoto (1990) that, with the decrease of product or function-specific relation, transfer possibility increases can be confirmed also for tourism where events perceived as not limited to certain areas, are quickly transferred to entire regions.

4.1.5.3 Similarity measurement

Various systems exist for the measurement of proximity between product and event, which is referred to as similarity and now includes the associations of the previously described 'fit'.

Mayerhofer's (1995) system for similarity measurement of image transfer in the wider sense makes use of the concept 'realm of experience'. This offers the possibility to use the extensive portrayal of the consumer's complex images by registering mutually objective and subjective assessment components (see Section 3.2.2). Problems that previously arose from a separated assessment can, therefore, be excluded to a great extent. Above all, the inclusion of pictures in image registration makes the recording of difficult to describe feelings easier (for the registration of feelings using pictures, see Weinberg and Konert, 1985). This is of advantage, on the one hand, not only for the subjectively assessed product in tourism but also for negative events. Those are, if not experienced directly, mainly communicated through pictures.

> **Correspondence analysis**
>
> The aim of correspondence analysis is to portray the connection between assessment objects and the assigned stimuli in a multidimensional manner. The advantage of correspondence analysis over other procedures results from the combined portrayal of assessment objects and criteria.
>
> Source: Backhaus et al. (1996)

Furthermore, the registration of similarities is improved by its indirect measurement. Both, the preliminary selection of product characteristics, which leads especially to problems when it comes to symbolic concepts as well as the fact that too much is expected of the test subjects, are excluded (Mayerhofer, 1995).

In the first stage of measuring similarities, relevant realms of experience are raised using picture and word stimuli; this is carried out separately for brands, product groups and regions. Using these three areas is also recommendable for tourism. As has already been discussed in the section about country image, in most cases, country image is greatly dependent on products and vice versa.

In the next stage, registered assessment values are transformed into multidimensional realms of experience with the help of correspondence analysis. In a first analysis between brand and product group image, it can be ascertained whether brand images have an independent realm of experience. This is the case if they are located correspondingly far from the positioning of the product group image.

The position within the realm of experience finally allows the assessment as to what extent it concerns similar realms of experience as well as the identification of the main dimensions responsible for this positioning. The further away an assessment object is from the centre of the illustration, the more distinctive is the corresponding image. On the other hand, no distinctive realm of experience can be assigned to an assessment object located nearer to the centre of the illustration.

Example 22: Similarity Measurement

As already mentioned, to record the realms of experience in tourism, the simultaneous use of brands, product lines and regions is recommendable as the country image is influenced by products and vice versa.

The following diagram gives through the positioning of the assessment objects: <u>BRANDS</u>, PRODUCT LINES and **REGIONS** in the two most essential dimensions (the horizontal axis portrays the first, the vertical axis the second dimension) a first impression of their spatial proximity to one another and to the assessment criteria used. These two dimensions explain 57 per cent of total variance in the case examined

(altogether, thirty-three dimensions contribute to the explanation of the total variance). On the one hand, this makes the multilayered effect of the image clear, while on the other, influential relationships become visible.

Realms of experience are recognizable in the concrete examples of Vienna or Salzburg, which are characterized by terms such as exclusivity, noticeable promotion and enjoyment as well as by pictures that show a theatre box and a couple embracing each other. These realms of experience also have relationships with product groups such as sparkling wine, chocolate and crystal, and with the brands Darbo, Riedel and Römerquelle.

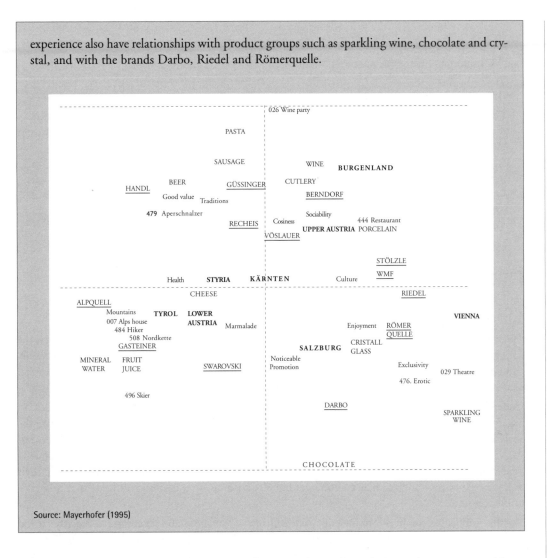

Source: Mayerhofer (1995)

These results are improved by similarity quantification and spatial proximity to the assessment objects. This is especially of interest in the identification of the transfer axis. The position data acquired in correspondence analysis is further examined in a cluster analysis. Both the graphic presentation within the dendrogram and the matrix of squared Euclid dissimilarity coefficients indicate clearly the image defining dimensions, the position with regard to other products and brands as well as association with the country.

> **Example 23: Not Involved, but Suddenly Affected**
>
> The importance of understanding negative image transfers, but especially to observe how surprisingly they affect third parties, is illustrated by the airplane accident of the charter company BIRGENAIR in 1996.
>
> A charter plane with 164 German tourists on board, crashed into the sea shortly after departure from the Dominican Republic. The investigations demonstrated later on that the pilots, who were of Turkish origin, had to be held responsible for the accident. Also the owner of BIRGENAIR, which was a typical low cost carrier used until then by tour operators, was of Turkish origin as well as the CEO of the tour operator who organised the tour. Not only did all the companies involved in the accident suffer in the aftermath from the absence of tourists, but surprisingly for most, also did tourism to Turkey in general, to the Dominican Republic and for nearly all business handled by all foreign charter companies.
>
> These consequences occurred although there were no objective reasons. However, they can be explained using the negative image transfer.

4.1.5.4 New opportunities using the image transfer

The use of image transfer offers new opportunities to identify relations and mechanisms between the negative events and the tourism products. Especially interesting is the fact that this instrument hardly requires the assessment of experts and complies fully with the need to use the consumer's perspective. This is particularly helpful in the analysis of new events.

Understanding the image concepts makes the fundamental estimation of potential threat as a result of negative events easier due to the different transfer potential. This also helps to limit and prioritize the analysis and protection of important areas and the events that might affect them. Furthermore, it offers the visual portrayal of the differences by means of the correspondence analysis and the following measurement of the similarity, the possibility to not only analyse the products comprehensively in their realms of experience and to their competitors but also to indicate the important areas that influence this perception.

Negative influences coming from these identified image factors should be classed as particularly critical in the same way as interference on these areas themselves. The transfer possibilities and probabilities of a negative event can be classed as greater the closer they are to the realm of experience of the respective tourism product.

Nevertheless, the identification of the factors influencing the image is generally not the task of preventive crisis management. Knowledge of the product positioning and the factors that influence this belong to the area of normal business management. However, in tourism, especially at the level of the destinations, there are still considerable deficits.

Evaluation

(+) Identifies relations and mechanisms between negative events and the tourism products and considers the aspect of increasingly important experience values.

(+) Hardly requires the assessment of experts and complies fully with the need to use the consumer's perspective.

(+) Suitable for the analysis of new events and important areas.

(−) Requires good knowledge of the product positioning and the factors that influence this, which is often non-existent.

4.2 Systems and methods of early warning

Apart from the analysis of potential events and important areas, preventive crisis management must identify latent events of importance in good time. This is achieved by generating information early, on emerging developments in the organization's environment, that is, to enable the analysis of effects on the organization. Three generations of such information systems are used to achieve these aims.

With early warning systems of the first generation, shortfalls and exceeded threshold values should be determined and warnings generated. These systems concentrate on result- and liquidity-oriented indicators that already exist. Through an extrapolation based on past data, the expected actual situation should be checked against determined targets. This procedure enables the introduction of certain countermeasures and planning corrections, but is not suitable for identifying latent crises, which means the company can only react to them. In this sense, first-generation early warning systems show shortcomings that considerably limit the scope for action of preventive crisis management. In spite of the disadvantages, these systems are still used as short-term information systems.

Systems of the second generation are based on the conviction that organization-internal and -external chance and risk areas can be covered by a series of indicators and, through observation and measurement of these, timely early warning information can be generated. As a consequence, efforts are concentrated on determining the relevant observation areas and on choosing suitable indicators. The latter must be sufficiently early in the cause and effect chain that the time interval allows a timely introduction of measures. Assuming stable environment conditions, these systems form a suitable basis for timely crisis management.

Through the early warning systems of the third development level, a new generation of systems has emerged that is based on the finding that it is difficult to ascertain complex environmental developments using systems of the second generation (based on causal relationships). Their main focus is strategic surprises, that is, future significant differences in information that influence strategic planning. Strategic surprises are based primarily on discontinuities, which are difficult to predict, but that have the quality of announcing themselves through the so-called weak signals. Systems of the third generation, therefore, concentrate on the timely detection and evaluation of these weak signals.

If these systems are assessed comparatively, it becomes clear that the objective is always the same: to provide the organization with information about changes in the environment as early as possible and

Information systems

105

to help to estimate the consequences. Although it became clear that early warning systems of the first generation cannot provide any suitable support for preventive crisis management, there is no doubt that the second and third generations are capable of this. Their applicability to crisis management should be made clear with the help of the situation matrix in the following diagram.

Diagram 26: Suitability of early warning systems in the situation matrix

		Events	
		Known	Unknown
Areas	Known to be important systems	1.\nSecond generation systems	2.\nSecond and third generation systems
	Not known to be important	3.\nSecond and third generation systems	4.\nThird generation systems

For situations within the first cell in Diagram 26, indicator-based early warning systems prove to be the most suitable tool. The choice of usable indicators is relatively easy to make, just as the timely indication of a negative event is also relatively certain.

For the cases in the second and third quadrants in Diagram 26, indicator-based systems are to be considered as partially suitable. In the case where the importance of the area is known, but it is not possible to put the threatening events in concrete terms, it depends above all on the type of area and the relevant environment whether an indicator-based solution is possible or whether third-generation systems must be used.

The situation is similar with known events, which as a rule can be detected by indicators. The special challenge in this case lies much more in the correct interpretation of the possible consequences. Therefore, the use of exclusively indicator-based methods would be insufficient here.

For the fourth quadrant, in Diagram 26 due to the high number of unknown components, only third-generation systems can be used.

This emphasizes the fact that both indicator-based systems and early warning achieved by the identification of weak signals offer a suitable preparation for promising preventive crisis management.

4.2.1 Indicator-based early warning

Indicator-based early warning systems use measurable indicators through which observable change should give timely hints about events that can otherwise only be detected at a later stage. The construction of those systems is carried out in a step-by-step approach.

Diagram 27: Development stages of an indicator-based early warning system

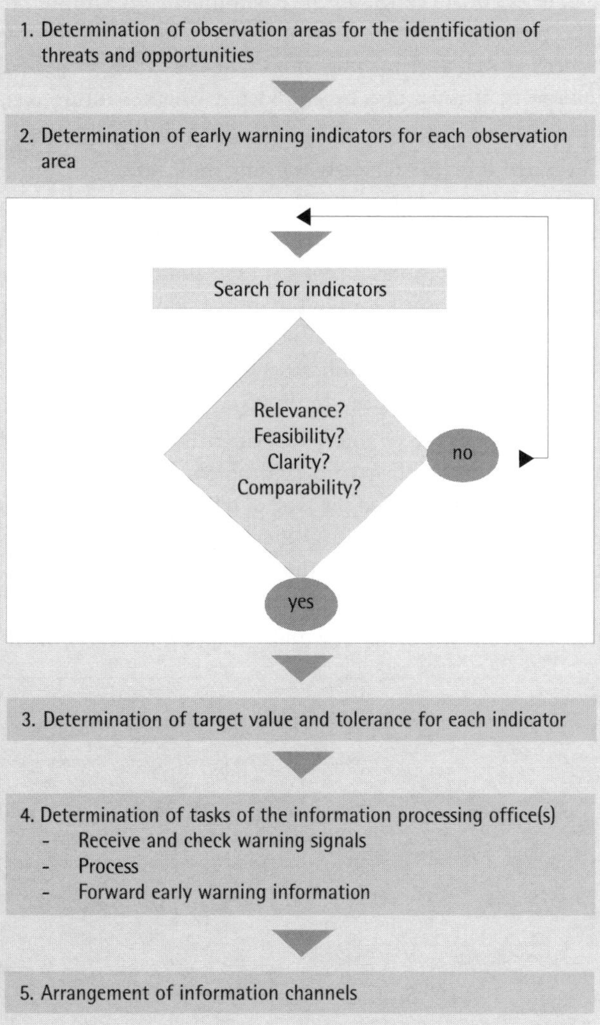

1. Determination of observation areas for the identification of threats and opportunities

2. Determination of early warning indicators for each observation area

Search for indicators

Relevance?
Feasibility?
Clarity?
Comparability?

no

yes

3. Determination of target value and tolerance for each indicator

4. Determination of tasks of the information processing office(s)
   - Receive and check warning signals
   - Process
   - Forward early warning information

5. Arrangement of information channels

Source: Adapted from Hahn (1979)

4.2.1.1 Determination of observation areas

Out of the huge array of possible areas for observation, those particularly important or critical for the specific aims and markets of the organization have to be selected. The determination of these areas has already been covered extensively, as has the fact that these observation areas can be both within and outside the organization (see also Section 4.1).

4.2.1.2 Determination of early warning indicators

In order to ensure that they have good early warning qualities, it is necessary to choose indicators that will point, in good time, to essential changes in the environment. In addition, they should allow clear statements to be made regarding the implications/consequences for the organization when the tolerance value is exceeded, as well as remaining important over a longer period of time. In addition, when choosing the indicators, it must also be considered whether future regular data collection is economically justifiable.

Various methods are suggested for choosing early warning indicators:

- Pümpin (1980) suggests the identification of suitable indicator cause and effect chains. By looking at the factors that precede a negative event, it is possible to work backwards systematically to the future indicators. An additional analysis at each choice stage by means of the cross-impact analysis is to be recommended so that only the most important preceding factors are included. The complexity of crisis situations and the multitude of possible dependencies mean that an exclusively causal determination of the indicators is only to be recommended to a limited extent.

- Another method is deduced from feedback diagrams. This, based on Gomez's (1981) system-theoretical approach, observes the symptoms as part of a complex system determined by diverse influences. To identify the causes of a particular problem situation, this is set firstly in relation to the essential influential factors and then the type of relationship is put in concrete terms. In addition to positive and negative relationships, other important aspects can be considered such as strength, long-term nature or cause area of the influence.

Diagram 28: Structure of a feedback model for analysing population growth in a holiday area

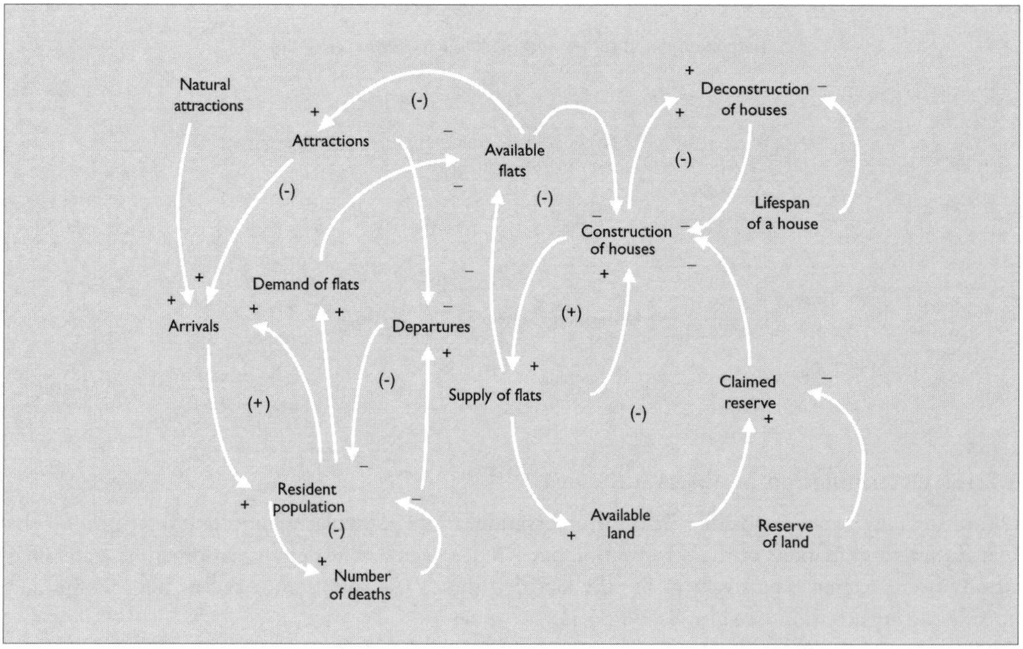

Source: Adapted from Gomez, 1981; Copyright by Paul Haupt Berne.

What is important is that effect relationships describe a cycle situation through which repercussions are likewise included in the analysis. The improvement of the feedback structure in further steps through the integration of additional cycles leads to a complete structure model of the problem situation. Not only is the relevant subject well structured but it is also easy to see if certain factors have a stabilizing or strengthening effect on the system as a whole.

For the final determination of indicators, the various identified, influential variables of the feedback model are examined and evaluated in the previously described interaction matrix. The variables identified as active and critical are especially suitable as early warning indicators.

4.2.1.3 Indicators for country risks

Those interested in foreign trade are traditionally interested in the evaluation of risks in foreign countries which influence their trade and investment activities. Therefore, typically the economic, legal, social and political situation are analysed and assessed by quantitative and qualitative criteria. Several specialized institutes, some public, some private, are working in this field and register, evaluate and publish regularly those risks commonly described as country risks.

The services have been recently extended and include specific information of relevance to the tourism sector. This is based on several influences. Foreign trade is very much linked with travel to establish and maintain contacts or for negotiations. Acting globally is not a privilege to a few but is rather becoming more normal even for smaller businesses. Thus, business travellers are seeking information to prepare better for their travel and to reduce the risks.

Below, a selection of important information services, their functioning and the usefulness of the indicators will be discussed.

4.2.1.3.1 Country @ratings – Coface

The Compagnie française d'assurance pour le commerce extérieur (Coface), a subsidiary of Natexis Banques Populaires and the Banque Populaire Group prepares several indices. The 'Country @ratings' monitors the risks of 150 countries and are published annually. Prepared as a classical index for foreign trade risks it assesses the extent to which the local business, financial and political outlook affects the financial commitments of an individual company.

The Country @ratings are based on information of the commercial missions of the French embassies. With staff in 168 missions, a total of 120 countries are directly covered and have taken regional responsibilities into account. Another 36 countries are covered indirectly. Another feed of information is received through the network of Oxford Analytica. The latter is a consulting company which, according to its own information, is supported through a network of 1000 researchers and academics from the University of Oxford and other research institutions.

Excerpt of the Country @ratings

Source: Coface

The indicators of the Country @ratings are organized in seven categories:

1. Political factors likely to interrupt payment or performance of contracts in progress;
2. Currency shortage risks resulting from a crisis in the balance of payments, which could lead to a transfer crisis and/or rescheduling of foreign debt contracted by public or private debtors;
3. Government capacity to meet commitments abroad;
4. Risks of devaluation following sudden capital flight;
5. Crisis of the banking system assessed by considering both the banking sectors soundness and the likelihood of financial bubbles bursting;
6. Economic risk, reflecting the likelihood of a slowdown in short-term growth independent of any external financial crises stemming from one of the risks described above;
7. Payment behavior on transactions payable in the short-term.

The first three indicators cover areas which have been typically reflected in indices for foreign trade risks. The categories 4-6 of the index monitor developments which were the origins of more recent crises. The seventh indicator is based on information which Coface and their partners in the Credit Alliance network gather through their operational activities.

The overall short-term country risk is summarized in two main risk categories:

- Ratings between A1 and A4 (with A1 being the highest rating) represents a short-term risk ranging from very low to acceptable,
- Ratings B, C or D, describe a highly uncertain economic and political environment, with middle to very high risk.

Furthermore, mid-term risks are evaluated on a 6-level scale and risk factors of special importance for the country are described.

The Country @ratings is the example of an index covering the country risks. Indices of this kind are also produced by other countries and institutions which provide export guarantees.

Evaluation

⊕ Suitable instrument for the evaluation of political risks for tourism.

⊕ As other countries with interest in foreign trade are also producing those evaluations, country specific indicators are available. Those independent evaluations of the country risks are of interest for internationally active tourism companies or destinations looking at different source markets.

⊕ Information is retrieved from a broad span of sources.

⊕ Economical.

⊕⊖ Although the index is from its composition not aimed at the tourism industry, its evaluation gives a neutral and not tourism sector-specific perspective.

4.2.1.3.2 Business Risk Service

The Business Risk Service (BRS) is a widely-known index in foreign trade based on a multidimensional concept. (There are single-and multi-dimensional point-evaluation systems. In the former, the evaluation only concerns a single criterion, whereas multidimensional methods cover individual components that are normally judged by country-specific panels of experts, evaluated according to the gravity of the problem and summarized into a total value.) The BRS predicts and evaluates business climate and political stability in more than 100 states. For a core group of 50 countries the data are collected, evaluated and finally published on 1 April, 1 August and 1 December. Another group of 50 countries is evaluated on an annual basis. The BRS comprises three components: the Operations Risk Index (ORI), the Political Risk Index (PRI) and the Remittance and Repatriation Factor (R Factor).

The ORI serves to evaluate business climate and concentrates on fifteen factors that impede the realization of profit abroad, that is, it indicates the investment climate. The index is based on the evaluation of over 100 experts from banks, industrial companies and government offices, whereby at any given time five to ten experts, with comprehensive lists, assess a country they know well according to set criteria. The scoring of the factors evaluated ranges from 0 (unacceptable conditions) to 4 (very favourable conditions). The ORI for each country is made up of the sum of the arithmetic mean of the criteria evaluated by the experts.

The PRI serves to assess political stability in a country. It covers ten criteria; eight describe the causes of instability and two describe symptoms. Political scientists and sociologists are predominantly enlisted as experts for the evaluation, whilst business people are consciously avoided. In this case, the possible scores range from 0 (extraordinary problems) to 7 (no problems). A further thirty points can be allocated to criteria of particular importance.

The R Factor covers a country's ability and obligation to pay and evaluates the possibilities of converting capital and profits into other currencies in order to transfer them. In contrast to the other sub-indices, the R factor is based on predominantly quantitative data.

The individual results of the ORI, PRI and R Factor are summed up, divided by three and result in the Profit Opportunity Recommendation (POR) which classes a country for the actual year into one of the following categories:

1. Business transactions not recommended. Advise against all business relationships.

2. Suitable for trade only. The situation in the country allows no investment. Only short-term transactions without movement of capital are recommended.

3. Suitable for profit-independent payments only. Realization of profit via the transfer of know-how or licences only is to be recommended.

4. Suitable for investment; investment of capital recommended. Problems in relation to conversion of currency or transfer of dividends are not expected.

A simplified form of the POR is also given for each country as a prognosis for the following year as well as for the situation in 5 years.

Excerpt of the BRS

PROFIT OPPORTUNITY RECOMMENDATION
2B. CONSIDER MEDIUM- AND LONG-TERM BUSINESS VENTURES, INCLUDING MANAGEMENT AND TECHNICAL SERVICE CONTRACTS.

Most Probable Political Scenario: President Gloria Macapagal-Arroyo fails to improve the fiscal situation despite adopting unpopular tax increases. Poverty and rising prices add to public frustration. Terrorist incidents weaken security and contribute to declining popularity of the government. Foreign relations with the U.S. are still captive to the country's decision to withdraw troops from Iraq. The administration takes advantage of its majority in the Senate and passes key measures to reduce corruption and bureaucracy. Consequently, foreign investment begins to increase and busy economic growth. The country increases its attractiveness as an offshore outsourcing destination but is unable to challenge India's dominance in the field. Relations with China strengthen in the next two years.

THE PHILIPPINES' RATINGS

	Combined Score	Political Risk Index	Operations Risk Index	Remittance and Repatriation Factor
1997	42	45	42	37
1998	41	44	40	39
1999	42	44	41	42
2000	43	42	42	44
2001	43	43	41	44
2002	43	43	41	44
2003	43	43	41	45
Present	43	43	41	46
+1 Year	43	43	41	46
+5 Years	45	45	44	48

THE PHILIPPINES' OUTLOOK

❖ Political risk is still high despite the reelection of President Gloria Macapagal-Arroyo. Mrs. Arroyo denied the possibility of a military coup d'état as corruption investigations into the armed forces intensified in October. The International Federation of Journalists (IFJ) recently criticized the lack of effort by the government to protect domestic journalists. The popularity of the government came into question when the lower house of Congress approved a proposed law to raise tobacco and alcohol taxes in October. The government will increase spending to strengthen the country's defense capability to the 2004-2010 Medium-Term Philippine Development Plan. A U.S. Senate Committee approved a nearly doubling of the foreign military assistance to the Philippines in 2005 (US$30 million to US$55 million). Public officials will promote technology-based entrepreneurship by upgrading current laboratories as well as underwriting new facilities in the next two years. The Chinese premier announced in November that China and the Philippines will enhance economic cooperation, particularly in trade and investment.

❖ Operating conditions are deteriorating because of power outages and terrorism attacks. Real GDP expanded 6.2% in the second quarter of the year, largely a result of the robust services performance (7.3%). Industrial production contracted 5.0% in August from a year earlier. Electrical machinery output decreased 7.0% during the period. The unemployment rate was 11.7% in August, down from 12.6% in that month in 2003. The number of unemployed contracted 4.4% to 4.207 million. Consumer price inflation was 6.9% higher in September than a year before. The strength of oil prices is creating cost-push factors and will contribute to a 5.5% average in 2004. In October, the government announced that the construction of Bacolod Airport is being placed on fast track. Once completed, the new airport will handle one million passengers and over 16 000 tons of cargo per year. The budget deficit was 4.2% of GDP during January-June. Government revenue increased 12.4% and expenditures rose 9.9% during that time, but an

Source: BERI. The data for each country are displayed on a two pages report.

Evaluation

(+) Suitable instrument for the evaluation of political risks for tourism.

(+) Information is retrieved from a broad span of sources.

(+) Individual requests to evaluate specific aspects of a country can be made.

(+) No distortion attributable to governmental interests.

(+)(−) Although the index is not from its composition aimed at the tourism industry, its evaluation gives a perspective which is neutral and not specifically for the tourism sector.

(−) Number of countries covered within the core group.

4.2.1.3.3 Risk Map – Control Risks Group

The annually published Risk Map from Control Risks is another product in the area of indices for the foreign trade. More than 130 countries are evaluated in respect of two criteria:

1. For the evaluation of the political risk, state and non-state political actors are examined and assessment is made on the activities that might occur and that could affect a company negatively. The extent to which the state is willing and able to guarantee existing contracts is especially looked at.

2. For the evaluation of the security risk the likelihood with which state and non-state actors are causing harm to the financial, physical or human assets of a company in analysed.

The sources of information for the Risk Map are manifold. According to information of Control Risks, the company has many primary sources in the countries (these are called 'stringers'; they carry out these tasks in addition to their main profession as for example lawyer, police officer or journalist). Those sources are complemented through secondary open sources such as news agencies.

The evaluation is handled exclusively through analysts of Control Risks. Both the political and the security risk are evaluated on a 5-level scale from insignificant to low, medium, high and extreme. The classification is of value for the whole country. However, often different assessments are also given for regions and even cities. The general assessment on this scale is complemented by an individual description and evaluation of the different risks.

Excerpt of the Risk Map

The government's pro-investment programme of low inflation and currency stability will proceed. Diversification will be another focus, particularly after a miners' strike in 2004 again highlighted the risks of dependence on the extractive sector. However, expected increases in diamond production will drive economic growth. Privatisation projects will again appear on the agenda and a more co-ordinated approach can be expected.

BURKINA FASO

Political risk: M
Security risk: M

President Blaise Compaoré is poised to win elections in 2005. He has consolidated his position and faces no serious threats to his position. His relations with neighbouring Côte d'Ivoire and Mauritania, which accused him of plotting a coup, remain tense. However, neither country is likely to attempt to undermine his position. The economy will remain stable despite the loss of revenue from labour remittances from Côte d'Ivoire; interest in the mining sector is likely to continue, with the prospect of significant investment.

BURUNDI

Political risk: H
Security risk: H

Burundi will enter a new political era in 2005 as a three-year transitional period draws to a close. Political tensions between ethnic Tutsis and Hutus will ease only when elections finally take place in April (delayed from November 2004), though attempts to disarm fighters and reorganise the army will consolidate the peace process. The elections will inaugurate a period when the power-sharing arrangements of the new constitution – to be ratified in November 2004 – will have to be secured. The new administration will face challenges from hardline opponents of the peace process and continuing ethnic tensions. Both will continue to pose a security risk in various parts of the country, but a return to serious conflict is unlikely.

CAMEROON

Political risk: M
Security risk: M; H in major cities

President Paul Biya will continue to keep a firm grip on power following his victory in the October 2004 polls; he faces no threat from the fractured opposition. There is little prospect of political reform; the country will remain stable, but undemocratic. Corruption will continue to plague business relations and poor infrastructure and governance will prevent any significant improvement in the economy. Crime will continue to pose a risk to expatriates. Armed robbery and other attacks are a problem in major cities such as Douala, Bamenda and Yaoundé. Corruption will persist among the security forces, which will also be used to harass Biya's opponents.

CAPE VERDE

Political risk: L
Security risk: L

Cape Verde will remain politically stable. It was acknowledged as a medium-developed country by the UN Economic and Social Council (ECOSOC), reflecting progress in economic management and its political

Source: Control Risks (2004)

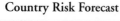

Country Risk Forecast

Source: Control Risks (2004)

A more up-to-date and complete form of the Risk Map is provided with the 'Country Risk Forecast'. This online-service provides continuously up-to-date ratings for the political, security, and terrorism but also travel risk. The before-mentioned 5-level scale is also applied to the two additional categories, i.e. terrorism and travel risk. This service is much more tailored to the needs of business travellers who also have to travel to regions in crisis or with an elevated risk of crisis. In that sense these evaluations have a direct link to tourism since with these ratings an evaluation of the personal risk for the traveller is made which can only be found in the travel advisories.

Evaluation

⊕ ⊖ While the configuration of the Risk Map is more aimed at middle-term and long-term activities, the more complete online-service takes also short-term developments into account.

⊕ Both products are suitable for the evaluation of the country risk.

⊕ The evaluation of the terrorism and travel risk is of direct importance for the tourism sector.

⊕ No distortion attributable to governmental interests.

⊕ Individual requests to evaluate specific aspects of a country can be made.

4.2.1.3.4 Travel advice

Travel advice is a specific information system for tourism. Publishers of travel advice are normally the governmental foreign offices in the most important tourism source markets. The information generated by them is aimed, in the first instance, at tourists and only secondly at tourism organizations.

Diagram 29: The system of travel advice in major source markets

USA	Consular information	Public announcement	Travel warning	
United Kingdom	Unclassified travel advice	Advice against all but essential travel	Advice against all travel	
Germany	Unclassified travel advice	Security advice	Travel warning	
Austria		Security risk		
	Good security standard	Alleviated security risk	High security risk	Very high security risk	Travel warning
France		Advice against travel except for imperative business reasons	Advice against all travel	

113

In the United States, information for tourists about other countries is made available through the U.S. Department of State's Consular Information Program. The so-called Consular Information Sheets are available in principle for all countries around the world. They are a regular and comprehensive description of essential topics to do with the country in question, such as political instability, criminality, terrorism, medical care, etc. The nature of the information as a recommendation is always underlined and tourists are therefore asked to make their own final assessments.

> **Consular Information Sheets**
>
> Consular Information Sheets generally do not include advice, but present information in a factual manner so the traveler can make his or her own decisions concerning travel to a particular country.
>
> Source: www.travel.state.gov

Travel Warnings and Public Announcements complement Consular Information Sheets. If, on the basis of the information available, the State Department judges travel to a specific country as too risky for Americans, travel warnings are published, which advise against travel to this country in general.

Public announcements are dependent on events and are given when a significant threat to the security of American travellers is triggered by unforeseeable events.

The Foreign & Commonwealth Office in Great Britain profoundly revised in 2004 the procedures and guidelines for the preparation of travel advice.

Travel advisories contain now, among others, information concerning safety and security, local laws and customs, entry requirements, health and other general advice. Normally, this information is not combined with a general grading. These advisories are prepared: '...to help travellers avoid trouble by providing information on threats to their personal safety arising from terrorist activities, political unrest, lawlessness, violence, natural disasters, epidemics, anti-British demonstrations and aircraft/shipping safety' (http://www.fco.gov.uk [9.9.2005]).

> **Homeland Security Advisory System**
>
> As the example of the United States illustrates, travel advisories are no longer focussing only on the territory of another country. The Office of Homeland Security, which was established following the attacks on 11 September 2001, issues regular warnings for security threats within their own country.

These travel advisories are regularly updated every 3 months or following any major incident. In the case of major incidents, they can be made several times a day.

Two forms of travel warnings are issued: they advise British citizens either against '… all travel …' or '… all but essential travel…'. In both cases, the general situation is described and the warning is explained in detail.

The German Foreign Office assesses the situation with both the help of its own diplomatic representations and other governmental sources of information as well as in close cooperation with the tourism industry.

The travel advisories inform about peculiarities of penal and custom laws, health and entry requirements as well as other important facts of the countries assessed. They are complemented through security advice and travel warnings.

Security advice is prepared on an individual basis and report on newsworthy risks in the countries concerned. It is only prepared if considered necessary and is consequently not available for all countries. Security advice is regularly revised and if needed updated several times a day. It can include the recommendation to avoid the travel or to limit the scope of the travel. A special form of the security advice is the 'Worldwide advice' with which, since the attacks on 11 September 2001 in the USA, the Foreign Office stresses the increased global security risk caused by terrorism. It also aims at avoiding the repetition of this general information for every country. However, naming certain countries has the purpose of indicating to the user which regions are particularly subject to the terrorism risk. In some cases 'Regional advice' has been used to warn for example about hurricanes in the Caribbean.

Travel warnings are more seldom issued unless they need to advise against general travel to a country or/and if it becomes necessary to advise their own citizens residing in this country to leave it.

The Foreign Office stresses explicitly that the information is only provided to help travellers assess the situation; it should not take away their personal decision. In particular, responsibility is not accepted for any legal consequences relating to the travel advice.

Example 24: The 2002 Bali Attacks in the Travel Advisories

On 12 October 2002, a bomb exploded in Bali's popular Kuta Beach area. It killed 202 people, among them: 88 Australians, 38 Indonesians, 26 British, 7 Americans, 6 Germans, 5 Swedish and 4 French. Hundreds of others were injured, most of them also foreigners. The following charts show how these attacks were seen and classified as dangerous by the respective ministries in major source markets.

Classification of Bali in the travel advisories of the different countries on 17 October 2002:

USA	Consular information	Public announcement		Travel warning	
United Kingdom	Unclassified travel advice	Advice against all but essential travel		Advice against all travel	
Germany	Unclassified travel advice	Security advice		Travel warning	
Austria	Good security standard	Security risk			Travel warning
		Alleviated security risk	High security risk	Very high security risk	
France		Advice against travel except for imperative business reasons		Advice against all travel	

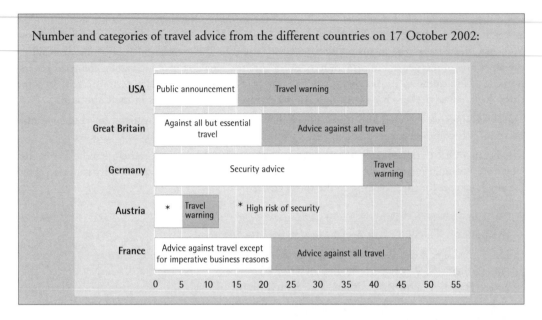

Number and categories of travel advice from the different countries on 17 October 2002:

The information from Foreign Offices has different advantages. First, with its direct relationship to tourism, it is much more in tune with the needs of travellers. In addition, the Foreign Office takes all national components, that is, the country of origin of the tourists, into account and bases its judgement on these points. In terms of the issue of terrorist threat analysed earlier, this interpretation is particularly valuable if the terrorist activities are aimed at the tourists' country of origin and therefore, contain a national component. Furthermore, the countries mentioned have a network of consular representatives that no other organization or company can provide.

The down side is that the assessments, despite the breadth and relevance of the information provided, are subject to political and geographical restrictions. There is no doubt that the assessment is subject to political control since the economic consequences of a warning can be considerable. Among the many factors which can influence are the following:

- Is it a friendly country?
- Do the companies from the own country have a strong interest in the other country?
- Are there significant parts of the population of the country assessed living in the assessing country and are elections close?
- Do historical constraints advise to proceed with special cautions?

This can lead to two types of distortions (Sharpley and Sharpley, 1995):

1. In order to punish the actions of a country, tourists are so influenced by a comparatively over-negative representation that they stay away from the destination.

Distortions

An approach to avoid these distortions in the assessment is to completely avoid classifications. Especially for lower risk levels, a purely verbal description of the circumstances would avoid to a large extent the unfavourable influence. It would still however inform the tourist comprehensively and avoid the problem of the 'objective classification'.

2. On the other hand, so as not to endanger good relations with the country in question, comparatively positive classifications are given despite an unfavourable security situation.

Both situations are disadvantageous and undesirable because they do not convey the objective facts correctly. This is particularly significant if, because of the given warning level, there is a higher signal effect, which may also bring legal consequences with it. In other words, the text version of the advice does indeed describe the circumstances but the classification of the advice is too high. However, a multitude of countries have committed themselves to conveying this information objectively, like, for example, the Member States of the WTO that adopted The Hague Declaration on Tourism, the Manila Declaration on World Tourism and the Global Code of Ethics for Tourism.

Travel Advice in the Global Code of Ethics for Tourism

The Member States of the World Tourism Organization adopted the Global Code of Ethics for Tourism in 1999, during their General Assembly in Santiago, Chile. The Code was later on also adopted by the General Assembly of the United Nations. The important role of governments when in comes to travel advice in times of crises and the necessity that the media reports as objectively as possible are pointed out in paragraphs 5 and 6 of Article 6:

5. Governments have the right – and the duty – especially in a crisis, to inform their nationals of the difficult circumstances, or even the dangers they may encounter during their travels abroad; it is their responsibility however to issue such information without prejudicing in an unjustified or exaggerated manner the tourism industry of the host countries and the interests of their own operators; the contents of travel advisories should therefore be discussed beforehand with the authorities of the host countries and the professionals concerned; recommendations formulated should be strictly proportionate to the gravity of the situations encountered and confined to the geographical areas where the insecurity has arisen; such advisories should be qualified or cancelled as soon as a return to normality permits.

6. The press, and particularly the specialized travel press and the other media, including modern means of electronic communication, should issue honest and balanced information on events and situations that could influence the flow of tourists; they should also provide accurate and reliable information to the consumers of tourism services; the new communication and electronic commerce technologies should also be developed and used for this purpose; as is the case for the media, they should not in any way promote sex tourism.

Example 25: The Revision of the Procedures of Travel Advisories in the UK

Travel advisories are frequently used by UK travellers abroad. Every week, the Travel Advice pages of the Foreign Commonwealth Office (FCO) get an average of 280 000 hits and 1600 people receive the Travel Advice through the Call Centre. The FCO Travel advisories are prepared with the assistance of its 259 embassies and consulates worldwide as well as 231 honorary consuls.

In 2003, as criticism of the FCO's travel advisories grew stronger, the British Government decided to revise and analyse its actual procedures to improve the service provided.

The first result of this analysis confirmed how travel advisories had become a significant information tool to the increasing number of international tourists: In 2003, an estimated 15 million UK citizens were living or working overseas and every year more than 60 million overseas trips were being made by UK citizens.

Second, there had been important changes in the circumstances of international travel: Low-cost air travel, opening of new air routes, more trips to exotic locations, more people travelling independently, more trips by 'at risk groups' (e.g. under-18s, backpackers, adventure travellers or the elderly).

Third, there were new security concerns: increased threat from global terrorist networks, greater risk of being caught up in other forms of international crime (drug trafficking, people-smuggling, cyber crime), etc.

However, it was also observed that the common risks travellers are in fact exposed to abroad are less dramatic than classically perceived, as the following table with the number of deaths in 2002 of UK nationals abroad shows:

Cause	Deaths
Natural causes	1 111
Non-natural causes	316
Total	1 427

The deaths from non-natural causes in 2002 of UK nationals abroad are as follows:

Cause	Deaths
Road accident	158
Committed suicide	57
Drowned	21
Air accident	14
Murdered (non-terrorist violence)	10
Murdered (terrorist violence) (of which 26 were from the Bali bombing)	29
Balcony related accidents	14
Skiing/Mountaineering accidents	12
Rail death	1

Taking all these elements into account, the FCO conducted a close examination of the process and threats assessments that other countries provide to their citizens (Australia, Canada, France, Germany and New Zealand). At the same time, an extensive consultation was carried out with the different stakeholders affected by the consequences of travel advisories. This included the UK travel and insurance industry and their customers, independent British travellers, UK businesses operating overseas, and tourism destinations outside the UK.

Although their opinions differed widely, the FCO was able to draw two main conclusions:

a) The different groups of stakeholders have mutually contradictory objectives and there is not therefore a particular approach that will please everybody;

b) What most stakeholders want is a definitive recommendation on whether travel is safe.

Consequently, the Travel Advice as such was a complex issue with an abundance of competing equities and stakeholders. Six alternatives were considered by the FCO to answer these challenges:

1) No travel advice at all;

2) Generic but not country-specific information (i.e. key messages on insurance, health);

3) *Information* only (i.e. presenting facts, leaving users to make their own decisions and never prescribing actions);

4) Prescription on non-terrorists threats (coups, civil unrest and natural disasters) / information only on all intelligence-based threats (i.e. international terrorism);

5) Continuing to prescribe against travel based on non-terrorist threats (coups, civil unrest, natural disasters), but confining such prescriptions in the case of intelligence-based threats to situations of extreme and imminent danger. British nationals would be expected to make up their own minds in all circumstances on the basis of information on the risks;

6) The status quo.

Following a thorough analysis, the fifth option was finally chosen as the most adequate form of travel advisories for the United Kingdom: The FCO's travel advisories would continue to provide travel advice, including prescriptions against travel in extreme circumstances, to keep British travellers as informed as possible about the conditions of a country before and during their travels. However, the FCO also considered that the ultimate decision on whether to travel (or continue travelling) was for the individual concerned. The FCO would not in this sense accept any liability for that decision.

Now, in addition to this new up-to-date travel advice, the FCO is encouraging travellers to consult the new *'Know Before You Go'* awareness communications. Taking more general information on countries out of the travel advisories and into these pages not only helped to keep the messages clear but also aimed at increasing the self-awareness of travellers and involvement of the tourism industry. The latter is now achieved through the close cooperation with a partner network of around 200 companies related to the tourism industry.

This case not only shows how the expectations of travellers have changed. It also demonstrates an important lesson learned: the importance of transparency in the preparation of travel advice as well as the need to prepare them in cooperation with the different stakeholders, both within the travel industry as well as the destinations.

In the end, it doesn't avoid a travel warning if considered necessary, but it limits the emotions and the long and medium term impact for tourists, tourism industry, states and other stakeholders.

A further point that must not be neglected is that the tourism destination cannot be comprehensively judged from the capital of each country, where the diplomatic representatives are based. This geographic restriction can, however, be remedied by the supplementary information provided by a company's own network of representatives, tour guides and incoming agencies.

Sisbo

Also worth mentioning are those information services which develop products directly aimed at companies working abroad. The British example is the 'Security Information Service for Businesses Overseas (Sisbo)' provided by the Foreign & Commonwealth Office which makes security information available. It is specially pointed out that the information is only complementary to the travel advisories which remain the main source of information.

OSAC

More comprehensive is the approach of OSAC (Overseas Security Advisory Council) that also aims at protecting investments, installations, employees and other interests of American companies working abroad. Founded 1985 as a consequence of the rising threats against American companies abroad, it intends at providing companies with security relevant information as fast as possible. The generated information is disseminated through daily emails (OSAC Daily News) or also on a country-by-country basis if newsworthy events happened (OSAC Consular Affairs Bulletin). The information is very complete and up-to-date. Especially interesting is the strong participation in the Council of companies with interests in tourism and the special reports for the hotel sector.

Besides the public and semi-public information services for travel advisories, there is an increasing number of private companies that produce such kind of information. These companies are mainly addressing business travellers. Their services include regular travel advisories similar to those prepared by the foreign offices as well as the risk evaluation of concrete travel itineraries up to individual travel assistance.

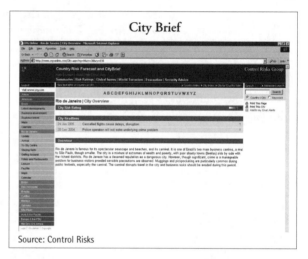

Source: Control Risks

Control Risks

The services of Control Risks have already been mentioned before. Besides the Risk Map, the online services of the Country Risk Forecasts have also been described. At this point the remaining part of the online service, the so-called 'City Briefs' are examined. Through these briefs, a detailed risk analysis of some 300 cities worldwide is made available. The cities have been chosen based on their importance for business travellers. The evaluation is carried out on a scale ranging from 1 (crime rates are low – there is no area of the city a visitor should avoid) up to 7 (high crime levels and/or terrorism and guerrilla violence demand extraordinary security precautions; the government is unable to maintain law and order). Furthermore, the typical risk for travellers to the city is listed in a short and up-to-date form.

iJet

iJet is another provider of services for the travellers. One of the core services of the company is their travel advisory called 'Travel Watch'. They are continuously kept up-to-date for more than 180 countries and 260 cities. Security risks are assessed with an overall rating ranging from 1 (very low) to 5 (very high). Furthermore, each of the 6 subcategories, i.e. crime, security services, civil unrest, terrorism, kidnapping and geopolitical risks, is rated individually on the same scale. Important security issues are described in detail together with aspects related to health, entry requirements and other information relevant for travellers. Altogether the travel advisories have 10 standardized areas of information. The information is according to iJet based on the work of more than 260 primary sources in the countries (so-called stringer) as well as on open accessible global and local news agencies. iJet's travel advisories are used widely in the tourism sector. Travel agencies have access to those advisories through the Global Distribution Systems Worldspan, Amadeus and Abacus/SABRE. Other users are Expedia and Orbitz or PATA; the latter used the service during the SARS-crisis in Asia as an alternative source of information for end-consumers (see Example 56).

The services of iJet and Control Risks have the advantage of being independent from governmental institutions. That makes in general a more objective evaluation possible, which is not necessarily followed by tensions on foreign relations. It is also possible to tailor the service much more to the needs of the users. Of disadvantage is however the difficult assessment of the source used by the companies.

Excerpt from the Travel Watch

The U.S. Consulate, Jeddah, Saudi Arabia
Palestine Road, Ruwais
Phone: 966-2-677-0800, ext. 4129, 4148, 4153, 4192
Fax: 966-2-669-3078 or 966-2-669-3098
Web: http://jeddah-usconsulate.gov/
Email: WardensCA@state.gov
P.O. Box 149
Jeddah, Saudi Arabia 21411
(or) Unit 62112, APO AE 09811-2112
Hours of operation: Saturday-Wednesday 0800-1700; U.S. Citizen Services - Saturday-Wednesday 1300-1530.

U.S. Counsulate General, Dhahran, Saudi Arabia
Located between ARAMCO Headquarters and the old Dhahran Airport at the King Fahd University of Petroleum and Minerals Highway exit.
Phone: 966-3-330-3200, ext. 3040, 3065, 3120, 3171
Fax: 966-3-330-6816
Web: http://dhahran.usconsulate.gov/
Email: ConsularDhahra@state.gov
P.O. Box 38955
Dhahran, Saudi Arabia
Hours of operation: Saturday 1200-1600; Monday-Wednesday 0830-1200 **NOTE:** Consulate General in Dhahran does not offer visa services.

Personal Security: Saudi Arabia nearly crime-free; be alert for petty theft.
Violent crime is rare in Saudi Arabia due to the immediate and severe punishments. While petty crime is on the rise as poverty rates continue to rise, individuals will encounter an almost crime-free atmosphere. Petty theft in crowded markets and public places is the most common crime, though reports of armed robberies targeting *Baqlas* (grocery stores) are on the rise.

In Jeddah, most incidents of crime occur in the Old City, particularly Al-Zahab Street, and the southeast neighborhood of Al-Jamal. In Riyadh, the Al-Bethaa area and locations south of Al-Hadinah Street are prevalent locations for petty crimes.

Immigrant laborers commit most petty crimes. Some criminals disguise themselves as police officers. If possible, avoid travel to areas dominated by foreign workers.

Police: Most police officers in Saudi Arabia speak only Arabic.
There are several types of security services in Saudi Arabia. Foreigners will generally only deal with the regular street police officers and the *Mutawwalin* (religious/moral) police. The religious police are officially known as *Hayat Al-amr Bilmaruf wa Al-Nahi an Al-Munkar*, or the Committee for the Propagation of Virtue and Prevention of Vice. Saudi police do not have a reputation for friendly or helpful service. Communication problems are the main hindrance when trying to work with local police or emergency units as the vast majority of Saudis only speak Arabic. Arabic is the primary language of the police force, and police investigative skills do not always meet Western standards. Any lack of response by local authorities should be reported to the embassy or consulate, as should any and all crimes involving a traveler.

To contact the police, call 999. To report complaints about illegal behavior by police, call 989.

Mutawwalin are constantly on the lookout for violations of Islamic dress, behavior, laws or customs. Most Saudis will not dare challenge the *Mutawwalin*. In all dealings with *Mutawwalin*, be courteous and responsive and be prepared to show identification documents if requested.

Road Travel Security: Roadblocks are increasingly common in Saudi Arabia. Exercise caution when driving.
Saudi security forces have made increased use of roadblocks on major highways throughout the kingdom to arrest terror suspects. These roadblocks may result in significant travel delays, especially in and near large cities, as authorities search vehicles and check identification papers. Several shootouts between police and Islamic militants have taken place at such roadblocks. If stopped at a roadblock, always be patient and cooperate with the police.

During the recent past, terrorists have made several attempts to assassinate Westerners in Saudi Arabia using bombs attached to the underside of a car. Do not leave your car unattended. Always lock your car. Carefully inspect your car, inside and outside - including underneath. If an unfamiliar or foreign object is found, do not touch it and immediately notify authorities. If there are no secure parking areas, select a well-lighted and non-isolated spot close to your residence.

Trips to isolated outlying areas can be dangerous. Drive a vehicle made and equipped for such a trip. Always travel in a convoy of two or more cars. Carry an extra supply of water and fuel and a second set of keys.

Source: iJet

Evaluation

⊕ Taken as a whole, travel advice is a suitable indicator of political risk.

⊕ The information is directly related to tourism.

⊕ The public's ever greater heeding of travel advice also means that travel advice is an indicator of public opinion and customer reaction.

⊖ Political influences have to be balanced out by comparing travel advice from different Foreign Offices and private companies.

⊖ Subject to geographical restrictions.

⊖ Sources are difficult to assess.

4.2.1.4 Indicators for ecological and health risks

Ecological and health risks are often the cause of crises in tourism. For the most part, these events were foreseeable. Despite frequently complex scientific contexts, causal dependencies are known that allow measurable indicators to be deduced, which point to the approaching changes in good time.

In addition, the technological progress makes a continuous and wide measuring of environmental indicators possible. Human beings were so far the limiting factor and one of the most important measuring instruments. Thus, useful indicators were limited to the capability of the person and the abilities of recognition. But this has changed in the meantime. Automatization now makes indicators feasible which would not have been measurable some years ago because of the enormous volume of data generated.

The different sensors used can be classified according to their location in satellite, ground, sea or atmosphere-based sensors. The practical examples of their use are manifold: Widely known is the use of sea and ground-based sensors for the collection of classical data such as temperature, wind speed, current or rainfall.

Less known are specialized sensors for the measurement of water pollution, pressure waves (for the detection of seaquakes) or atmosphere and satellite-based systems. The latter gained enormously in importance especially in the recent past. They are of particular use to monitor and collect data in extensive areas.

In the framework of the 'Earth Watching'-project of the European Space Agency (ESA), which was initiated at the end of 1993 as a consequence of the flooding in Germany, several satellites are used to monitor natural catastrophes. Radar satellites are mainly used for the detection of flooding and oil spills since they are able to draw even at night or with foggy weather conditions a clear picture of the situation. Optical sensors on the other hand are used to detect and monitor wildfires.

More focussed on early warnings than with 'Earth Watching' is the 'Epidemio'-project that the ESA is working on together with the World Health Organization (WHO). Both partners are concentrating on the early detection of Ebola and other epidemics. Satellites are also used worldwide for the detection of volcano activities and hurricanes but also for the alert of skin cancer as in Australia.

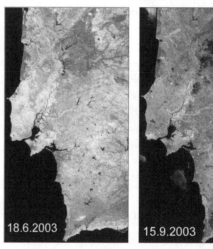

Fires in Portugal 2003

18.6.2003   15.9.2003

Pictures: ESA. These pictures show the devastating wildfires in Portugal in 2003. Taking pictures using bands in the Near Infrared (NIR) the full spectrum of the fires in the Algarve and in the north-east of Lisbon become visible.

Among the indicators for health risks two other systems which issue alerts for health risks are worth mentioning: The Centre for Disease Control and Prevention (CDC) and the World Health Organization (WHO). In addition to the travel advisories of the U.S. State Department, the CDC, also a U.S. governmental institution, issues for a great number of destinations specific warnings about actual health risks and explains the measures which can be taken to protect and prevent from them.

Similarly, the WHO, a specialized agency of the United Nations, makes regular communications on health risks and protection measures for the travellers. In addition, travel warnings can be issued. This instrument was until now only used by national states with the purpose of informing their own citizens. Such a warning was issued for the first time on the occasion of the SARS crisis. In the future a more active role of the WHO is to be expected. This is based on the fact that the WHO is strongly convinced that contagious diseases are currently spreading around the globe through tourism in just a few days. This makes an early and resolute handling of the situation necessary.

Example 26: The Use of Laser Scanner

St. Anton is a small village in the Austrian Alps with a population of some 2500 permanent inhabitants. Every year, especially during the winter season, many tourists arrive for winter sports in the village. With more than 1 million nights of stay, the guests are one of the most important sources of economic welfare.

Back in 1969 the first measures for the protection of the inhabitants and tourists were taken. Since 1988, an additional 17 million Euros were spent on avalanche protection which reached its peak with the Alpine Ski Championships in 2001. The devastating avalanches in Austria during the winter of 1999 shocked the population of St. Anton so much that further measures to improve the avalanche protection were decided on.

A result of these improvements was the first-time use of the laser scanner. Until its implementation, it was only possible to punctually measure the most important indicator for snow avalanches: the depth of snow. This changed dramatically with the laser scanner. The technological progress made

More protection from avalanches through laser scanner

Picture: Dibit Geoscanner System

available an instrument which could not only measure the depth of snow punctually but also without interruption up to a distance of 2300 meters.

Further improvements are scheduled. To attempt to control the situation even further and allow warnings to be generated during times of bad visibility, as they occur with snowfall and fog, the first tests with ground radar systems were undertaken.

Source: Sailer (2001)

For ecological and health risks it is especially important to analyse in good time important events and areas. For the area of ecological risks the use of indicators is especially recommendable if known negative events such as avalanches, volcano eruptions etc. need to be monitored. Through the triggered warning announcements, countermeasures or other steps can be taken to protect the population and the tourists. Health risks can usually be observed only through indirect indicators such as the warnings of the CDC or the WHO. However, one should not forget that the majority of health problems for typical travellers is diarrhoea which can be observed through indicators within critical areas such as restaurants and hotels (see also WTO, 1992).

It must, however, be noted that some ecological risks, those caused by human beings, for example, a ship disaster, are not foreseeable either by means of indicator-based systems or third-generation systems. However, since the consequences in this case are easy to judge, the direct observation of the events is less important than the perception of this area as critical and the introduction of appropriate planning measures in the form of contingency plans (see also Section 6.2).

4.2.1.5 Collecting and analysing information

Once the indicators have been chosen, regular collection and analysis of data must be guaranteed.

Basically, there are two possible ways of collecting the data: first, the data can be obtained from someone else. This is particularly suitable when the data has already been collected for other purposes. Since this form of data collection is, in principle, better than personal collection, the only thing left to check is whether the collection intervals meet the needs of early warning systems.

If it is not possible to get someone else to collect the data or if the collection intervals are too far apart, personal collection of the data is the only option available. This is more expensive and is caused by the initial establishment and acquisition of the necessary procedures, staff training, and maintaining the equipment in the future. In addition, the data collectors need to have the necessary abilities in order to ensure the validity and reliability of the data.

Regardless of the form of data collection, target values and tolerance thresholds for each indicator must still be assigned before the first collection of data. Measurements can then move within these limits without a warning being triggered (Hahn, 1979; WTO, 1996b; WTO, 1996c; WTO, 2004a). If these limits are exceeded, the reports are forwarded to the appropriate management level in a manner agreed beforehand.

It is to be recommended that warnings be classified in terms of exceedance level so that management can interpret the forwarded warning announcements more quickly. Both the target and tolerance values and the classification of the warning announcement must be decided upon when the indicator is chosen.

4.2.2 Early identification of weak signals

An essential prerequisite for the use of indicator-based systems is the presence of causal relationships between the observed indicators and the events. If this causal logic is not present, systems of the second generation normally fail. As a consequence, the events are classified as surprising and unpredictable. This situation appears increasingly more often in an environment that is becoming ever more complex and turbulent and it hinders the initiation of countermeasures.

Most of these surprises can be traced back to the so-called discontinuities. These are changes of direction, that is, new phenomena, for which there is no experience available. This hinders their detection and assessment considerably, but does not make it impossible. The suddenness of discontinuities affects rather less their occurrence and rather more their perception and assessment.

In principle, it is assumed that discontinuities are embedded in a longer-term development process and that they are influenced by human actions and interests. This is what the early identification systems of the third generation are based on.

In this context, Ansoff's (1981) concept of weak signals is of central importance. The aim was to show that even at a very early stage there is an opportunity for the management of a company to be proactive. It is, therefore, necessary to interpret and handle information in good time in an ongoing process of reality construction regarding peculiarity and effect. For the introduction of successful reaction strategies, it is imperative not to wait until the information has been well defined and its meaning assessed beyond all doubt. By that time, the affected organization is usually left with limited possibilities for reaction.

Ansoff (1981) clarifies this surprise problem for the organization by differentiating between available and used information, which he presents in three levels:

- The first information level concerns all of the information available – the 'general knowledge' – in the environment of the organization.

- The second level refers to the information available within the organization. This can be identical to the first level in terms of quantity, but differs qualitatively as a rule, because the organization does not pay attention to part of the information. The difference between this information and that of the first level comes from the abstractness, uncertainty and the lack of context of the received information, which does not permit a logically consistent assessment of the information. This so-called 'reaction gap' is a result of the fact that information is processed but not correctly classified as relevant to the organization.

- The third level describes information that is finally only used by company management. Despite its availability, information may still be discarded as too abstract, without correlation to the experiences and without relevance for the type of problem in question. This difference between available and used information is called the 'decision gap'.

According to Ansoff (1981), it must be a consistent aim of management to analyse and reduce both types of information gaps. The concept of weak signals, however, focuses specifically on the deficiencies from the first to second information levels, that is, on the increase of information from the corporate environment of importance for the organization.

There has been fundamental criticism of the concept, however. This focuses predominantly on the practical realization of the recognition of weak signals. On the one hand, the knowledge from problem-solving psychology is cited, according to which weak signals cannot be recognized due to the reduction strategies that a person uses because of his limited capacity to process information (Konrad, 1991). On the other hand, the concept is criticised in relation to knowledge from perception psychology that a person basically observes only those stimuli whose content and relevance he can judge.

Both criticisms are justified in terms of normal human behaviour. However, the systems evaluated in the following text try to overcome these human deficiencies. This means that even ways of thinking and interpretations, which seemed irrelevant and deviant at the time of the analysis, should be paid consistent and systematic attention (this is in accordance with the aim of creativity techniques, that is, to develop new ideas, thoughts and solutions to problems, in order to overcome thought barriers for unstructured information).

4.2.2.1 Discontinuities survey

In a discontinuities survey, experts are questioned on the probability of occurrence and effects of particular events by means of a questionnaire. The aim is the assessment and classification of these incidents as threats or opportunities for the company. Whilst the probability of occurrence is collected as a percentage, the experts class the effect using an interval scale from -4 for very unfavourable to +4 for very favourable. The two assessments must be carried out independently of each other.

Following the survey, the results are presented two-dimensionally and calculated '95 per cent probability ellipses and rectangles' are added. In this way, possible 'runaway' opinions can be identified. It is these opinions that are of particular interest. Through ensuing examinations, it is attempted to discover whether these deviations from the majority of the estimates should be put down to a consciously made new interpretation of the circumstances – a possible weak signal – or to another source of error, such as lack of understanding or expert knowledge. To do this, the motives of the outsiders must be examined more closely through individual deep analysis.

A further result of this analysis is the interpretation of the spread of the presented opinions. If this is high, this means that the opinions vary greatly and that there is great uncertainty about the possible effect of the events. In this case too, deep analyses must be used for further clarification.

Evaluation

+ The particular value of the discontinuities survey lies in conveying outsider information, which does not sink without trace in a condensed value.

− A minimum of twenty to thirty qualified experts is required.

− The selection of events through the pre-formulation of questions makes the quality of the results dependent upon the specific selection of events included.

− The separation of outsiders' opinion is practically impossible if the spread of the statements is high overall.

4.2.2.2 Portfolio analysis

In practice, portfolio analysis had already been well disseminated when it was further developed for analysing weak signals. All variations of this analysis were based on the system-theoretical finding that the development of an organization is dependent on the particular interrelation of different internal factors with the corporate environment. Further development took place under the conviction that no new subsystems needed to be introduced in order to locate weak signals.

The general aim of portfolio analysis is to assess, in a comparable way, the delimited 'strategic business units' of a company in various situations with regard to their opportunities and threats. The expert

Diagram 30: Area positioning in the portfolio analysis

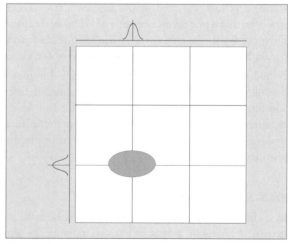

Source: Adapted from Kirsch and Trux (1979)

126

assessments are finally portrayed in a portfolio matrix. However, since an accurate determination of the position requires a consensus from the participants in the assessment process, the uncertainties and dissenting opinions are normally lost.

At this point, further development begins. In place of an exactly accurate determination, the deviations in the assessment are consciously emphasized, by carrying out an area positioning. In this way, the assessment discrepancies are no longer hidden from the management, which can process them further in a much more targeted way.

The size of the relevant blurred areas allows conclusions to be drawn about the degree of uncertainty in the estimations. These blurred areas can be interpreted as weak signals. To analyse them more closely, however, management must discuss the causes of the dissenting assessments. Only this deep analysis can provide information about what is causing the weak signals, how they are to be assessed and what effects are to be expected.

Evaluation

⊕ In contrast to discontinuities surveys, portfolio analysis has the advantage that it avoids the necessary pre-selection of events. In this way, an early restriction on the alternatives considered is prevented.

⊕ A probability assessment, which is quite problematic, in particular with regard to events that are dependent on many influences, is spared.

⊕ In practice the wide application of the portfolio analysis and, therefore, the available knowledge, is useful.

⊕ A disadvantage that stands out is the need for duly qualified experts. This problem is reduced at least in the case of already practised portfolio analyses. Nevertheless, deep analyses are still necessary and these require a thorough knowledge of the company on the part of the interviewer.

4.2.2.3 Structural trend lines

The development of structural trend lines as an instrument for early detection of weak signals goes back to diffusion theory and paradigm change findings (Krampe and Müller, 1981). Thus, new findings and models of behaviour spread in a kind of infection process, at the beginning of which there is an innovator or an event, and at the end, a widespread impact. The decisive point is the assumption, upon which the considerations are based, that distribution processes follow a specific pattern, which is shown as diffusion function or structural trend lines. In these patterns, which are not universally applicable but rather area-specific, the starting point for the formation of entrepreneurial early warnings can be seen.

Diagram 31: Structural trend lines for triggering events

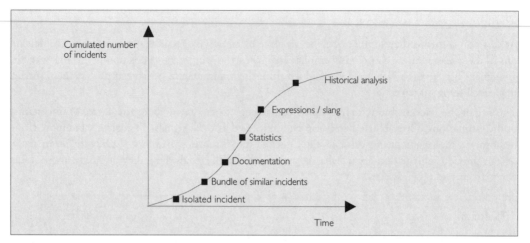

Source: Adapted from Krampe and Müller (1981)

Through the observation and analysis of the important observation spheres of the company, representative distribution functions are developed. They can be improvised in the beginning, when there is still little experience available. Diagram 31 shows a visualized trend line for the effect of accidents, in this case, tanker accidents.

Using the forerunner of events and developments of interest discovered in this way, an observation system can be installed, which recognizes, earlier than before, similar events or developments or those from the same area of origin. The aim is to detect the change in the phase from isolated to cumulated incidents. Due to the purely qualitative nature of the information at this stage, this is not easy, but a later identification would barely still permit promising measures.

Example from the social legislation

Normally, Scandinavian countries play a leading role in social welfare legislation. They, and in particular Sweden, therefore, come in the first position on structural trend lines for this area. If draft bills are introduced in these countries, this gives the first signal for similar processes at a later date in other countries. It should be noted, however, that in tourism, this national leading role – in particular, in terms of consumer protection – is attributed to Germany.

Evaluation

(+) Structural trend lines help to identify in good time a multitude of events in the environment through the observation of forerunners.

(+)(−) The quality and reliability of this system depends to a large extent on the adjustment of the trend lines to the specific peculiarities of the organization.

(−) The system is time consuming and the ongoing observation of the changes requires experienced and trained personnel.

4.2.2.4 Defining the contextual conditions of matters of social concern

The social environment of a company is, to a considerable extent, responsible for determining which events trigger a crisis at the affected organization. This influence is strengthened by the fact that companies ever more frequently have to justify themselves concerning social problems and this means that they themselves become a topic of debate.

In order to have a better understanding of the underlying processes and to develop helpful courses of action for the affected companies, models that analyse matters of social concern are produced. They do not really focus on the prediction of events, but rather on classifying whether or not these events pose a threat to the organization.

The various scientific approaches that deal with matters of social concern are all part of a development process that is split into phases. In these phases, an examination is carried out to determine which influence factors are beneficial or harmful to development. The development of a matter of social concern will be described using Dyllick's (1992) five-phase lifecycle concept.

Triggered by an event that is in discrepancy to predominant expectations, a matter of social concern (need for action) is established in the latency phase. It is generally assumed that social matters of concern exist when '… there is a difference between the expectations about the state of reality and the perceived reality of a social area, which is considered to be intolerable' (Dyllick, 1992). In the following emergence phase, the events occur increasingly often whilst, because of this, scientific discussion certainly increases. This discussion remains limited to experts. Only in the upturn phase is the matter taken up by interest groups which have now become stakeholders and brought to the attention of the public. These groups pursue the goal of achieving public awareness of the matter and influencing public opinion. In this phase, politicians join in with the opinion-forming process and the mass media also becomes active. Apart from setting the exact aim, the discussion revolves around the 'politically valid version of the matter'. In the maturing phase, the political/normative regulation of the matter is pursued, whereby expert opinion is once again at the fore. At the same time, media interest diminishes and public awareness stagnates. Finally, in the downturn phase, the completion of the regulations clearly moves back to the fore and public interest decreases.

The lifecycle model is, in this form, predominantly a tool for determining the current status of a matter of social concern and estimating its dynamics. The state of development, that is, the phase in which a matter is, can only be determined by indirect criteria such as the type and size of the participating groups, the social or political status of these groups or the dissemination and frequency of media reports that influence the degree of public awareness. Whether and how the organization should react is derived from these findings. It is generally true that the more important and urgent the matter, the higher the degree of public awareness reached.

It is clear that, with this procedure, the focus is on the analysis of contextual conditions and not on the prediction of events. The basic conviction is that a current event cannot be considered in isolation from its background variables when attempting to estimate its possibility for development. The basic contextual conditions, which result from a combination

---

Positive terms of reference

For the 1988 mine accident in Borken (Germany) this approach proved to be extremely helpful. The positive terms of reference for coal as a source of energy explained why the accident and risks were classified as unavoidable and acceptable. The otherwise normal demands, that is, to improve security or even to abandon coal mining, were omitted.

Source: Mathes, Gärtner and Czaplicki (1991)

of social value position, public sensitivity and the agenda of relevant stakeholders, are to be considered much more.

In this context, Mathes, Gärtner and Czaplicki (1991) speak of the terms of reference according to which an event is classified. In concrete terms, they recommend that general coverage for all important company areas be analysed using quantitative content analysis in order to define these terms of reference. In this way, by means of separate encoding, news items, reports and commentaries are evaluated as to whether they contain positive or negative assessments, whether positive or negative characteristics or consequences are attributed to them, whether the events can be influenced by people and whether the experts are credible or not. Surveys, scenario techniques or regular contact with and observation of the interest groups are also suitable methods for determining the terms of reference.

Example 27: Terms of Reference

The significance of the terms of reference is also highlighted by the events relating to the sinking of the Brent Spar oil-loading rig in 1995.

Although Shell, owner of this oil-loading rig, worked at that time with various early warning systems, none, however, indicated the upcoming conflict with Greenpeace nor could generate a warning. Even the additional analyses that were undertaken at a later stage would have changed this assessment.

This can be explained, above all, by the fact that it concerned an action planned by humans as a surprise, which, similar to terrorist actions, can only be identified with difficulty, but which can be predicted as theoretically possible.

By the cessation of the events in their terms of reference, however, whereby the North Sea – as a polluted area – has already often been the subject of environmental-political discussions, another conclusion would have been reached after the onset of the action. The so-called terms of reference were clearly recognizable and classified as negative; consequently, the later effects of the events were foreseeable.

Herein lies a particular problem for most organizations because it is difficult for people who are directly involved to recognize such slowly developing terms of reference and to assess them correctly.

Evaluation

⊕ The analysis of contextual conditions differs from the previous models because its approach is geared towards observed events. This procedure is of practical relevance because, for many crises, it is less about the timely perception of events as unfavourable incidents than about the correct prediction of further effect developments.

⊖ The system is time-consuming and the ongoing observation of the changes requires experienced and trained personnel.

4.2.2.5 Computer-based early warning systems

Automatic early warnings have made enormous advances in the recent past. Especially since the attacks of September 11 in the USA, many public and semi-public institutions were encouraged and backed with enormous financial support to develop better early warning systems. New and old approaches were looked at, improved and developed further. Different approaches can be distinguished.

Some approaches tried to automize the techniques for the identification of weak signals already described (see for example Schulten, 1995; Kelders, 1996 or Jossé, 2004). Now they use the advantages of computers to overcome the problem of complex observations and analyses, which come together with continuous monitoring. These systems require a human interface to provide the necessary information about the social environment or try to import it through text-based sources from news agencies or newspapers. Although the process of importing and collecting the information is solved, 'understanding' the information is still the major problem for these systems.

> The trading on the Hollywood Stock Exchange is a reliable indicator of the nominations for the Oscars. In 2004, 29 out of the 39 nominations were forecasted. The years before similar results were achieved:
>
> 33 out of 40, 2003
>
> 35 out of 40, 2002
>
> 33 out of 39, 2001
>
> 31 out of 39, 2000
>
> 32 out of 38, 1999
>
> Results of this kind are also conformed from other markets. It is said that the trade of futures on orange juice gives a better forecast on the weather in Florida than the forecast from meteorologists.

Simulation models

Simulation models for modelling social and economic systems try, based on historical, actual or hypothetical data, to forecast future developments. Although simulation models for social systems still cannot replicate human living conditions in all detail, useful results can be achieved through the use of mathematical models for the collective instead than for the individual behaviour. To obtain these results, a general knowledge about what shall be observed as an event is required. Thus simulation models are used partly to forecast natural catastrophes such as hurricanes or flooding. However, the main field of application for simulation models lays in the identification of the further course of action, e.g. to optimized escape routes, or to identify important areas, e.g. when especially threatened areas are identified or places for sensors are determined for indicator-based early warning systems.

Artificial markets

Artificial markets also gained in importance when it comes to forecasting events. Already existing in the 1980s, the Iowa Electronics Market was used in 1998 for the forecasting of the outcome of the presidential elections in the USA. Artificial markets are not designed for the exchange of real goods or services. They exist for the sole purpose of obtaining information. They are used to forecast elections, the weather, demand or the winners of Oscars.

The American 'Defense Advanced Research Projects Agency' (Darpa) presented in 2003 an artificial market (FutureMAP) for the prognosis of future events of importance for the U.S. administration. The core problem of the weak signal analysis, the identification of those signals out of the enormous amount of information was planned to be resolved with the market mechanisms of a stock exchange. As political events, which are planned or influenced by human beings are going through a development process, early informed persons and experts would have the chance, using the market mechanisms, to trade this information for their personal benefit. The following market changes would serve as a weak signal and indicate appearing changes. Although this approach was seen by the scientific community as useful, the project had to be cancelled due to political concerns before the market was officially launched.

Structure of the IDOL Server

Source: Autonomy (2005)

Significant progress was achieved in the field of filtering and interpretation of information. The British/American Company *Autonomy* is using for this the Bayesian Interference Theorem and Shannon's Information Theory and has developed the software, IDOL Server. Based on the assumption that 80 per cent of the digital information held available in the environment and within one's own organization is only accessible in an unstructured format, the system aims at becoming as much independent as possible from classical and manual processes.

Information can be imported by the system in text, audio or audiovisual forms. Information in foreign languages is only causing limited additional effort. As words in languages are interpreted in their context and not in their grammatical structures, the language barrier is only of minor importance.

The data is analysed in its context by the 'Dynamic Reasoning Engine' in such a way that the relation to topics is made possible. This happens even if the topic is not mentioned as a word within the information piece. This is possible because of statistical probability modelling. The programme analyses existing 'information pieces' which already belong to a certain category; the new 'information piece' is then added to the category based on similarities of the contexts that they are used in. As the assignation to one category does not exclude the assignation to another category or even to several others, a comprehensive approach is possible. This is the main difference in comparison to other software products that still require manual categorization or metadata and thus have only limited possibilities to overcome the main problem of weak signals, information overflow and limited resources.

The software offers different interfaces and allows a wide range of applications. In call centres for example, the software can identify topics that are discussed between clients and call centre personnel more frequently, although all parties are acting independently from each other. That way arising problems can be identified at an early stage, which would otherwise only be available through intricate surveys. As the software also examines the tone of the voice of the caller (e.g. tense or relaxed), an analysis, until now impossible even with content analysis, is becoming feasible.

The wide use of this system within governmental administrations for the generation of early warning signals confirms that this procedure of information analyses is promising. With its application for the early warning of security events during the summer Olympics in Athens (Greece) in 2004, the programme had already experienced its first important employment in the field of tourism.

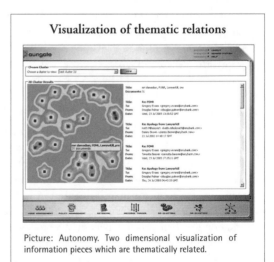

Picture: Autonomy. Two dimensional visualization of information pieces which are thematically related.

In general, it is to be expected that in the field of early warning, further significant progress will be made. The technological progress allows us to make these approaches possible, which up to now were unthinkable. Nevertheless, the element of surprise will still exist. Similar to the surprising and fast rising success of some companies in this field, it is unavoidable that some negative events will be discovered only once a certain effect has already unfolded.

Evaluation

⊕ Only way of collecting and processing a large quantity of information without limiting it beforehand.

⊕ Typical human deficiencies in the perceiving of information, which actually hinder the detection of weak signals, are almost completely eliminated.

⊖ Developments are in the early stages although enormous progress was made in the recent past.

⊖ Human beings are still required to make the final assessment based on their knowledge, intuition and experience.

4.2.3 Limitations and possibilities of early warning

A prerequisite for successful crisis management is the timely recognition of negative events. This requires a systematically-operated and well-functioning early warning system.

The analysis of various early warning possibilities reveals that both indicator-based systems and those based on weak signals are appropriate. Already in 1992 Krystek and Müller-Stewens point out that certain environmental events are, therefore, only interpreted as weak signals, because no indicators have been determined for this early warning area. This observation is still correct.

The particular advantage of indicator-based systems is that they are simple to apply and to maintain. In addition, they offer the possibility, to a certain extent, of determining automized measurements. This form of early warning seems suitable for the area of ecological and health risks. For the social and political environment, the usability of indicators is determined by the time horizon of the early warning. If this is more towards the short term – which is true for tour operators without direct investment in foreign countries – indicators offer completely useable early warning information.

The observation of weak signals is particularly important for the social environment. It is to be noted that, for destinations and international tour operators, these are in the source market of the tourists. The low use of third-generation systems is basically due to the high amount of time required and their complex handling. Furthermore, classic methods have been shown to be deficient in evaluating rapid changes in the social environment. As most of the methods were developed for the strategic planning of the organization their usability for processes with shorter development cycles is considerably limited. In particular, quick changes in the social environment, which are shown to be responsible for many crises in tourism, can only be recorded with difficulty. This is surely the reason why, in practice, such early warning processes are only used to a limited extent. Still one of the oldest instruments of early warning dominates the consultation of one's own employees who work at the forefront of the organization.

Computer-based systems have to be seen in practice as the preferable alternative for the identification of weak signals. It is the only way of collecting and processing a large quantity of information without limiting it beforehand. Moreover, typical human deficiencies in the perceiving of information, which actually hinder the detection of weak signals, are almost completely eliminated. Artificial markets and software developments as from *Autonomy* are relatively young products but very good examples of the possibilities already available nowadays and – above all – indications of what developments are to be expected.

However, it must be noted that in the near future all these systems will still have to do the preliminary work for human beings, who with their knowledge, intuition and experience make the final assessment.

Questions for review and discussion

- How does a scenario analysis work?
- Which areas are suitable for the use of indicators?
- What has to be taken into account for the selection of indicators?
- What are the problems when formulating travel advisories?
- What importance do the contextual conditions of matters of social concern have?
- Explain the effects of a negative image transfer.
- Why are weak signals so difficult to detect?
- What are artificial markets?
- Name promising techniques for the detection of weak signals.

Suggestions for further reading

Ansoff, H. I. (1981), 'Managing Surprise and Discontinuity – Strategic Response to Weak Signals', *Zeitschrift für betriebswirtschaftliche Forschung*, 28(1), pp. 129-152.

Autonomy (2005), *Understanding the Hidden 80%*, Autonomy, Cambridge.

Coface (2004), *Risque Pays 2004*, Sedec, Paris.

Control Risks (2004), *Risk Map 2005*, Control Risks Group, London.

Mayerhofer, W. (1995), *Imagetransfer*, Service Fachverlag, Wien.

Sharpley, R. and Sharpley, J. (1995), 'Travel advice – security or politics?', in *Security and Risks in Travel and Tourism (Proceedings of the International Conference at Mid Sweden University)*, Mid Sweden University, Östersund, pp. 168-182.

VisitScotland (2005), *Avian Flu: A Pandemic Waiting to Happen (A Briefing Paper)*, VisitScotland, Edinburgh.

World Tourism Organization (2000), *Global Code of Ethics for Tourism*, WTO, Madrid.

World Tourism Organization (2004), *Indicators of Sustainable Development of Tourism Destinations*, WTO, Madrid.

World Tourism Organization (2005), *Document A/16/22 – Recommendations on Travel Advisories*, WTO, Madrid.

Yeoman, I., Galt, M. and McMahon-Beattie, U. (2005), 'A Case Study of How VisitScotland Prepared for War', *Journal of Travel Research*, 44(1), pp. 6-20.

Useful websites

Travel advice
Australia: www.dfat.gov.au

Austria: www.bmaa.gv.at

Belgium: www.diplomatie.be

Canada: www.voyage.gc.ca

Centre for Disease Control and Prevention: www.cdc.gov/travel

France: www.france.diplomatie.fr

Germany: www.auswaertiges-amt.de

Italy (only in Italian; published by the Italian automobile club): www.viaggiaresicuri.mae.aci.it

Japan (only in Japanese) www.pubanzen.mofa.go.jp

New Zealand: www.mft.govt.nz

South Africa: www.dfa.gov.za

Spain: www.mae.es

USA: www.travel.state.gov

United Kingdom: www.fco.gov.uk

WHO: www.who.int

Artificial Markets
Hollywood Stock Exchange: www.hsx.com

Tradesports: www.tradesports.com

Wahlstreet: www.wahlstreet.de

Others
www.autonomy.com

www.beri.com

www.coface.com

www.esa.int

www.ijet.com

5 Strategic measures of crisis management

Objectives

- To understand the possibilities of preventive crisis management both within the framework of corporate strategy as well as through strategic actions
- To recognize the advantages and disadvantages of strategic actions
- To be aware of the necessity of an early and critical examination of crisis handling strategies

Key terms and concepts

- Corporate strategy
- Competitive advantage
- Strategic actions
- Crisis handling strategies

5.1 Preventive crisis management within the framework of corporate strategy

All those responsible for the success and failure of organizations have to tackle with the different aspects of their corporate strategy if they want to achieve lasting success in the market. This includes timely analysis of the possible consequences that negative events have on these strategies.

The aim of generic strategy is to lay the foundations for the long-term success of an organization. Competitive advantage, which must be considered from the customer's point of view, embody a meaningful customer benefit, which ensures that the company, or product, permanently and clearly distinguishes itself from its competitors. Competitive advantages have, in order to be strategically significant, to fulfil three basic requirements:

- they must provide an important performance feature for the customer,
- actually be perceived by the customer, and
- be sustainable, that is, difficult for competitors to imitate.

In their basic form, there are two types of competitive advantage: cost advantage and differentiation advantage. Whilst the former achieves advantage by charging a lower price in comparison with the competition, for products with the equivalent benefits, differentiation advantage requires the company to create a unique benefit that justifies a higher price in the eyes of the consumer (Porter, 1998a).

Based upon the competitive advantages, cost advantage and differentiation advantage, and taking into account the scope of activities, three generic strategies can be distinguished:

- cost leadership,
- differentiation and
- focus strategy.

Porter (1998a) points out that a company can use strategies of cost leadership and differentiation at the same time completely successfully, if it is in a position to keep the different company units strictly separate. The essential criterion for this separation is the consumer's perception.

5.1.1 Cost leadership

With a cost leadership strategy, the company offers a comparable standard product at a lower price than its competitors. It is important that the product attributes are perceived by the customers to be identical or equivalent to that of the competition.

The basis of this strategy is the company's ability to produce at a lower cost than its competitors. The causes of this are diverse and can be based on the learning curve effect, particular preference conditions or technology exclusive to the firm. When following this strategy, the company must be aware that there can only be one cost leader in the sector, unless a focus strategy is followed for a certain segment of the market.

As a consequence of the necessary comparability of the products comes interchangeability. This possibility for substitution could be a considerable problem if there is a negative event. If one of the basic product characteristics is harmed by the negative event, the basis for cost advantage – comparability – is lost. Substitution products would be bought in place of the affected product. The same effect occurs when personal safety is threatened by a negative event. In this case, the perception of risk increases and the tourism product in question is – after the exceedance of a certain threshold value – no longer seen as comparable.

Since in both cases the necessary requirement of the comparable standard product is no longer fulfilled, the effect of cost advantage is lost. The only way to keep up this strategy in the long term and to make the product still saleable is with a price policy. This instrument can balance out the higher sensitivity by lowering the price. The leeway is, however, restricted because of the given cost structure. The consequences of lowering the price are short- and medium-term collapses in profit (there are also further consequences that limit the use of price instruments; see a discussion on this in Section 7.3).

The long-term problem lies in sustaining the cost advantage, since this is based as a rule on higher relative market shares. A change can cause a vicious circle effect: diminishing market shares, and disappearance of cost advantage, leading, in turn, to a limitation of the price policy. This effect can finally lead to the stage when a cost leadership strategy is no longer sustainable and must be changed completely.

The great susceptibility and limited possibilities for action in the framework of coping crisis management illustrate how important crisis precautions are in this case. They must be used to prevent the onset of such events, or to bring them to an end in good time.

5.1.2 Differentiation

With a differentiation strategy, the company's aim is to differentiate itself from its competitors through the characteristics of the product in such a way that it allows the firm to charge a premium price for it. Differentiation strategies are very important in tourism because the majority of products are interchangeable and there is little room for improvement in terms of objective differences. In contrast to a cost leadership strategy, several companies in the same sector can successfully follow a differentiation strategy.

The differentiation can be achieved both by material and immaterial changes to the product. The decisive thing is that as many customers of the sector as possible perceive the differentiation as unique and important. Only then is it possible for the organization to achieve long-term above-average profits that exceed the additional expenditure on differentiation.

While the aspect of material differentiation occupies an important position in the business travel market the immaterial differentiation is very important for holiday tourism. The exact immaterial differentiation is carried out by developing and implementing an experience value strategy. This strategy gives the product an image profile that has unique, distinctive and sustainable advantages over competing products. A clear dividing line has to be drawn between this strategy, which normally goes along with a 'Total Quality Management' strategy, and active publicity, which, in contrast to the experience value strategy, does not build 'company-specific preferences' (Konert, 1986; Kroeber-Riel, 1992).

To be relevant, experience value strategies must take the values, lifestyle and experiences of the target group into consideration. According to Kroeber-Riel (1993a) it must be checked whether the experience profile:

• has psychological relevance,
• is not in conflict with the company philosophy,
• appeals long-term to the target group and therefore keeps up with lifestyle trends,
• makes an effective positioning possible in comparison to the competition and
• is able to be introduced not only through advertising, but extensively.

Since image profiles can only be generated and established through ongoing and long-term conditioning, experience value strategies must not only be valid in the long term, but also developed with an eye to the future. This means that the development must be accompanied by a serious discussion of future social trends.

A point not considered until now is the demand for consistency and freedom from contradiction of experience-oriented positioning, also from the point of view of future negative events. Even at the conception and assessment of possible experience profiles, it is important to think about certain events that are more likely or more threatening than others. This can make a considerable contribution to preventive crisis management.

Example 28: The Experience Value Strategy of Liechtenstein

With only 34 000 inhabitants on 160 square km, the image of Liechtenstein has been suffering for decades from the fact that it is sandwiched between its two big neighbors Switzerland and Austria. Only the financial sector contributed to a diversification of the image of Liechtenstein, whose people lived off primarily of agriculture some 80 years ago, and helped to make the country known beyond the European boundaries. But this fame was of doubtful quality as it came together with the reputation of a paradise for letter-box companies and tax heaven. Finally in 2000, the OECD raised concerns that Liechtenstein had become a centre for money laundering. This was not only counter-productive for the tourism sector but also for all other economic activities as well as the self-understanding of the people of Liechtenstein. The culminating point was a rather emotional confrontation after the Prince won the right to veto laws and elect judges.

It became obvious that there was need for change. In 2001 the government decided not only to focus on those allegations but also to prepare the ground for attracting more foreign investments, companies and tourists. In March 2002 the 'Image Liechtenstein Foundation Group' was founded. Chaired by the prime minister, the group was composed of representatives from the government, state agencies and leading trade associations. The members started to assess the domestic and foreign perceptions of Liechtenstein and in May 2003, they submitted their recommendations to overcome the identified weaknesses.

It was especially proposed to fundamentally improve the Internet presence of Liechtenstein, followed by the recommendation to expand the foreign missions from 2 to 8, besides Bern and Vienna also in Brussels, Berlin, New York City and Washington, D.C. It was also particularly recommended to develop a new positioning for Liechtenstein and to launch it as a brand.

For this, in November 2003 an international contest took place, and the winner was the international branding consultancy Wolff

Source: Foundation Image Liechtenstein

Olins. This company which also produced the widely known campaign 'I love New York' systematically developed the elements which shall shape the image of Liechtenstein in the future. Unknown in its consequent approach, the country developed a differentiation strategy and symbols, which will not replace the existing official emblems but complement them.

140

> On 20 September 2004 the Prime Minister officially launched the campaign to the world public in London.
>
> The case of Liechtenstein is a remarkable example that destinations not only look after their image but also evaluate their positioning from scratch, plan and finally construct the new image through experience value strategies.

A further point to consider is based on the finding that destinations are strongly influenced by typical clichés and over-generalizations. This must likewise be considered while developing conceptually the image profile. The spillover effects of a regional image on those destinations that have not been affected by events will cause them to suffer indirectly from it. Indeed, in a normal situation, independent positioning goes hand-in-hand with increased expenditure; however, this effort pays off through a certain crisis resistance. In the practical implementation, the image dimensions, which are responsible for the whole region's image in the source markets, must be included, analysed and finally changed in such a way that an independent sustained positioning is achieved.

> **Example 29: Egypt and its Beach Destinations**
>
> Although while developing the product of beach holidays as a new product area, Egypt did not explicitly consider it under the aspect of strategic crisis management, the later consequences proved that these decisions had positive results seeing it from the point of view of strategic crisis management.
>
> The various terrorist attacks of 1992/1993 led to a negative overall image of Egypt. However, consumers in the various source markets did not perceive the beach destinations 'Sinai' and 'Red Sea' related to this image. This strategically unplanned separation of the two products, independent from each other as far as image was concerned, was quickly recognised and used by the destinations and tour operators alike.
>
> Since then, the destinations on the Sinai and the Red Sea have been offered without making reference to Egypt. All textual and pictorial information was removed from advertising to prevent a connection between Egypt and the beach destinations.

This means that experience value strategies and experience profiles should be designed from the start in such a way that they can only be spoiled with difficulty by potential events. Even if as a consequence of negative events crisis circumstances cannot be totally excluded, there is the possibility of ruling out certain susceptible concepts in good time.

It remains to be emphasized that it is, above all the long-termness that demands a cautious and considered planning of the experience value strategy also from the point of view of negative events. Investment in the development of immaterial differentiation is considerable and the company only makes a return on its investment in the medium or long term, in the form of higher profits. Developed experience value strategies and built-up image profiles are not really changeable in the short term. Likewise destroyed and influenced image profiles mean the loss of considerable investment. For the tourism market, in which the number of products with interchangeable benefits is increasing and which is, therefore, more and more dependent upon immaterial differentiation, this kind of prevention is becoming ever more important.

5.1.3 Focus strategy

The focus strategy concentrates on a narrow segment and within that segment attempts to achieve either a cost advantage or differentiation. While the basis for the first strategy variation is different cost behaviour, the latter requires the existence of special customer needs. When there is sufficient structural attraction of the segment within the sector, several companies can, as with the differentiation strategy, follow a concentration strategy, as long as their target segments are different.

Typical for tour operators is concentration on segments of the supply market – destinations – or on segments of the sales market. From the point of view of a destination, the concentration strategy refers to the choice of certain customer segments.

Since concentration strategies go back to cost and differentiation advantages, observations made above are valid here too. However, in this case there is also the fact that a concentration on a particular segment follows. Dependence on the choice of this segment limits the leeway for action considerably.

Example 30: Risk of a Focus Strategy

The risks of a focus strategy are shown with the example of the German tour operator 'OFT Reisen'. This tour operator concentrated on study trips to Egypt. Therefore, there was considerable dependency on the development of this customer segment and of the destination.

As a consequence of the attacks in 1997, participant numbers fell from over 30 000 to just 10 000 customers per annum. In the same period, turnover fell from 31.6 to 10.6 million Euro. This effect was softened by changing the emphasis to other customer segments. Pure beach holidaymakers, whose share rose from 20 to 82 per cent, replaced the normal 80 per cent share of student tourists.

However, as a result of these developments, the tour operator had to give up some of its independence.

In spite of the risk that goes with a focus strategy in terms of negative events, this strategy is becoming ever more important as an answer to the individualization of consumption. In order to introduce measures in the framework of crisis management, it is recommendable to use the international dimensions of these developments. Since this fragmentation of segments also happens internationally, there are intercultural target groups, which show similar needs structures and can be appealed to in the same way. If it is considered that negative events are also judged differently due to national and cultural differences, it makes it clear that there are reaction possibilities. These require an appropriate international capability for action, which, if it is not yet given, can be a preventive crisis management measure.

Finally, it must be emphasized that especially for this strategy variation, the extent of the precautions must increase in relation to how small the market basis is. If this is not done in an area as sensitive as tourism, unforeseeable negative events lead with greater probability to an abandonment of business activity.

5.2 Preventive crisis management measures through strategic actions

It is already known in risk management that there are possibilities to limit the risks through strategic actions.

The aim with strategic actions such as the configuration of the company, the contractual relations to other companies and its own appearance, is to contribute to limiting, or rather easing, the effects of negative events. In addition, these measures are intended to make the causal areas of negative events at least jointly responsible in economic or legal terms, as this will effectively limit the sources of negative events.

Next, several approaches are looked at and their applicability to tourism is evaluated. They do not exclude, but rather clarify the different directions of possible measures. Since the actual success is basically strongly determined by the type of event and specific situation, the following discussions can contribute to a choice decision, but they are not universally valid. The variations are:

- diversification,
- transfer,
- cooperation,
- insurance and
- self-bearing.

5.2.1 Diversification

Diversification is understood to be the preventive measures that serve the distribution of company activities with the aim of scattering and keeping the consequences of negative events low. Through the distribution of activities on several profit sources, a balance is created that can compensate for the harming of one source. The strength of the counterbalance is determined, above all, by its perceived complementarity to the event in terms of crisis susceptibility.

Example 31: The Case of Gambia

Gambia is a country of West Africa with 1.2 million inhabitants. As a former British colony, the country became an independent State within the Commonwealth in 1995. Gambia's economy is poor and depends almost entirely on the cultivation and exportation of groundnuts in the form of nuts, oil and cattle cake.

Tourism has rapidly grown and reached in 1994 more than 78 000 international tourist arrivals, thus becoming an important foreign currency earner. However, the distribution of this tourism has proved to be quite uneven.

From the beginning, Gambia depended heavily on tourists from the UK. At this time, more than 60 per cent of all charter flights originated in the UK and resulted in 52 000 out of the 78 000 arrivals into the country in 1994.

This special dependency proved to be fatal for the economy. By November 1994, the Travel Advise Unit of the British Foreign and Commonwealth Office issued the third travel advice

---

within half a year concerning Gambia. Due to a military coup five months earlier, the political situation was considered unstable and travellers were recommended to postpone their travel plans, if possible.

As a result, all British tour operators except one, cancelled their operations immediately and ceased the entire scheduled winter programmes. The Scandinavian operators followed quickly and also left. Finally, only the Dutch and German tour operators continued to act normally. The number of British tourists dropped by 73 per cent down to 14 000.

This loss had an enormous impact not only on the tourism-related sectors but on the entire Gambian economy. More than 1000

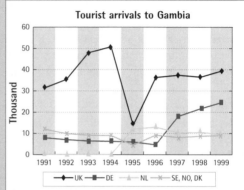

jobs disappeared in the hotel industry and at least eight hotels had to be closed. People indirectly dependent on tourism such as taxi drivers and souvenir sellers also lost their primary source of income. The sudden drop in revenue from tourism-related sources such as sales-tax, airport departure tax and import duties led to a serious lack of foreign currency. In addition, with the abandonment of charter flights that used to serve as freight carriers, products could no longer be taken out of the country and an additional thousand jobs were lost in the country's largest horticulture business. Besides this, other sectors such as agriculture and brewing also suffered severe economic declines.

These heavy aftermaths of the issued travel advice can mainly be traced back to the particularly strong focus of Gambia's tourism industry on the British market and its dependency on few tour operators. While in times of tourism growth this strategy is highly successful, in times of crisis the problems rise disproportionately and can create a very serious situation. To prevent this, a further diversification on markets and products is recommendable. As the above chart shows, the arrivals of German and Dutch tourists remained stable during this travel warning, but nevertheless their share was too small to compensate for the withdrawal of the British visitors.

Source: Sharpley and Sharpley (1995)

Horizontal Diversification

For the horizontal diversification, that is, changing the sales programme through products that are complementary to the organization's existing activities, the viewpoint of the tourists must be taken into consideration for this balance assessment. What has been considered a balance from a risk-political viewpoint is determined by the event, or rather by how the event is perceived. If it has a regional reference, another destination creates the balance and, if it has a functional reference, then the balance is achieved by the type of product. If the negative event shows a reference typical to the company, switching to another company is suggested. The diversification means, in this extreme case, the buy out or new formation of the company.

> **Example 32: Diversification in the Hotel Portfolio**
>
> The classical hotel business is subject to strong competition. This is also the case for the Kempinski Hotel Group whose origin goes back to the year 1896 and which nowadays specialises in hotel management.
>
> Traditionally the group was strongly dependent on the German market, which contributed until recent times with 90 per cent of the company's profits. To reduce this dependency and to minimize its exposure to crisis, the company took the strategic decision to diversify systematically.
>
> In the first place the company now aims at geographical distribution of its activities. Interestingly, this does not always lead to classical destinations but also to areas which have been classed as risky. The company seeks a good mix of risks and revenues. While hotels in traditional destinations such as London, Madrid and Paris are constantly suffering from low margins, hotels in Mali and Chad have high occupancy rates and revenues. Still the aim is that four out of five hotels are located in areas with little risk. However, every fifth hotel is allowed to be a financial risk if above-average revenues are produced.
>
> Diversification across the different possible future crises is also carried out through the types of hotels. City hotels have proved to be more crisis resistant than holiday resorts. Consequently, a mix of 60 per cent city hotels to 30 resorts and 10 per cent airport and congress hotels is the future goal of the company.

Vertical diversification, which refers to the preceding or succeeding stages in the organization's production process, is recommendable when dependencies on external suppliers, which are of existential importance in a crisis, come to light. Through vertical diversification, self-sufficiency (autarky) is achieved, which helps in the avoidance of crises. The completed relationships must not lead to a complete takeover of the other company. They can also be carried out in the form of strategic alliances. Through this interconnection, economic dependencies are achieved which serve the same purpose.

The downside of a diversification strategy from a risk viewpoint is that the company's resources are not used efficiently in a normal situation. In addition, there is a danger that a distinctive personal image achieved through specialization will be watered down. Above all, it is important to note that diversification, particularly when it should create a balance as horizontal diversification, is a dynamic, never-ending process. This is to be carried out in close coordination with early warning systems.

Vertical Diversification

5.2.2 Transfer

The activities of transfer aim, even before the onset of a negative event, at transferring the consequences onto another economic subject. This basically requires that there is an object as target for the complete or partial unloading of the risk. This object can, on the one hand, be part of one's own group of companies, by which the risk is transferred through a spin-off. On the other hand, the consequences can also be externalized, by transferring them onto an economically and legally independent object.

145

5.2.2.1 Spin-off

The aim of the spin-off of certain identified risk areas in one's own company is to transfer the risk to a subsidiary company. If this activity has already been performed in the company, this happens in the form of legal independence. If the activity is new, a new establishment takes place. Spin-offs come into question particularly when activities are considered to be especially risky, but nevertheless important for one's own group of companies.

By maintaining the ownership function, the established company keeps essential company controlling functions over the spin-off. At the same time, the economic risk as a consequence of negative events is primarily limited to the assets of the spin-off.

Another advantage is that through the transfer of consequences a higher personal responsibility within the spin-off company is achieved. This is especially justified when the effects are influenced by the reaction of this area. Consequently, the spin-off offers the possibility of a more flexible crisis management determined by the area, from which the whole group can profit.

It is, however, not recommendable to use this strategy in order to get rid of easily solvable, generally known problem areas. In such a case, the measure can be identified and judged as a deliberate ploy and finally become the subject of social concern. As a result, the financial and legal consequences remain limited to the subsidiary, but damage to the image of the parent company cannot be ruled out.

5.2.2.2 Externalization

Through externalization, there is the possibility of transferring the consequences of the negative events onto an area that does not belong to the group, or rather, to the company's area of influence.

This can happen through measures of risk sharing and contractual risk limitation. Risk sharing includes the alternatives of splitting the risk or of risk alliance. In both cases, several companies share the financial consequences. While this sharing only concerns the negative deviation from aims of splitting risk, in a risk alliance, financial success is also shared.

In the framework of contractual risk limitation, attempts are made to transfer the consequences of a negative event silently onto the business partner using additional contract conditions or special contracts. While there are no explicit contractual references for silent transfer, the other two forms go into risks in detail.

Regarding the basic contractual rules for risk adoption in tourism, the different aspects of the effects of negative events need to be considered. Above all, it must be taken into consideration that, when it involves basic benefits that can be substituted, negative events cause customers to buy substitute products relatively quickly. Therefore, the use of non-binding agreements, that is short-term terminable contracts, is the goal. The possibly unfavourable contract conditions that result are preferable to a future, possible complete loss of revenue. The latter is to be suspected, since the interchangeability of the products leads to a 'ruled out – not put off' decision regarding concrete choice of product.

The consequences will be different for tourism products that form their competitive advantage on basic benefits and cannot, therefore, be substituted. Here, a higher risk threshold value can be observed as can the existence of a 'putting off – but not ruling out' behavioural pattern. The latter ensures that the desire to travel will be made up at a more favourable time, which accounts for a quicker 'recovery possibility'. The higher risk threshold would also mean lower initial consequences. In this case, longer-term contracts are a possibility, which pays off above all when more favourable conditions about the contract period can be achieved.

Ruled out-not put off

Putting off-but not ruling out

146

To what extent it finally succeeds in transferring the risks onto a market partner is determined by general competition conditions; above all, the market power and negotiations strength of the company that is interested in externalization. In addition to the advantages of transferring the economics risks, it is also true in this case that by completely or partially adopting the risk, the market partner's interest and efforts strengthen the onset possibility and keeps the consequences of negative events low. In this respect, this action is especially justified and sensible when the contract partner has influence over the developments.

5.2.3 Cooperation

Cooperations can be founded with the exclusive aim of shouldering risks among the members of the group. If this is done in grand style, this forms a mutual insurance company. Cooperations of this form still do not exist in tourism. Nevertheless, many tourism companies decided to form cooperations to improve their competitive capacity and benefit from scale effects, e.g. on the supply side or to carry out more efficient marketing.

These cooperations, seen from the perspective of crisis management are also of use. Many preventive measures do not have company specific characteristics. Thus, existing cooperations could offer crisis management measures to the partners of their cooperation without the risk of weakening one's own competitive position. An example is the International Air Transport Association, a group to which the majority of the worldwide active airlines belong. Their members which are traditionally exposed to a high risk have access to a wide set of training tools related to security and crisis communication. Another example is the Caribbean Hotel Association which produced together with the Caribbean Tourism Organization the 'Hurricane Procedures Manual'. As Hurricanes are a regular phenomenon in the Caribbean, especially during the hurricane season from July to September, the Association decided, following Hurricane Hugo (1990), to put together a comprehensive manual for its members. With this master plan all important phases and measures related to prevention and coping with a hurricane were illustrated. Based on this master plan, member hotels finally developed their fine-tuned individual plans.

Existing cooperations

Cooperations formed only under the aspects of crisis management are the call centre which will be looked at in more detail at a later stage. As the set-up and maintenance of these call centres require significant financial resources and that the punctual needs during an emergency go very fast beyond the possibilities of the affected organization, cooperation in this field is a logical consequence. An installation of this kind is the call centre GAST/EPIC at the Munich airport (see Example 40). Not too long ago the Centre was only the product of a cooperation of airlines. However, recently TUI and FTI, two major tour operators, also joined.

5.2.4 Insurance

Insurance against the possible consequences of a negative event is a special form of transferring risks. The basic consideration of insurance is the combination of risks, which threaten a single person or company, in a contractual solidarity committee, in which it is balanced.

With the completion of an insurance policy, the insurer obliges himself to bear the financial consequences of a particular risk. For this, the policyholder pays a regular premium. From the point of view of the policyholder, this means that a risk that is difficult to calculate and prevent can be transferred into firmly calculated costs. A special form of cover can be observed repeatedly in practice, namely the intervention of the state. Destinations or large companies can almost always count on the fact that extensive damage or extraordinary events are at least partly covered by the State. This behaviour of the State – a kind of insurance for the organization – is difficult to predict as it is based on political considerations and the feeling of solidarity. Even if this form of insurance cannot be concluded in advance, it can be observed that the probability is determined by the profile of the organization or destination, the type of events and the political-economic situation.

If the effect of a negative event can be borne by a solidarity committee, the risk concerned must meet various requirements, for example randomness of the onset and extent of the damage, measurability of the extent of the damage, sufficient number and independence of the damaging event which guarantees that a risk balance within the group is possible and unambiguousness of the damage obligation.

Besides the traditional property insurance, insurances against business interruptions are in use. These are used by companies to insure against the financial risk of breakdown of operations and the loss of earnings as consequences of a negative event. Normally, compensation from this kind of insurance is always then paid if the installations of the company are directly damaged.

Diagram 32: Checklist for insurance coverage

1.	Have all installations that should be insured been listed? (software, hardware, tennis courts, swimming pools, etc.)
2.	Have all installations been described correctly? (Number of rooms, floors, property boundary lines, etc.)
3.	Are the quoted values accurate and up-to-date? (otherwise only portions of the damages will be refunded)
4.	Is the removal of damaged installations also insured?
5.	Is the business interruption insured?
6.	Determine liability levels and ascertain whether you need local or international jurisdiction clauses.
7.	Are the insurance number, the telephone and fax numbers of the insurance company easily available?
8.	Are the insurance records stored safely and will not be harmed by the negative event?
9.	Have the questions in dispute and unclear clauses with regards to the insurance contract been recorded in written form?
10.	Are photographs or videos of the installations before the occurrence of damage available?
11.	Work closely together with your insurance agent and the responsible insurance company to record and settle the claim.
12.	Ensure that you contract a leading insurance company. Not the price but the cost/performance ratio counts!

Source: Based on information of CHA/CTO

Example 33: Cover Your Event Insurance

Hurricanes are not new to the Caribbean and the Gulf Coast of the United States, but the strength of the recent hurricane seasons have had a wider and deeper impact on the infrastructure and on the perception of tourists more than ever before.

For this reason and to encourage companies to continue their activities in the state, Visit Florida, the official destination marketing organization of Florida, has presented in 2005, for the first time, a free insurance for events that take place in Florida during the hurricane season. The aim is to minimize the risk for the event organizer and to ensure that the lucrative convention business does not move away from Florida, especially during the hurricane season, i.e. August to October.

Convention cancellation coverage is a type of insurance which has been available to the conventions and meetings industry for quite some time. It covers risks such as curtailment, cancellation or postponement due to all types of adverse weather conditions, strikes, terrorism, power outages and physical damage to show facilities. However, offering this type of insurance as an incentive by a Destination Marketing Organization is new.

Visit Florida introduced this programme in cooperation with Marsh Affinity Group Services, a company specialized in insuring the events and meetings industry. To be covered by this 'Cover Your Event Insurance' the organizers must apply for it and the event has to meet criteria such as taking place between August and October, bringing a minimum of 100 room nights over a minimum of two nights, etc. Within a limit of 10 million US$ of total exposure each month, meetings are then approved by Visit Florida. In case that an event or meeting needs to be rescheduled because of a hurricane, the extra expenses of rescheduling the event at the same or nearest available venue in Florida and within 12 months as well as the room differential, are covered.

As a result of the initial success of the programme, Visit Florida has extended it up to the year 2007.

To insure in the field of tourism against the risk of terrorism has become one of the most difficult tasks since the terrorist attacks of September 11 in the USA. In many instances, this type of insurance was no longer offered for new contracts, or in most cases the offered maximum insurance sum was no longer sufficient. Although in the meantime the situation was easing especially because of the intervention of the state, the premium to be paid increased in such a significant way that many companies decided to bear these risks again by themselves.

One of the new instruments of insurances in the wider sense are weather derivates. The idea of insuring against the influences of the weather is not new to tourism. Already several decades ago insurance companies were selling contracts to travellers which compensated the tourist with a fixed

Weather derivates

The Chicago Mercantile Exchange (CME) has been trading weather derivates since 1999.

The traded futures and options on 'Heating Degree Days' HDD and 'Cooling Degree Days' CDD insure the buyer against changes in temperature using a baseline temperature of 65° Fahrenheit (18° Celcius).

amount for every raining day during his holidays. Weather derivates are now going far beyond this initial approach. Nowadays they are still mainly used by energy suppliers or in agriculture. In these cases the weather derivate primarily provides protection against the occurrence of the event, which is measured against a parametric trigger. Different to the classical insurance, material damage is not necessary. The payment of the contractually agreed compensation is due with the occurrence of the event. The kinds of events offered for insurance are widely spread. They can be based on a specific wind speed, amount of rainfall, temperature, depth of snow or magnitude of earthquakes.

Weather derivates are also an interesting instrument for tourism, to insure in an intelligent way against extreme weather changes and the ensuing losses of earnings. For instance, they are useful for winter sports tourism destinations but also for companies which are following a country or segment specific focus strategy. Nevertheless, it should be taken into account that the insurance of events other than extreme situations is always having an important impact on the profitability.

Example 34: Insurance Coverage for Political Risks

In many cases insurance coverage is difficult to obtain. This is especially true for the coverage of political risks (country risks) where coverage is usually only offered by institutions which provide export guarantees in the exporting countries.

To also cover investments in their countries, several African countries have founded with the support of the World Bank the African Trade Insurance Agency (ATIA). Through this insurance agency investors can insure against the political risks in the participating African countries.

The functioning of this insurance is rather simple. Member countries make their payments to the ATIA fund, which is administered from London (UK). Together with Lloyds London, the CEO of ATIA decides whether a claim is justified. The affected countries have no influence on the decision taken. If a member state is not settling the justified claim, payment to the injured party is made against the money that was previously paid into the fund. Furthermore, a refusal will result in no further loans being obtained from the World Bank.

In addition to this mechanism the premium and the duration of the insurance contracts are very attractive; investors have a useful instrument at hand to insure their investments in this region.

Above all, it is to be taken into consideration that the so-called speculative risks, which also include the entrepreneurial risk, cannot be the subject of an insurance contract. The loss of a possible future market position is, therefore, not insurable. Furthermore, the fact that some negative events due to legal conditions or narrow distribution of the risk are not insurable must be taken into consideration.

In addition, it should also be noted that through insurance neither probability of occurrence nor the magnitude of damage of a negative event is reduced. It is also important to note that the general insurance of all possible risks is contrary to the profitability goal of a company. In this respect, it is, above all, risks with low occurrence probabilities but serious consequences that should be covered by insurance, as long as it is possible to insure against them.

5.2.5 Self-bearing

Despite all the precautions that the company can introduce there remains an area that – in the end due to the novelty of the event – can only be borne by the company itself. On the part of the company, security measures can be made by forming liquid reserves. However, it should be taken into consideration that it concerns purely passive measures, which are also cost-intensive.

Besides, self-bearing is always of interest, if the necessary flexibility is available. The means of air transportation are in this sense of high relevance for international tourism. Seen from the perspective of a destination, national airlines offer the chance to react fast to problems arising in source markets and to establish connections to other destinations. From the perspective of a tour operator those means of air transport allow them to take tourists to other destinations if problems occur in certain regions. Flexibility is also an issue for the hotel sector, so far considered a tourism activity mostly related to a given permanent place. The increasing use of cruise liners for mega events – like for the Olympic games in Athens – is not only of interest from the point of sustainability but also from crisis management. As a result, with such a flexibility of the offer, tourism can also be an opportunity in those regions which could not find investors for hotels and resorts as the Return of Investment (ROI) is normally only reached after a period of 10-15 years. This is often too long for a safe investment.

Apart from this, proactive action is also possible in terms of an acceptance strategy. The aim of this strategy, which originates from the stakeholder management is to have a good and anticipating look at possible events and the position of the organization in the social sphere. To do so, the environment of the organization is examined for potential events and themes of importance for the company. Even before these matters are the topic of a debate, they are picked out as a central theme by the company and contact with the main stakeholders is sought. The significance and classification of and the solution possibilities for this event are discussed in the form of a 'real dialogue', at which the differing viewpoints of the stakeholders are considered to be legitimate. This form of discussion of the possible negative events should finally increase the understanding and with it the acceptance within society. At the same time, it should be shown that for certain events only limited solution possibilities are known or in existence. But, nevertheless, the interested company underlines, like TUI did this for years with the environmental forum, its high interest in cooperating with stakeholders to improve the situation.

It should also be considered that it is not about a purely communicative concept. The acceptance strategy should be understood much more as a fully comprehensive management task, which goes far beyond the announcement of viewpoints. The approach is less aimed at eliminating information deficiencies, but rather at eliminating credibility deficiencies. This also makes it clear that this central task of the organization cannot be delegated to the powerless and ineffective public relations department. On the one hand, it is the task of the company to represent these events in the relevant contexts. On the other hand, the company must also be ready to actively put in place its own resources in order to work out practical solutions. In principle, this course of action is not without risk, because once initiated communication processes are no longer controllable by the company in their advanced stages. Nevertheless, the initiative function, with the contribution of functional solution approaches, contributes considerably to preventing an emotional discussion and allowing the company to keep the initiative. In this way, a considerable contribution to the limitations of the effects of negative events is achieved, which is of advantage for both the company and the public.

5.3 Basic forms of crisis handling strategies

A further area of strategic considerations concerns the determination of the basic courses of action for crisis handling. The aim of the crisis handling strategy is the influence of the developments of the effects caused by the negative event with the aim that a neutralization of the effect is achieved. At the same time, or as soon as possible, the crisis causing problems should be gradually eliminated. The target area of the strategy should be wide and include all spheres of activities.

In literature, there are various approaches for handling strategies. A fundamental distinguishing feature is the form of coping behaviour, which has influence over the choice of instruments, problem solution orientation and the point of time when the activities start. The forms of a crisis handling strategy can lie between two extremes, proactive (offensive, oriented towards finding a solution) and reactive (defensive, oriented towards resistance).

In addition, it should be taken into consideration that strategic handling strategies embody the fundamental moral and ethical position of the organization. Since these are subject to particular attention in a crisis situation, their design should receive appropriate consideration. Independent of which position is finally chosen, the determination of the strategy should be seen important enough to be done at a calm moment and weighing-up all the possible consequences.

Moreover, it should also be considered that the crisis handling strategy, as only a temporary strategy variation, is reasonably compatible with long-term corporate strategy. Despite the necessity to realize short-term advantages within the framework of crisis handling, deviation must be kept as low as possible. A clear limit can finally be seen where the guiding function of the chosen competitive strategy is affected.

5.3.1 The proactive approach

The aim of a proactive handling strategy is the timely implementation of measures that eliminate and contain the causes and related effects of an identified problem area. This requires a functioning early warning system, which aids, even with vague and imprecise information circumstances, the implementation of reaction. In addition, the organization must be prepared, voluntarily and independently, to admit to all spheres of activities, especially customers, stakeholders and the state that something has not worked as expected.

A not necessarily occurring but often initial result of a proactive handling strategy is an immediate increase in public interest and media coverage. Since the affected company is right in the middle, the result is an unfavourable intensification of the crisis. This intensification is accompanied by a negative influence on the image, which the company must accept.

A proactive handling strategy does have some advantages:

First, it should be noted that a negatively influenced image does not necessarily mean a loss of credibility.

Mea Culpa?

The proactive handling strategy is clearly to be distinguished from an approach of 'mea culpa'.

A proactive approach includes the confession that something did not go as planned. However, that does not necessarily mean that this is exclusively or partly the responsibility of the concerned organization.

Credibility

152

Credibility becomes important when the facts of the case are confusing and complex. The recipient of the information can then, because of the existing credibility, do without the complete information, that is, overcome uncertainty. Since credibility is the preliminary stage for trust (credibility stands for content-wise pure conveying of information, trust for agreement as regards content) continually credible company communication is of considerable importance in attaining trust in a crisis situation. These two areas, image and credibility, should be considered separately. The credibility of a proactively acting organization rises, or at least stays the same, in large parts of the public, among its customers and the media, especially because it acts. This is the basis for the future use of the marketing instrument, whose effectiveness is essentially influenced by credibility.

Second, it should be taken into consideration that, in spite of the short-term intensification of the crisis situation, the company still has strong communicative control. The facts provided by the company are used to a relatively large extent and speculation is mostly avoided.

Communicative control

Third, this type of strategy contributes essentially to shortening a crisis since there is no staggered publishing of 'new revelations' that stimulate public interest.

Shortening a crisis

In order to implement a proactive handling strategy in good time, the distinction of influences on the image and credibility loss, but also the future value of credibility, must be recognized. Only then is it possible to overcome resistance within the organization, which is based on the following consideration: *'why should an intensification of the crisis and a negative influence on the image be brought about by ourselves and consciously when it is possible that the incident will go unnoticed?'*

Example 35: Air Berlin

On 18 November 2003 a passenger aircraft of Air-Berlin was forced to conduct an emergency landing in the military part of the airport Rome-Ciampino (Italy) because of an alleged kidnapping. Once the aircraft landed, Special Armed Forces made their way on board of the aircraft. No kidnappers were found, not even the slightest indications of a kidnapping could even be seen. Instead of waiting, Air Berlin – seeking the public – immediately issued a press release on the incident.

It used this proactive approach to avoid any speculation but also as it was deeply convinced of no wrong-doing. Instead however, the company was immediately put into the media spotlight and the crisis intensified. The results confirmed that this 'spectacular intervention', later explained by the Italian authorities as a 'communication misunderstanding' with the pilot, was not justified.

Air Berlin decided to take the initiative and cover the cost of safekeeping the voice-recorder and the analyses through the German Federal Bureau of Aircraft Accidents Investigation (BFU – Bundesstelle für Flugunfalluntersuchung). This office would have normally only acted if an airplane accident would have taken place. The analysis of the recorded conversation confirmed fully the initial position of Air Berlin. There had been no misunderstandings and no indications of a kidnapping on board.

With this proactive approach Air-Berlin contributed actively and at a very early stage in the dissemination of the news on the incident. Although this has caused an intensification of the crisis, the company ensured the accurate reporting and was able to preserve and even extend its credibility.

A proactive crisis handling strategy must be initiated at a specific moment in time. This point in time is normally related to the 'voluntary nature of the decision', i.e. that the decision to inform the public is still taken voluntarily by the affected organization. However, once state institutions intervene, the social environment will no longer adjudicate the benefits of this strategy to the organization.

An essential part of the proactive handling strategy is the effort to eliminate the causes of the problems. Despite huge efforts, there will always be some problem areas for which this is not possible; for example, natural catastrophes. In such cases, a long-term organized proactive strategy can be used to accept and capitalize on the event. The aim is to change negatives into positives.

Example 36: Turning Negative Events into Positive – The Wildfires in Yellowstone and Glacier National Parks

In 1988, the most severe wildfires in the entire history of the Yellowstone Park broke out. A total of 50 fires started in the National Park together with 198 fires in the greater Yellowstone area. More than 25 000 fire fighters could not avoid the burning of more than 1.2 million acres and 36 per cent of the entire park's area. Hundreds of animals died, park facilities and infrastructures such as roads, campgrounds and cabins were destroyed.

As fire seasons and the peaks of visitor arrivals to National Parks coincide in the months of June, July and August, visitors usually suffer heavy restrictions such as closing of roads and campgrounds to avoid wildfires. These limitations and the intensive media coverage of the fire disasters have regularly led to a shortening of the tourism seasons.

Now, the affected National parks, such as the Yellowstone or Glacier National Parks, put heavy efforts into changing the visitors' awareness regarding fires. People mostly consider fire as a destructive and powerful force, an unpredictable enemy to plants, animals and men. For many, the aftermath of a fire is a blackened landscape that represents death and destruction. However, wildfires have occurred in the northern Rocky Mountains region at regular intervals since the last Ice-Age. Fires have shaped most of the natural beauty of landscapes, diversity of vegetation and wildlife. They are very important within a functioning, balanced ecosystem and have very positive impacts on the evolution and natural stimulation of plants and forests. Many plants and animals cannot even survive without the cycles of fire to which they are adapted. Fires break down organic matter into soil nutrients and rejuvenate soil with nitrogen from the ash, thus creating a new fertile seedbed for plants. With less competition and more sunlight, seedlings grow quickly and vegetation recovers fast.

The interpretation of the phenomenon and understanding of the impact and importance of fires within the ecosystem moved to the centre of the parks' objectives. The park managers succeeded, indeed, in turning the bad image of the destroyed landscape and fear of fires into a new attraction for visitors.

The Glacier National Park, for instance, has set up an exemplary educational programme for its visitors. It includes detailed exhibitions on the role of fire in the ecosystem in the Park's Visitor Centres, road-side exhibits in areas that have recently been burned as well as evening slide illustrated and non-illustrated talks at campground amphitheatres. Rangers discuss the impact of fires on all hikes and offer special trails into burned areas so that tourists can see and get directly in touch with the aftermaths of a fire. In the event of a fire, special activities and information are set up. Various publications, which describe the pros and cons of fires in ecosystems are sold at the visitor centres. Television and radio spots inform and create awareness for this topic, even for people who are not visiting the park themselves.

These educational segments create not only a new consciousness, but also lead to the acceptance of further restrictions connected with fires. When in the year 2000 new heavy fires broke out, visitors could easily understand the managers' regulations and according to the Glacier National Park statistics, there was no real decline in numbers of visitors. Although some visitors cancelled their trip to the park due to the fires, others were encouraged to visit the affected area and were keen to learn about the fires.

Comprehensive surveys document generally consistent visitor use patterns of the landscape before and after the fires of 1988 in the Yellowstone National Park. With a total of 2.7 million recreational visits to the Yellowstone Park and 1.6 million to the Glacier National Park in 2001, visitors provide an inevitable economic income to the communities, their businesses and their employees. Therefore, the Parks not only continue to work on shaping the new awareness of fire but are also interested in establishing a long-term relationship with their visitors, as the following slogan of the Glacier National Park proves:

'Come along! There are many discoveries to be made in a post-fire area. And, come back again – next year, in five years, ten, in a different season – and witness the transitions, the increasing diversity.'

This idea of capitalizing on an initial image problem is not so far-fetched and this is illustrated by the development and current importance of destinations such as Pompeii, Waterloo or Verdun, which are today places of contemporary history. In all cases, the negative events created a competitive advantage whose basic benefits were not interchangeable with another destination.

It is very much a question of time that determines the transition from voyeurism to contemporary history, from horror and shock to interest and culture. Titanic-trips or trips to the battlefields of Korea and Vietnam show that these time intervals are becoming ever shorter.

Example 37: The Southampton Titanic Walk

The sinking of the luxury cruise liner R.M.S. Titanic in 1912 can probably be considered as one of the earliest and best-known disasters in tourism. Only 3 days after leaving the port of Southampton for its maiden voyage, the liner struck an iceberg and sank in the freezing Atlantic. About 1500 people lost their lives.

Until today this tragedy is remembered and has not lost any of its mysticism and fascination. It has become a source for innumerable novels, stories and films. The success of the film Titanic produced in 1997 and starring Leonardo di Caprio and Kate Winslet shows the ongoing world interest in this accident. With more than 17 million spectators in Great Britain, 18 million in Germany and even about 104 million in the United States only during 1998, it became the most successful film in the entire history of cinema.

Southampton, a city in the south of England with some 211 000 residents, was the Titanic's port of departure. As the city lost more than 500 inhabitants, mostly crew members, it felt and continues to feel very strongly related to the disaster. Numerous memorials dedicated to those who perished were built shortly after the incident throughout the city. But neither tourists nor tourism planers thought about converting the incident into a tourist attraction. The sorrow and shock as much as the close time relation of the disaster prevented all imaginations of this kind. In addition, tourism destinations and objectives differed at that time very much from those of today.

Today, as tourists' habits and perspectives have changed, Southampton has discovered the benefits and the potential of this past tragedy and uses successfully the advantages of its world-known fame to attract more tourists to the city. The visitors are encouraged to experience the original setting and review the beginning of the famous story. Southampton's City Council designed the self-guided Titanic Walk, which leads visitors to all key memorials and landmarks related to the story of the doomed liner. During a one-hour walk, tourists pass more than ten points of interest, among them a first-class hotel, where some Titanic passengers spent their last night before boarding or the pub where many had their last beer before going on board.

The Titanic Walk brochure of the Southampton City Council

5.3.2 The reactive approach

With a reactive handling strategy, it is attempted, despite the knowledge of the circumstances, not to act upon them, but to wait to react, in order to then bring the situation under control. The aim is to evade the crisis as far as possible and not to intensify the situation with one's own actions.

The activities of the affected organization are put off until the post-active point in the crisis. They can, for example, concern product modifications that eliminate the problems afterwards or leave the product as unrecognizable. Particularly important in this context is also lobbying, which helps, above all, to reduce the consequences in the political sphere. In an extreme case, the situation is resolved completely and comprehensively by quitting the market. Quitting the market is particularly to be recommended where business development was unsatisfactory, no kind of improvement could be counted on in the future or market position is too weak.

> **Points in time**
> The post-active point is defined as the time when the actual event is no longer in conflict with the general, public interest.
> See also Section 7.1.1

The essential advantage of a reactive handling strategy is that an intensification of the crisis by the company's own actions is avoided. On the downside, a reactive strategy cannot only result in loss of image but also – in contrast to a proactive strategy – loss of credibility. The reason for this is that if a company reacts reluctantly and only when it is forced to do so, it is not believed that there is really an interest in finding a solution to the problem. In the end, the negative influence on the image and loss of credibility is determined, apart from the peculiarities of the events, above all, by the behaviour of stakeholders. If they prove – more or less conclusive assumptions are sufficient – that despite knowledge of the circumstances and the possibility to act on them, that inaction prevailed, the damage will be considerable.

Furthermore, it is important to realize that by using a reactive handling strategy the company gives up its natural role as leading information provider (see also Section 7.5.2). In this way, the company loses a fundamental advantage and boosts the importance of other information sources. It should also not be neglected that the duration of the crisis will tend to be lengthened by this, namely when the successive leaking of new information continually ignites public attention.

In practice, the reactive handling strategy can often be observed. This is certainly also affected by the fact that proactive handling strategy and information providing come with unfamiliar attention in the initial period. In this respect, the behaviour is really a natural reflex reaction that values the initial negative influence on the image higher than the long-term loss of credibility which is probably not considered. The frequency of its use does not, however, correspond with its success. Therefore, using a reactive handling strategy is only to be recommended in few cases. This is, for example, the case of situations in which there is conclusive proof that the negative event occurred, but it can neither be explained nor eliminated and the company is sure that criticism will be limited and will soon pass.

The greater scope with regard to handling and structuring but also the sensibleness of voluntarily taking on social responsibility means that a proactive handling strategy has a lot going for it. It not only promises bigger chances, but it is sooner paid off in the long-term (Berger, Gärtner and Mathes, 1989; Wiedemann, 1994; WTO, 1998b). If the crisis is understood in such terms, it offers the chance to develop the organization further and ensures the influence in the various spheres of activity.

Questions for review and discussion

- Explain what a differentiation strategy should take into account from the crisis management point of view.
- Explain the circumstances which support the use of a reactive handling strategy.
- What is the latest moment in time to decide for a proactive handling strategy?
- How does the transfer of risks through 'spin-off' and 'externalization' work?

Suggestions for further reading

Kroeber-Riel, W. (1993), *Bildkommunikation*, Vahlen, Stuttgart.

Porter, M. E. (1998), *Competitive Advantage*, Free Press, New York.

Porter, M. E. (1998), *Competitive Strategy*, Free Press, New York.

Smith, V. (1998), 'War and tourism', *Annals of Tourism Research*, 25(1), pp. 202-227.

Useful websites

www.visitflorida.com
www.expoplus.net

6 Crisis planning and organizational measures

Objectives

- Learn to identify the important areas of crisis planning
- To distinguish the different phases of the planning process for crises
- To understand the organizational measures of crisis management
- To take decisions regarding the use of external experts

Key terms and concepts

- Planning
- Generic planning
- Contingency planning
- Preventive planning
- Crisis committee
- Experts
- Information centre, management centre
- Care teams

Planning describes a structuring process that defines how the decision-makers want to see a future process developing. Planning is, therefore, the opposite of improvisation, ad-hoc decisions that are dependent on chance. The fundamental aim of corporate planning is to assure the existence of the business, which is constantly threatened by the uncertainty of future events, for as long as possible. This type of planning allows negative events to be taken into consideration as far as it is possible and sensible. The result is a strategic configuration of the business that reduces proneness to crises. While this aspect has already been touched upon (see Chapter 5), the focus here is on the further possibilities of preventive crisis management. For this, a separate planning and implementation process, the so-called 'crisis planning', is used.

Since the number of conceivable negative events can be very large, there must be limitations put on the eventualities considered for crisis planning. Crisis planning should, therefore, concentrate on those events that are particularly destructive but rather unlikely and on those that are extremely time-critical. The aim of crisis planning is to reduce the element of surprise and, through prepared measures, to gain a head-start in time. This early consideration of crises should also incorporate a fundamental review and evaluation of the chosen steps with regard to generic strategy and other possible consequences. (Above all, the interaction between liquidity, success and factors of success must not be underestimated.

Short-term liquidity measures must always take the long-term consequences for success factor into consideration.) Such a review is rarely possible in a situation of crisis, but is extremely important due to long-term influences.

Within this crisis planning and implementation process, there are three distinct stages: generic planning, contingency planning and preventive planning.

6.1 Generic planning

Generic planning lays the planning basis for possible situations. The aim of generic planning is to determine fundamental requirements and potentials. In addition, the ensuing planning stages should be simplified and speeded up. In this sense, generic planning is rough contingency planning, in which the specific scenarios for the crisis situations remain purposely vague and determinants are consciously left unspecified. Besides, it is in many cases impossible to predict all those determinants (WEU, 1995). Questions related to the organizational structure of the company as well as to the workflow organization are as much the objects of the planning process as the results are influenced and determined by it.

6.1.1 Determination of structures and responsibility

A fundamental part of generic planning is determination of responsibility and authority. Subsystems for planning and future executive functions within crisis management are, as a rule, set up within the organization. Since these subsystems plan, and in the case of crises, manage highly important processes, they are usually located at the highest management level or directly assigned to them.

It is commonly agreed that a project organization can best face the challenges that are timely, limited and irregular. In concrete realization, these are either organic sub-unit 'working groups', which have no authority to give instructions, or crisis committees, which are composed of representatives from several departments, but do not form a department on their own.

Advisory group

It is particularly advantageous to have an advisory group that should do the groundwork for management when it concerns the elaboration of different contingency-planning measures. By being assigned to top management and thus breaking free of the specific interests of different parts of the organization, distorted exertion of influence is avoided. As from the moment of a negative event, if not before, the limited legitimization to put their ideas into action will be problematic. A call is, therefore, often made to increase the authority of such advisory groups to allow them to impose their will. However, this makes an advisory group become more like a crisis committee.

Crisis committee

In addition to members of management, a crisis committee is also made up of other relevant decision-makers such as a marketing manager, legal advisor, press spokesperson, etc. The composition is easy to vary depending on the type of event. In this way, not only is the specialist's knowledge of the members used, but it is also ensured that the decisions reached will be implemented by the people responsible under normal circumstances. This form of functional similarity in cases of crisis and in normal situations has proved to be an important factor of successful crisis management (Höhn, 1974; Mileti and Sorensen, 1987).

160

Example 38: Lufthansa's Crisis Management

They can be called experienced or well prepared, but airlines have, like no other sector, done a lot already to prepare for the unlikely possibility of an airplane accident. The high emotional judgment when it comes to flying but also the companies' interest to demonstrate their compromise with quality and service, even in those exceptional situations, were the major forces that led to establishing a well-thought crisis management concept and team.

In the case of the Star Alliance Partner Lufthansa, crisis management has played an important role for many years. Their case is thought to explain how such a system of strategic and functional responsibilities works.

Lufthansa defines the responsibilities and the organizational structure in its Emergency Response and Action Plan (ERAP). This plan is prepared and updated under the supervision of the Manager for Crisis Management Planning, a permanent position, which in the event of a crisis becomes the Head of the Special Assistance Team Centre. Under him, the different departments of importance in times of a crisis, as for example, Medical Services, Communications, Personnel, Governmental Affairs and Security, etc., deliver their specific input to this ERAP.

The organization of crisis management at Lufthansa

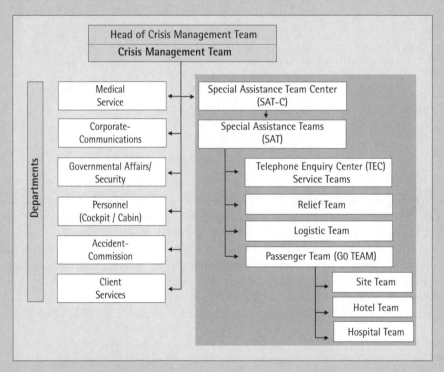

In the event of a crisis, the so-called Crisis Management Team (CMT) is assembled. This Team is led by a high-ranking manager who represents the Board of Directors and is responsible for the overall Crisis Management of the company. He is assisted by the different departments participating in the ERAP, which send a previously designated representative to the Crisis Management Team's room, based at Frankfurt's Rhein-Main Airport. Special Advisors, who are selected according to the specific needs of the situation, join the Crisis Management Team. The main functions of the Crisis Management Team are the pooling of information, the situation analysis and strategic decisions.

The Special Assistance Team Centre (SAT-C) is supporting the CMT (as a working group) and is assembled simultaneously in rooms prepared at Frankfurt's Rhein-Main Airport. The SAT-C manages and coordinates the different Special Assistance Teams.

Tasks and responsibilities of the Special Assistance Teams

Telephone Enquiry Center (TEC) Service Teams	True and complete information for the external enquiries • Handling of communication • Telephone service for families, friends, and relatives of the victims
Passenger Team (GO TEAM)	Caring for air passengers, relatives, persons at the site, persons affected • Listen • Inform • Help
Relief Team	Support to the station concerned • Take-over of routine activities • Maintenance of station service • Management of tasks assigned by the local head of station
Logistic Team	Handling of administrative tasks • Air tickets for relatives • Hotel reservations • Providing financial support • Answering further administrative problems

The Special Assistance Teams (SAT) are the operational arm within the company's crisis management and reflect the typical operations an airline may be confronted with in times of crisis. These teams, which are available worldwide, are only activated in case of a crisis but they can also be easily deployed to the place of emergency. The SAT members are volunteers who are recruited from different departments within the company, trained for their emergency function and activated on demand. The responsibilities of the Special Assistance Teams (SAT) are defined in a Special Assistance Team Centre (SAT-C) manual.

Example 39: TUI's Crisis Management

Crisis management has already become for some tour operators part of their overall quality strategy. That includes the establishment of departments exclusively responsible for crisis management and called accordingly. However, the management of extreme situations is not a new field for most tour operators and is often one of the reasons why holidaymakers decide to choose a package holiday. The European tour operator TUI for instance is managing some 200 cases of death and 1000 difficult health cases such as strokes among all their guests every year.

The organization of crisis management at TUI

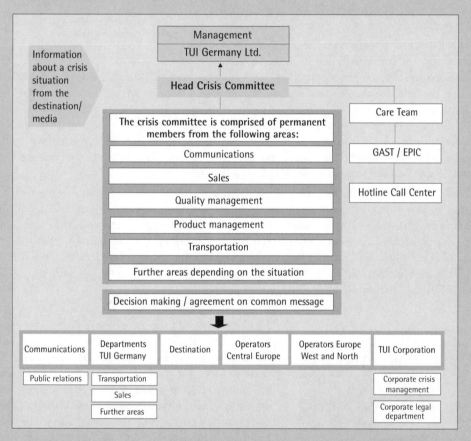

TUI has a department permanently headed by the Manager for Crisis and Event Management. He is responsible for the corporate planning and operational activities of TUI's emergency and crisis management. He is also in charge of establishing and maintaining a wide network with all relevant areas within the company, as well as with governmental institutions and associations. He reports directly to the Management of TUI Germany Ltd.

The Crisis Committee is assembled in the event of a crisis. Besides, the already designated members from the departments of communications, sales, quality management, product management and transportation, other members are requested to join the group depending on the needs of the situation.

The crisis management activities are centralized and managed from TUI headquarters in Hanover (Germany). Actions are always coordinated and consulted with the affected areas / destinations but only the members of the Crisis and Event Management department have the necessary market overview and competence to decide on special flights for evacuation, ambulance services, etc.

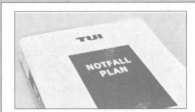

Picture: TUI. The crisis manual is available in all main departments and destinations

The TUI crisis management comprises several core activities. In the first place, it includes the development of contingency plans for typical situations resulting from negative events. In those plans, the field of duties, responsibilities and rules of conduct are defined and, information and decision procedures are also determined. The contingency plans are updated continuously. Furthermore, typical important data such as names of key personnel, telephone and fax numbers are also kept permanently up-to-date. Another important result of this planning is the preparation of checklists for evacuations and aircraft accidents. Those checklists are standardized and do not focus on the specific details of a destination.

In addition, special rooms are kept available. This includes the air traffic control centre which is open all year-round, 24 hours a day, and monitors and coordinates all air traffic related to the company. Furthermore, there is a crisis management centre equipped and prepared for running a crisis situation. Client contacts, an increasingly vital factor during times of crises, can be handled with their own resources for situations of the extent of an airplane accident. In addition, TUI is as a member of the GAST/EPIC centre (see also Example 40) allowed to use the GAST/EPIC installations at Munich airport (Germany).

The crisis management centre of TUI

Picture: TUI

Besides, Care teams have been established. These teams are already known from the airline industry where they have been used for several years to look after those affected by an incident and their relatives. Since the beginning of 2002, TUI counts on some 230 staff who volunteer to help in crisis situations. After the selection of staff, which focussed on mental strength, tact, understanding and talent for organization, they are trained in a three-day basic course with special emphasis on psychology for crisis situations. Annual one-day courses aim at keeping the state of readiness high.

TUI's Care teams can be moved and have occasionally been sent in the past to destinations (usually one-person missions). However, trained members of the care team are ideally already working in other main functions in the destinations. To improve the situation even further, TUI aims now at extending these staff in double-functions in all destinations.

While determining the structures of crisis management, ideally detailed job descriptions of all those persons involved in crisis management are produced. That way, duties and responsibilities are defined clearly, at an early stage. Replacements are made easier through a clear definition of duties and responsibilities and, the need for further training becomes clear. This not only helps to fill the posts in the first place but is also of benefit to find the adequate replacement if the incumbent is temporarily or no longer available. For instance, the post description of a head of communications could cover the following points:

Diagram 33: Job description (head of communications)

1.	Ensures the designation of the first and only official spokesperson
2.	Coordinates communications with public authorities, associations, etc.
3.	Monitors the public opinion
4.	Prepares press conferences
5.	Prepares press releases for discussion with the head of the crisis committee
6.	Organizes and chairs telephone conferences after the occurrence of a negative event
7.	Participates in the morning meeting of the crisis committee (if possible, at 7.30 a.m. for a short briefing)
8.	Participates in the meeting of the department heads (8.00-8.30 a.m.)
9.	Holds daily press conferences (together with the head of the crisis committee) at 11.00 a.m.
10.	Participates in meetings of the crisis reaction centre (if possible, 1.00 p.m.)
11.	Gives press briefings to management
12.	Participates in meetings of the stakeholders or sends a deputy (at least once a week)
13.	Is responsible for internal communications
14.	Appoints deputy

As the above-mentioned job description already indicates, the different fundamental meetings should be determined as well as their time and those who will be participating. Fixing this basic working rhythm at an early stage also sets the framework for internal and external communications and the control mechanisms. This allows an immediate start of the activities, defines the workflow and the coordination systems and is a helpful way to make use of the 'lessons learned' especially for people new to this process.

Diagram 34: Daily Communication Advisory Meeting

Title:	Daily Communication Advisory Meeting
Purpose:	Daily forum, to examine facts and background information of the event. Determination of essential communication objectives and uniform wording for internal and external communications
Activation:	As soon as possible, after the head of the crisis committee ordered the activation
	Head of the communications department informs the participants
	Time: 8.00–8.30 a.m. (after presentation to the crisis committee)
Report to:	Crisis Committee
Permanent members:	Head of communications, head of concerned region, head of quality management, head of call centre, head of library
Other members:	On invitation by head of communications
Receive information from:	Daily report from the press office, exceptional event report from the call centre, stakeholders meetings, library
Instruments:	Morning press-clippings, overnight reports of the situation room
Objectives:	Forward findings to the head of the crisis committee
	Identification and determination of essential communication objectives and uniform wording up to the press conference at 11.30 a.m.
Output:	Agreement on common message for press conference (by the head of communications) at 11.30 a.m.
	Report of important news to the head of crisis committee
Meeting place:	Room 2005, communications department

6.1.2 Use of external experts

A further aspect of generic planning must deal with the fundamental willingness, whether, when and to what extent the company will fall back on external experts in a crisis. The basis of this consideration is the fact that handling a crisis, on the one hand, is an exceptional situation, but, on the other hand, coping with it successfully requires experience and specialist knowledge. Although for the most part the latter is available today, getting access to this information is still very difficult. Accessing personalized knowledge in the form of experts is usually preferred. Experts can either be part of the organization or brought in from outside.

The number of companies offering crisis management services has constantly increased in the past years. Most of these companies offer their services for business travellers in crisis situations or assist destinations, tour operators or other service providers in their crisis communication efforts.

Reverting to external experts has the advantage that they only need to be around in an exceptional situation. The organization, therefore, only incurs costs for the duration of the possible service. In addition, due to their extensive personal experience of dealing with such situations, external experts have developed a capability to reduce complexity that enables them to come to decisions more quickly and with more certainty. There is also the fact that they are not directly affected by the events and as such they can work more rationally.

Diagram 35: Checklist for the use of external experts

1.	Analyse which areas should be strengthened during times of crisis and which are not covered through internal experts
2.	Which handling strategy shall be adopted?
3.	Is a generalist or a specialist desired?
4.	Examine, whether this expertise is already available by means of existing partnerships like insurance companies, banks, (tourism-) associations, national or international institutions
5.	a) Examine possible external experts evaluating their qualification for points 1, 2 and 3
	b) Consider in particular previous references for these activities. In case of unknown experts there is the additional risk that they may try to gain a reputation and promote themselves on account of the parties involved
6.	Ask the expert to convince you why he is the right person for this job. If he fails now, it will be even more difficult for him at a later stage
7.	Make sure that the corporate culture of the expert is not that different from that of your company or your destination

The use of external experts does, however, also bring disadvantages. Above all, this is true for those negative events that affect success factors or important areas of the business. In order to work effectively and to avoid long-term damage to the chosen competitive strategy, the not so obvious interrelations and facts must be known. External experts do not have such knowledge, as the specifications of the respective corporate culture are not fully known or, indeed, not known at all. In addition to this, it must not be forgotten that external experts are not immediately available. This poses a considerable risk, in particular, in the case of fast developing crises.

It is clear that, on the one hand, using external experts presents an opportunity, above all in special areas, to fall back on knowledge and crisis-specific experience. At the same time, giving external experts sole responsibility is risky and not sensible, when a successful crisis management should be guaranteed. For this reason, timely decisions need to be made as to which areas should be strengthened by external experts, should the need arise. This includes availability analyses, establishing contact, as well as preliminary negotiations about remuneration and performance.

The hidden expert

Although this function exists in many companies and destinations, the head of the library is seldom used or even considered to be useful when it comes to crisis management.

Librarians, who are more and more often also called information managers, are perfectly prepared to research facts, reports and other information. They know the sources where to find the information and the ways to retrieve it fast.

Considerations regarding a reinforced extension of computer-supported information systems seem sensible, since they can help to reduce complexity and pressure of time by preparing internal and external information suitable for the user.

6.1.3 Measures in the area of infrastructure

There is also a high infrastructural component involved here as a result of how unusual the circumstances are. This covers special spatial requirements that come along with a crisis situation but also changed information technology needs.

First, the affected or responsible organization must consider the spatial requirements, which must satisfy two different needs. The respective management personnel must be able to gather together in a suitable place, that is, a management centre, so that they can manage the crisis from a central place. The rooms should be equipped with all command, control and communications means. In addition meeting rooms are becoming necessary where the advisory group or crisis committee can carry out discussions and take decisions. The demands differ from normal circumstances, in particular, in terms of the number of people involved, the necessity to work round-the-clock and additional security measures.

Meeting room of the crisis response centre of the German Ministry of Foreign Affairs

Picture: German Ministry of Foreign Affairs. Chancellor Schröder, Minister of Foreign Affairs Fischer and other representatives from the administration and the tourism industry during the Tsunami-crisis in 2004/5.

In addition, an information centre is required to deal with the multitude of outside contacts both within affected consumers or the media and those unaffected. The extent of this unit reaches an unusual size for the organization and is often underestimated. Like the management centre, the information centre must be prepared for a round-the-clock operation. This should reflect the necessary spatial requirements whilst at the same time making clear the number of staff required.

Management centre

Meeting rooms

Information centre

The concepts used in practice are geared towards a kind of 'reserve concept', whereby employees and other special staff like psychologists, police officers, pastors, etc., are trained and prepared for their role and, are only called into action at the time a negative event occurs.

Both infrastructural measures can also be implemented on an industry-wide level. Good examples of this are the EPIC and GAST crisis centres.

During the tsunami crisis in the Ministry

Picture: German Ministry of Foreign Affairs. The Crisis Management Centre.

Example 40: GAST/EPIC Centre – Example of an Information and Management Centre

EPIC (Emergency Procedures Information Centre) in London Heathrow (UK) and GAST (Gemeinsame Auskunftsstelle - Common Information Centre) at Munich Airport (Germany) are the two best equipped and most experienced accident information and communication centres in Europe.

Crisis information centre

Picture: GAST/EPIC

The EPIC at London's Heathrow airport was established in the 1970s and acts as a shared crisis centre for more than 70 different airlines. Its main function is the management of direct communications with the general public, both with the affected or unaffected by aircraft accidents. Its major test was the airplane accident of Lockerbie, when within 72 hours some 100 000 telephone calls had to be handled.

GAST was established in 1995 at the initiative of the Munich Airport Authority, the Munich Airport Police and British Airways, as a non-profit organisation financed by German airports and various airlines. The main objective of GAST is, similar to the EPIC-Model, the fast distribution of reliable information to the public. It serves as the central information point within a network, where passenger data from the appropriate institutions (e.g. airlines) and information from police investigations, rescue teams, hospitals and the public are gathered and evaluated.

GAST only works in case of a negative event. However, it does not necessarily have to be a civil aircraft accident or take place within the borders of Germany. In an emergency situation, GAST becomes operative within 10-15 minutes by calling upon more than 500 trained volunteers, recruited from the police and airlines staff. With their help and the latest technical equipment in a permanently prepared and secure office, GAST offers a 24 hours telephone-hotline for as long as it may be necessary and in up to 20 foreign languages.

Some examples of situations when GAST became active are:

- Train accident in Eschede, Germany (3 June 1998, 1000 calls)
- Airplane accident of the Concorde in Paris, France (25 July 2000, 800 calls)
- Fire of the Glacierexpress in Kaprun, Austria (11 November 2000, 2700 calls)
- Air accident in Überlingen German-Swiss border region (1 July 2002, 350 calls)

The telephone pool for incoming calls

Picture: GAST/EPIC

Diagram 36: Checklist for the IT equipment

1.	Are there enough phones and extension numbers available? a) Telephone numbers should not be assigned for regular business b) Is there a sufficient pool of reserve-numbers for overloaded extensions? This aims especially at the extensions of key personnel for crisis situations which take longer than expected
2.	Are preparations for conference calls known and arranged?
3.	a) Is an adequate number of stable internet connections available? b) Is the access information for the own server available and does it include the right to modify files and pages (writing rights)? c) Are special e-mail addresses set-up?
4.	Are fax machines available? (further questions see points 1a and 1b)
5.	a) Is a sufficient number of computers available? b) Are they connected to a network? c) Are soft- and hardware up-to-date and are they compatible with new standards (e.g. USB)? d) Are Laptops available for temporary staff?
6.	a) Is a sufficient number of mobile phones available? b) Are reserve-numbers for key personnel available? (see point 1b) c) Have enough batteries been charged and are enough reserve batteries available? d) Consider during the planning process that mobile telephone systems are frequently jammed in crisis situations. Therefore, if possible, ensure a preference access to the mobile telephone systems or alternative communication channels such as short-range two-way radio communications (walkie-talkies) e) If necessary use satellite telephones for key personnel
7.	a) Are digital cameras available? (for internal communications or website) b) Are web cameras available? (for video conferences) c) Are video cameras available? (for the transmission of situation reports to the control and command centre and for documentation purposes)
8.	a) Ensure power supply b) Keep batteries available c) Prepare for power loss (generators)

9.	a) Are manuals up-to-date and in sufficient numbers available?
	
	b) Are all telephone lists up-to-date?
	
	    i. Do they include all internal numbers?
	
	    ii. Do they include all, also the now activated, emergency numbers (normal and cell phones)?
	
	    iii. Are important and necessary external numbers available (public authorities, associations...)?
	
	    iv. Can they easily be updated and extended during the crisis (ideally numbers are available through the intranet)?
	
	c) Is the list to alert staff – ideally to be sent via SMS – prepared and up-to-date?
	
	d) Are email lists prepared and up-to-date? (it is recommendable to define in advance the different groups)

10.	Arrange, where necessary and useful, crypto measures for telephone, fax and mobiles
11.	Is access to the finance and accounting department ensured? (this point matters especially for long crises)

Management and information centres do not have to be attached to a certain place. Depending on the type of event or the development, it is sometimes advisable to be on the spot. In these cases, the British airline British Airways, for example, sets up a 'Relief Aircraft', which is used to transport not only the necessary personnel, but also all kinds of infrastructure and communications resources.

IT requirements must also be taken into consideration – a quick supply of information is the prerequisite for quick processing of information – these differ from those in normal situations in terms of obtaining and disseminating information.

By obtaining information, a reliable and comprehensive picture of the situation must be drawn up quickly and presented to the decision-makers. The information channels should therefore establish a connection as direct as possible between the location of the events and the decision-makers. Ideally they will allow visual communication which enables decision-makers to receive even complex information much faster than with the traditional means of communication. Nevertheless, traditional telephone lines still play a very important role. Numbers for those telephones should already be available and assigned, but only made public in case of emergency. Since the information exchanged is highly sensitive, the question of security must also be borne in mind. Larger organizations keep crypto machines available for this reason.

The ability to disseminate information, not only outside but also within the company, demands further infrastructural measures. Lack of knowledge is dangerous as it provides scope for incorrect information and thus loss of trust. Besides the emergency numbers which allow the direct contact between the concerned person and the organization, the Internet became another very important tool (see also Section 7.5.6.1 and Example 54).

The management and information centres must be constantly equipped with extensive information technology. Especially, for the information centre, the proportion of direct communication has to be taken into consideration. This means that the necessary number of communications equipment (telephones, etc.) is available and that the additional telephone lines can also be made available quickly. The high importance of the Internet in the dissemination of information makes the necessity clear to provide direct Internet access in this area in order to provide information in as short a time as possible.

Obtaining information

Disseminate information

6.2 Contingency planning

Generic planning is followed by the anticipative analyses of certain crisis scenarios. The aim is to work out and evaluate different options in order to keep them available as plans of action. This form of planning is also known as 'alternative planning' or 'emergency planning'. In principle, contingency planning for anticipated events enables the organization to get a considerable head-start that essentially helps them to be more sure about their decisions in complex situations and when under pressure. The planning process, especially its detailing, is limited by financial and human constraints as well as restrictions of imagination.

It is, therefore, recommendable to carry out the basic efforts among similarly concerned entities and to continue fine-tuning the basic plans to the individual needs. This can be achieved, for instance, through associations such as the previously mentioned Caribbean Hotel Association, which produced together with the Caribbean Tourism Organization the 'Hurricane Procedures Manual' for the members of the Association.

On the other hand it is important to pay a lot of attention to the details when it concerns situations for which there is only a short reaction time available. Also for standard situations, it is important to strive for a high level of detail. In this way, the focus is more on the reaction to the situation and less on the event. Furthermore, situations in which the strict following of certain steps is required must be covered in detail in order to avert damage to the organization. For the last two cases, formulated planning modules are the result. They can be brought into use in a crisis situation and leave only the need to concentrate on minor adaptations.

Diagram 37: Checklist for the preparation against tropical storms

Natural disasters such as tropical storms leave little or no time to prepare for the onset. The preparation of checklists is therefore of major importance and should not be neglected by resorts in areas which are likely to be affected. The following example gives an idea of how a checklist can be prepared:

I. Activation of management	
Identify a person who will take on each of the following eight major responsibilities	• Building (resort) • Emergency shelter coordination and supplies • Communications • Employee coordination • Guest roster maintenance • Evacuation coordination • Travel assistance and transportation coordination • Security coordination

II. Preparing the resort	
(a) Verify the status of:	• Emergency communications equipment, including walkie-talkies and mobile telephones • Fire protection systems • Lightning protection systems • Water-level monitoring systems • Overflow detection devices • Automatic shutoffs • (Rechargeable) batteries, emergency power generation systems • Fuel supplies (full if possible) • Hazardous materials storage
(b) Define shutdown conditions	• Determine who can order shutdown of major resort elements (including evacuation) • Determine how a partial shutdown would affect other facility operations • Verify the length of time required for shutdown and restarting • Specify the conditions that could necessitate a shutdown and provide this information to the decision-maker in conjunction with information on what parts of the facility would be affected and the time needed to shut down and restart • Determine who would carry out shutdown procedures
(c) Preserve vital records	• Secure vital records not needed during the emergency. Store computer tapes and disks in insulated and waterproof containers • Initiate back up of computer systems • Ensure the your own web services are redundantly available on servers outside storm area • Arrange for evacuation of records to back-up facilities

(d) Secure outside facilities	• Move equipment to protected areas • Move furniture inside buildings • Remove banners, flags and vulnerable potted plants and artwork • Relocate livestock and move pets to indoor facilities • Secure materials to shutters or protect windows
(e) Prepare shelter facilities (if appropriate)	Clear and organize interior rooms for: • Guest and employee occupation • Food, fuel and luggage storage • Food distribution • Sanitary needs • Communications Provide for emergency heat, lighting and cooking

III. Emergency shelter coordination and supplies

Determine for whom the facility will be used as an emergency shelter site (i.e. guests, employees, essential operational employees). Base action on the items below on this decision:	• If the facility is NOT intended to be a shelter, identify official shelters and evacuation sites and prepare directions to them • If the facility WILL provide shelter, verify the accessibility and adequate provision of fuel, food water, blankets, pillows and first aid supplies to the sheltered areas of the facility. Verify telephone and backup communication lines to civil authorities and emergency assistance

IV. Communications

- Move communications equipment to the shelter space and test it to verify it works. This should include radios and, where possible, telephones and televisions
- Distribute portable short-range two-way radios to managers, coordinators, critical facility locations and security staff
- Establish back-up communications procedures which might include human messengers (runners)
- Activate automatic call divert to specialized call centre in the event of disrupted phone lines (important for the communication with relatives)
- Coordinate with civil authorities regarding facility intentions and status
- Establish a 'Message Board' for posting announcements on the status of the storm, warnings, evacuation notices, travel advisories and telephone numbers for assistance and emergencies
- Ensure that your own web services are redundantly available on servers outside storm area (mirror servers)
- Arrange for web maintenance during and after storm to disseminate important information to relatives and stakeholders (transmit important server access information to headquarters and to other (company) resorts outside the storm area)
- Copy and distribute checklists and advisory notices for tourists and guests

V. Employee coordination

- Identify and notify critical employees needed at the facility for the preparation or maintenance and operation during the storm
- Provide checklists and advisory notices to employees and their families
- Determine the need for employee sheltering and inform shelter coordinators

VI. Guest and employee roster
• Provide a log for guest and employee sign-in and sign-out
• Prepare and maintain a roster of current employees and guests
• Establish a file in which to maintain data provided by guests about their home addresses, emergency family contacts and travel plans
• Upon evacuation, update the roster with information on departures and intended destinations

VII. Evacuation coordination
• Determine evacuation conditions for the various categories of tourists, guests, non-critical employees and critical employees
• Verify who makes the decision to evacuate the facility
• Determine and post the evacuation routes and destination points
• Establish notification procedures to announce an evacuation
• Upon the decision to evacuate, contact civil authorities on facility intentions and evacuation progress

VIII. Travel assistance and transport coordination
• Identify commercial and emergency travel coordinators for airline, train and bus lines
• Announce the availability of emergency travel assistance
• Contact tour directors and determine transport requirements and the availability of any additional seats, if they have their own transport. Post the availability of such opportunities

IX. Security coordination
• Determine security requirements during emergency preparations, onset of the storm and immediately after the storm
• Establish when security resources should be brought to the facility and when they should be deployed
• Identify a coordination centre for security resources and supply it with appropriate emergency communications equipment
• Coordinate with communications in the event of security problems and the need for civil assistance

Source: Based on WTO (1998b)

If the modules from standard situations are not considered, planning must be interpreted again as situation bound, which requires adjustments over the course of time. Nevertheless, the ongoing planning updating must not lead into a permanent planning process that quickly exceeds the resources and can obstruct awareness of the essentials. It is much more advisable to carry out a review at regular intervals. The assessment of the actual threat, which is a result from the real environment, determines the appropriate rhythm.

Once developed, key personnel are to be made familiar with the contingency plans, especially the parts under their responsibility. For events with a high likelihood of onset, it is also in the interest of the guests to use an active approach of risk communication (see also Section 7.5.1.1). In the case of tropical storms, guests should already be informed upon their arrival about this natural phenomena and basic information about emergency procedures given. However, the details of the contingency plans should be handled more restrictively and only be made available to those involved in the emergency activities.

The results of the contingency planning are plans of action, normally in the form of files, that have been drawn up for different situations according to a certain scheme (in spite of the advantages of computer-supported systems, printed crisis instructions dominate in practice). They contain all information required for the situation, checklists and contact data for internal and external decision-makers and critical personnel.

Need for a wide view

When preparing a contingency plan, it is important not to underestimate that most situations are not only a threat to the tourists but also to the locals in those destinations. As Hurricane Katrina showed in September 2005 in the United States, both of these groups were affected and the enormous threat to the lives and belongings of the local population caused prioritization for the needs of the latter. Incidents were reported where originally chartered transportation capacities organized for guests by hotel management had been confiscated by local authorities for 'higher needs'.

Example 41: The Service Handbook of TUI

The Service Handbook of the tour operator TUI comprises some 200 pages. It complements the crisis manual described in Example 39 and is at the disposal of all the 1500 TUI travel guides worldwide.

In this Handbook, major negative events of importance for the tour operator are listed, among other things, and detailed binding instructions are given for the travel guide on how to handle a situation, what to prioritize first, what to be taken into consideration and whom to contact. The conceptional responsibility of the handbook lies with the department of Destination Support Services (ZUA) which regularly updates it.

6.3 Training

The results of the crisis-planning circle are in practise often disregarded or intentionally ignored when a crisis occurs. This can be explained by the need for decision-makers to reduce the complexity of the situation whereby personal experience is preferred to other knowledge. This underlines the need to get this level of decision-makers already involved during the crisis-planning phase. Management that takes part in crisis planning before an evolving crisis, tends less to reject those plans than those using the plans for the first time.

Furthermore, an early acceptance and internalization of the procedures of crisis plans should be achieved through regular training. This avoids on the one hand that the belief of invulnerability continues to exist, as it can cause extremely damaging situations during a crisis. And, on the other hand, a feeling for crisis situations gradually develops and helps those responsible, through the experience they have collected, to respond more successfully in the event of a crisis.

Generally, the willingness of staff to participate in training increases with the personal perception that such an event will likely repeat. For this reason, the preparedness of an organization must be increased by using scenarios tailored to the specific circumstances of the organization (see also Example 21). Through this reflection on the possible negative events and the consequences for one's own organization, the vulnerability becomes something real and not that far fetched. Thinking about concrete costs and financial losses makes very clear to both staff and management what is at stake and what happens if they are not prepared.

As it concerns the training, two different groups need to be distinguished. One large group of people have to be prepared for activities that are considered exceptional tasks. Those specific abilities must be

Abilities in times of crisis

One of the abilities that needs to be trained especially for situations of crisis is the prioritization. Most incidents significantly exceed limitations known from normal situations. The available resources are not sufficient to concentrate on all affected persons or all consequences at the same time. For example, within the sphere of emergency medical treatment the approach necessary is described by the term 'triage'. Originally this French term was used by cotton traders to distinguish the different qualities. Later, Napoleon's military doctor Larrey used this term to set treatment priorities when dealing with wounded soldiers in the battlefield.

learned and kept regularly up-to-date. The aim of the first training session is to learn about the 'unknown activity' in such a way that the person can carry out this activity in a sound manner and without delay. This kind of training is useful for care personnel, machine operators, telephone operators, etc. Management does not form part of this kind of training with the exception of media training, i.e. learning the correct way of interacting with media representatives.

Example 42: Care Teams

Care Teams in times of crisis look after those affected and their relatives. They need to train regularly and most of the time they are recruited from the staff members of one's own organization. They therefore carry out these duties in second function.

After a careful selection based on mental strength, tact, understanding, talent for organization and ability to take decisions, they follow a first training course learning the fundamental principles. This includes legal, financial, medical and other practical issues as well as psychology for crisis situations. Through regular training sessions these skills are practised and kept up-to-date to ensure an adequate level of preparedness for the care unit members.

Care Teams are one of the most important functions of crisis coping for an organization. It's the interface to the client and the relatives and therefore one of the key functions that also determines whether or not the crisis management efforts will be seen as successful.

The other group of people are circled around the management of the organization which becomes responsible for the crisis management. The training of these decision-makers offers the opportunity for these people to gain a deeper knowledge of the existing crisis plans, get acquainted with the aims and procedures of those plans. This training might also as a result encourage them to suggest further improvements for the plans. The main aim of the training is the step-by-step introduction to the particularities of a crisis situation. That includes dealing with complex decision situations with normally unimportant factors, time pressure and heavy stress. Through situations which are just played at management level, those factors and consequences can be well simulated. Practice shows that especially those situations are extremely helpful to train control and decision procedures, channels of information and the interaction between the decision-makers. They also help to identify at an early stage possible problems of competence and responsibility and to resolve them consequently. The latter is still one of the major problems for crisis coping.

6.4 Preventive planning

When a negative event is looming on the horizon, that is, early information points to the increased likelihood of a negative event, then preventive planning is used. Depending on the urgency with which the task must be completed, that is, depending on the speed with which the crisis is developing, this can happen through the formulation of various option plans. These consider – in contrast to contingency planning – the immediate and probable negative event. The aim of these option plans, drawn up in the framework of preventive planning, is the formulation and preparation of actual possible solutions for overcoming the developing crisis situation. As high a level of detail as possible should be striven for, through which the pros and cons of the various options are made apparent.

In addition, it must be checked that the data, which the current plans have been based upon, are still valid in order to increase the certainty of the planning and the success of future actions. This is to be done with current planning too, which is to be constantly updated on the basis of the constant monitoring of the threatening situation. For all planning measures of preventive planning, the findings and results of previous planning steps, above all, the contingency planning, are used as a starting point. Even though this rarely results in the formulated contingency planning being used in its entirety, the likely use of at least parts of the contingency plan considerably shortens the preventive planning process.

Questions for review and discussion

- Explain the purpose of generic planning.
- What are contingency plans?
- What are the typical functions of Care Teams?
- Why is training so important for crisis management?
- What are points in favour and against the use of external experts?

Suggestions for further reading

Sexton, J. B. (ed.) (2004), *The Better the Team, the Safer the World: Golden Rules of Group Interaction in High Risk Environments: Evidence based suggestions for improving performance,* Gottlieb Daimler and Karl Benz Foundation and Swiss Re Centre for Global Dialogue, Ladenburg and Rüschlikon.

World Tourism Organization (1998), *Handbook on Natural Disaster Reduction in Tourist Areas,* WTO, Madrid.

World Tourism Organization (1998), *Guide for Local Authorities on Developing Sustainable Tourism,* WTO, Madrid.

Useful websites

GAST/EPIC: www.gast-epic.de

7 Crisis management instruments

The marketing instruments employed in crisis management require no change or innovation in themselves. The instruments and fundamental decisions still remain the same. Only the different framework caused by the negative event has to be taken into account.

The following considerations use the differentiation of instruments predominant in literature into the following levels: product, price, communication and distribution policy. These instruments are not used separately but always combined. This is the reason why particular attention should be paid to this interaction.

The effect of the instruments is determined by the selected competitive strategy, which, conversely, influences also the selection of the instruments in times of crisis. Before an in-depth consideration of the different instruments takes place, a few important questions arise that need to be clarified before selecting instruments, determining the marketing mix and finally employing the instruments. Under normal circumstances, the form in which the market is targeted has to be determined. In times of crisis, the question must be answered once again regarding the sphere of 'interested' people and of activity change. In addition, there is the timing aspect, that is, the temporal implementation of instruments, which includes not only their sequence and duration but also their relation to the event.

7.1 Basic decisions

Objectives

- Learn to distinguish the different points in time for the employment of instruments
- To recognize the different factors influencing the determination of the budget in crisis situations
- To understand the pros and cons of a standardized or differentiated strategy of employment of instruments

Key terms and concepts

- Timing aspects
- Marketing budget
- Employment strategies

7.1.1 Different points in time

The temporal dimension of the use of the instruments has an important function. Even under normal circumstances, the effect of the marketing instruments differs depending on the time factor.

The onset of a negative event strongly influences the different points in time when the marketing instruments are to be employed. This external influence is a very important difference compared to the normal situation, when time plays a far less important role.

In a first step, the crisis has to be identified. This is accompanied by the previously discussed problems of perception and assessment. From the point in time a negative event is noticed, the employment of each instrument has to be seen from a changed point of view, even if it only concerns the continuation of marketing decisions taken previously. From then on, all the organization's activities are interpreted and understood as the result of conscious decision-making. At the same time, however, it becomes clear that the point at which instruments are employed in crisis management is divided in at least two parts. A first pre-active point in time can be seen where decisions are taken about the interruption of the marketing measures that were initiated under normal circumstances. In the first place, this has to do with the assessment as to whether the use of instruments is still appropriate. Therefore, the important variables of the communication policy – advertising, type of exhibition participation, etc. – and also of the product policy – for example, the introduction of new products – have to be checked against the negative event for contradictions.

Active point

A second, active point in time comes when the instruments are selected and knowingly employed as the result of a negative event. The determination of this moment is particularly influenced by the chosen reaction strategy. In this active phase of the instrument's employment, market and environmental conditions change constantly and to a far greater extent than usual. For this reason, instruments should be put in place during a crisis, which constantly monitor such changes and indicate whether strategy changes and/or corrections might be necessary (see the explanations in Section 7.5.6.4).

Post-active point

A post-active point in time can also be observed where the event is no longer of general public interest. Nevertheless, the negative event is still present as long as it can be remembered. The employment of instruments in this phase can trigger undesired memories and, therefore, cause intensified negative effects such as contradictions. Also in this case, the chosen reaction strategy determines how seriously the problem will be dealt with or whether it is preferred that the events should be buried in oblivion.

Seasonal aspect

The seasonal aspect of the affected product has the strongest influence on the time that lies between the negative event and the different points in time. The overall period of time available for the employment of the instruments has to be defined in relation to the traditional peaks of the product's demand curve. Within this time span, the individual points in time must be determined. It is absolutely possible that the post-active point in time must be placed in a phase in which irritation cannot be avoided, that is, the product presentation is in contradiction with the negative event. This instrument employment must consider this inconsistency and aim at minimizing it.

Micro-level of the point in time

Another peculiarity of marketing in times of negative events is the micro-level of the point in time. This describes the determination of instrument employment within the course of the day. Changing consumer attentions and product-technical peculiarities of the mass media show, for instance, that this micro-level is more important in times of negative events than under normal circumstances.

Diagram 38: Points in time

Points	Normal circumstances	Pre-active point	Active point	Post-active point
Macro-level		Affected by the seasonal aspect		
Micro-level		Affected by changing consumer attentions within the day and product-technical peculiarities		

The moment the negative event is noticed

7.1.2 Duration of employment and budget determination

Besides the determination of the point in time of a particular marketing activity, the duration is another important influential factor for the marketing mix. Normally, the duration of the marketing activity is marked by the improvement of the actual situation and the achievement of new objectives, such as higher sales, etc. In a situation of crisis, the main aim is the regaining of the positions kept before the crisis. Because the majority of marketing activities are related to cost, the available budget imposes an essential restriction when determining the duration of instrument employment.

Budget

Due to the crisis situation, the determination of the marketing budget must take cost and profit into account from a changed point of view. In the present case, no additional profit is gained by the investment of a particular amount but a loss of profit is avoided. This means that the estimation of future losses is an important criterion when determining the budget. Therefore, it must be the uppermost aim of company management to analyse medium- and long-term consequences as quickly as possible. This should describe the loss that would be expected if counteractive instruments were not employed.

Analyse of medium- and long-term consequences

The estimation of the loss of earnings, determination of the budget and actual allocation of financial resources is in practise one of the biggest challenges. On one hand, as the resources and positions of the budget are generally determined for mid- and long-term and even if earmarked positions of the marketing budgets are reallocated, they would only last for a short period of time. On the other hand, they require a thorough knowledge of crisis management, as without it an estimation of the losses, strategy selection and a suitable determination of the

Estimation of the loss of revenue

$$LR = (ETA * ADS * ADE) - MC$$

LR =	Loss of revenue for the destination
ETA=	Expected change of tourist arrivals
ADS =	Average duration of stay
ADE =	Average daily expenditure
MC =	Material cost

instruments and their costs are hardly possible. The process of determination of the budget must be carried out fast, as only after completion can it be ensured that a chosen strategy can be carried out successfully, that the instruments can be employed consistently and that future activities can be financed against stabilizing revenues. In practise it can be observed that destinations and companies which had undergone this process once and gained experience with crisis management, are completing this process of budget determination faster than those affected for the first time.

Furthermore, the time at which a negative event occurs has an influence on the determination of the overall duration of instrument employment. The duration is longer, the further away the onset of the negative event is from the normal booking time. As there is more time available, the emphasis of instrument employment can be placed on the post-active phase. Thus, potential consistency problems are avoided. Conversely, the duration of instrument employment decreases if the negative event occurs in temporal proximity to concrete travel decision and, therefore, demands a quick reaction.

7.1.3 Standardization and differentiation aspects

The decision whether to target a market in a standardized or differentiated form is taken by the company under normal circumstances in view of markets with their current and potential customers. Whilst a standardized approach targets all spheres of activity, similarly, differentiation aims at the differences between segments. In times of a crisis this question has to be answered again. This comes because of the different reactions towards the negative event but also as the marketing activities will now be observed by a much larger audience.

Low costs are an argument in favour of standardization, even in times of crisis. Because instruments are used in the same way towards all spheres of activity, no additional planning or adjustment costs and quantity advantages can be obtained. There is also the fact that time advantage can be gained by a standardized use of instruments. Furthermore, the employment of instruments is less complicated because the segments must not be dealt with individually. The non-optimal satisfaction of needs of the different spheres of activity is of disadvantage. This way, an important opportunity for crisis management, which is based on differing needs and reactions to a negative event, is wasted.

The necessity of differentiation first arises in the area of operative activity. Here, it is important to ensure the protection of the individuals' sphere. In concrete terms, this means that those directly affected by the negative event and their relatives, especially if so desired, are kept separate from the uninvolved. For this reason, generally the distinction between: those affected (uninjured), injured, collecting relatives and media representatives are made. This operative aspect of differentiation follows a strategic one. With regard to the segments of the sales market, a revision of differentiation criteria appears to be appropriate. Depending on the type of event, segmenting characteristics used under normal circumstances should be extended to risk-relevant behavioural characteristics. Various individual factors with influence over different reactions have already been determined.

The cultural circle membership factor through which differing reactions to one and the same event can be explained is particularly noticeable. It suggests that segments should be targeted differently depending on their risk perception. This means that, in the initial phase, those markets that react less sensitively and have a more stable image of the service should be concentrated on. In other segments, the employment of the marketing instruments should be planned and carried out with a medium- to long-term perspective. At the same time, other influential factors discussed previously, such as the dismay of a national group, can be useful differentiation characteristics.

Furthermore, travel decision phases were identified as important criteria. Within these periods of time, the tourist goes through various stages of involvement and, therefore, has different information needs.

Consequently, it would seem to be sensible to differentiate the employment of the instruments over these phases. This poses a particular challenge as it must be ensured that no contradictions arise.

Apart from this segment differentiation aspect within the consumer sphere of activity, it should be assessed whether the remaining spheres of activity should be handled differently. In the first place, it must be ascertained what ranking the other spheres of activity should be granted and what their specific needs are. The resulting differentiation refers predominantly to the scope of information made available and less to the differentiation of the instruments themselves.

It generally applies both under normal circumstances and for crisis management that only as much differentiation as necessary but as much standardization as possible should be practised. This is not simply due to high costs that are the consequence of differentiation but also the risk of the different strategies interacting. The latter means that differentiation, especially when used in crisis management, must be carefully thought and applied. In practice, the use of personalized instruments, which offer certain differentiation possibilities, must be taken into account more often than in normal situations. It should also not be forgotten that differentiation, an essential influential factor for crisis management, takes more time to implement. Therefore, standardized behaviour is to be recommended at the start of a situation.

Example 43: Egypt's Marketing Plan

Egypt's marketing budget amounted to 586 000 US$ in 1991, which, if converted, equals to 0.28 US$ per international visitor. The Ministry of Tourism asked, even before the first negative events occurred, to increase this relatively low international marketing budget to at least 1–3 per cent of the tourism receipts generated.

The budget, which was step-by-step adjusted to 815 000 US$, was later extended to 21 million US$ for 1994 and 1995 due to the events of 1992/93. It was to be distributed among the following source markets: USA, Great Britain, Germany, France, Italy and Japan.

In this way, there was no fundamental change in the selection of contending countries as these markets already existed in the selection of 1991, before the first negative events took place. There were changes, however, in the selection of Egypt's contending product areas. In 1994 and 1995, activities concentrated on the independently perceived beach destinations of the Sinai and the Red Sea. These alone received 25 million out of the 42 million US$ budget for advertising.

The distribution of financial resources was divided as follows:

Advertising campaigns in the general and specialist press of the 6 core markets	7 million US$
TV spots in the 6 core countries	22.4 million US$
Conventional advertising in the remaining source markets	2.6 million US$
Trade shows, conferences, Egyptian nights and receptions	3 million US$
Road shows	1.2 million US$

The increase in the budget was maintained the same way as with the concentration on electronic media. This end consumer advertising was to continue the newly trodden paths of advertising for the new beach resorts on the Red Sea. In addition, the diminished cultural tourism of Nile cruises was strongly encouraged once again. Tour operators welcomed this form of marketing which stimulated demand.

The period of time which went by until financial resources were made available and which, as a result, formed the starting point of a new marketing offensive, progressively decreased over the various events which shook the tourism industry in Egypt.

If the events of Luxor in 1997 are considered, estimations of the expected costs were made available in the shortest possible time. The International Monetary Fund (IMF) estimated this at a maximum of 500-700 million US$, which proved to be extraordinarily precise. It can be assumed that, under the circumstances, the decision for an early post-active point of employment of the marketing instruments, scarcely three and a half months after the event, was encouraged. Without doubt, this was also influenced by the traditional purchasing period for trips to Egypt in its most important source markets which begins in March and ends in May.

With its stronger orientation of the marketing activities since 1994 directly towards consumers, where Egypt itself saw its biggest mistake in the past, the most standardized market treatment was aimed for. A differentiation took place only between the European and the American market, on the one hand, and the Arab market, on the other.

Sources: Sayed (1997), Wahab (1995), Peymani and Felger (1997), WTO (1996a)

Questions for review and discussion

- What are the factors influencing the determination of the budget in times of crisis?
- Explain the concept of the 'pre-active point in time'.
- Name the advantages of targeting the market in a standardized form.
- What has to be taken into account when using an approach of differentiated form?

Suggestions for further reading

World Tourism Organization (1994), *Marketing Plans & Strategies of National Tourism Administrations*, WTO, Madrid.

World Tourism Organization (1996), *Budgets of National Tourism Administrations*, WTO, Madrid.

World Tourism Organization (2003), *Evaluating NTO Marketing Activities*, WTO, Madrid.

7.2 Product policy

Objectives

- To be familiar with the short-, mid-, and long-term possibilities of product policy for crisis management
- To be aware of the importance of product accessibility
- To recognize the importance of personnel
- To realize the potential of guarantees

Key terms and concepts

• Product development	• Product accessibility
• Product positioning	• Scheduled and charter-flights
• Product variation	• Guarantees
• Combined effects	• Personnel

The task of the product policy as an instrument of crisis management is to form or adjust the product in line with the reaction strategy in order to alleviate the consequences of negative events. All spheres of activity of the negative event should be taken into account. Nevertheless, the consumer sphere of activity is generally paid more attention to due to its function in ensuring the existence of the organization.

7.2.1 Product development

The first task of product development is the elimination of the event's negative effects on the services on offer. Against this background, measures of product development aim at re-establishing the original condition and benefits on offer. For a negative event that would endanger a tourist's personal safety, steps should be introduced that prevent or curb this threat. In the case of beach pollution, beach cleaning or the immediate readiness of alternatives, such as swimming pools, could be an action of product development. This cause/event-oriented behaviour must be introduced immediately because consumers follow them with increased interest in all the various travel phases. Tourists in the holiday phase take an immediate interest in the speed with which the measures are introduced.

In the active but mainly in the post-active phase of instrument employment, the question must be answered as to whether the product positioning can be maintained in spite of a negative event. If this is affirmed for the long term, various short-term product development measures can be taken to lessen the consequences. Product positioning

One possibility is the temporary or lasting use of combined effects. By linking the negatively affected product with other important services, the product can be still sold. It is conceivable, for example, that the destination becomes the venue for music concerts or other events. This draws attention away from the affected product, which, as a result, is no longer the main object of purchase interest. Subsequently, Combined effects the event takes on the travel trigger function. Furthermore, such events are suitable for imparting certain communication content, assuming an appropriate selection. Because the realization of many events is accompanied by media reports, a bridge is formed between the event and the venue (see Section 7.5.9).

Variation of the products on offer

The variation of the products on offer is also an option. With the launch of new products – for example new destinations within the affected country – the actual special attention of the media can be used effectively to launch the product to a wide audience. This approach is always recommendable if the newly launched products differ significantly from those affected by the negative event.

Temporary product variations

Temporary product variations were recommended by WTO (1991a) to the countries affected by the Gulf War. The aim was, by means of temporary product changes, to reach segments of intra-regional and domestic tourism, which reacted less sensitively to the events. The success of short-term product variation depends above all on whether the segments approached have a comparable readiness to pay. If this is not the case, it does not only reduce profit but also the 'scenery effect', with its long-term consequences, comes into place (see Section 7.3.1).

Product variations, which are aimed at improving the quality of the product, can often be observed in practise. They are as a rule the result of a period of lower occupancy which is used to advance modernization plans or additional training of staff. Many hotels in Indonesia chose this approach after the attacks of 2002 in Bali. Nevertheless, whenever these measures are started, it has to be born in mind that they require liquidity in times when the occupancy, and thus the regular revenues, are particularly low. Thus, a rather prudent approach should be followed.

Example 44: H.I.S. – A Japanese Tour Operator Proves the Unthinkable

Japanese tourists are normally known and aimed for because of their high spending habits. When it comes to negative events however, tourists from Japan are considered as one of the most sensitive national segments. They disappear fast after a negative event and it takes destinations a long time to recover and convince Japanese tourists once again that their attractions are safe and back in place. Japanese tourists usually start returning only when everyone else has returned.

It is very important for this reason to understand that not every nature-given thing is insurmountable. H.I.S., a Japanese tour operator with headquarters in Tokyo and 171 offices nationwide, faced the challenge after the attacks of September 11 in a way so far unknown. Rather than cancelling all its activities in the United States, H.I.S. launched shortly after the attacks a product that can be best described as 'Solidarity Trips' and labelled it with the slogan 'We love New York'. This new product was fully aimed at supporting the tourism industry in New York City by continuing the visits to the city rather than staying away. In addition, H.I.S. showed its solidarity with the families of the victims and conveyed to its customers that 5 per cent of all income generated by these Solidarity Trips would be donated to NYC ex-Mayor Giuliani's Twin Towers Fund. With these Solidarity Trips, H.I.S. was able to encourage Japanese tourists to travel in times of fear and insecurity, as no other product had done before.

A total of 1600 bookings were generated during the promotional time, 2 October until 19 December 2001, and proved its success not only in commercial terms but also in showing that tourism is a form of expressing emotions. These emotions do not necessarily have to have a pleasant origin, as it is very often assumed.

The H.I.S. press release

Translation:

The re-establishment of New York

Special project: 'We love New York'

The company H.I.S. (central office in Tokyo, Shibuya-ku, Executive Manager: Mr. Hideo Sawada) will organize a special project 'We love New York' in order to collaborate in the re-establishment of New York City. Part of these benefits will be donated.

The terrorist attacks of September 11 plunged the entire world into grief. First of all we want to transmit our condolences to the families and friends of the victims of this act of terrorism.

The United States mean a lot to Japan and at an individual level it is one of the countries that developed the closest relationship with our country. The decrease of tourism after the terrorist attacks has damaged the economy, starting with the tourism sector.

Consequently, wishing a fast recovery for New York, H.I.S. has organized a special project called 'We love New York'. In its own view, the most important thing for New York is that people perceive that the city and the United States are trying to recover their brightness and to receive the energy of tourism to regain dynamism. This tour operator wishes that the visit of tourists will encourage citizens of the United States and wishes to go on and give complete support as a first step to peace.

H.I.S. will donate 5 per cent of the income of this project to the foundation 'Twin Towers Fund' created by the ex-Mayor Giuliani for 'the families that have lost their loved ones'. Details can be consulted in our web page (www.his-j.com) and in our 171 national offices.

The products related to the project 'We love New York' are identified with this label.

Tour operators can, by means of a change to the contracted quantities, balance temporary fluctuation and shift the burden of the event. This opportunity is limited by contractual developments and economic relationships. The increasing vertical integration of services, such as flight or accommodation services, formerly contracted by the tour operator, has, from this point of view, a restrictive effect on action possibilities. At the same time, this makes clear the particular significance of preventive measures, which must be introduced to make these investments safe. Apart from the purely contractual perspective, the aspect of future cooperation must not be neglected because, in spite of short-term necessities, long-term success is decisive. **Contracted quantities**

If, however, the analysis indicates that the product positioning can no longer be maintained, other steps must be initiated. Whilst a destination itself could initiate a difficult repositioning, in this case, the tour operator carries out an assortment adjustment, by which the affected product is removed from the programme on offer. More difficult is the situation for the provider of the core service. He can already **Repositioning** achieve a first limited success with a simple renaming. This is recommendable for example when the negative event did not have its origin in the sphere of one's own organization. In practise such renaming is used for cruise-liners but can also be applied in some cases to the hotel sector. However, together with the change of the brand name, a new experience value strategy must be put in place and in the case of a destination, a rather difficult process of reposition starts.

7.2.2 Product accessibility

The accessibility of the product is a problem primarily to be found in the tourism sector. It appears mostly in the area of mid and long-haul destinations. These are reached mainly by using aircrafts for transportation (see also Diagram 16). If those accesses cannot be provided, the tourism products of the destination cannot be reached and consequently they will, most likely, not be called upon anymore. This is a regular problem to be observed following negative events.

Charter flight companies

Holiday destinations usually have a high dependency on charter flights. But also charter flight companies highly depend on holidaymakers. Different to regular scheduled flights, the 'estimated customer demand' is taken as a basis for the seasonable preparations and there are only few possibilities to compensate the demand of holidaymakers with business travellers. Consequently, charter flights are regularly cancelled to destinations where negative events took place or re-routed to other or new destinations. In this sense, already at an early stage, a decision is taken on the short-term recovery possibilities of the destination.

From the point of view of a destination, this problem can be solved by using national carriers which continue to ensure the accessibility of the destination or at least fly to other or new source markets. However, this form of maintaining the accessibility is very cost intensive and in liberalized markets rarely feasible. But it can be tried through strategic actions to reach long-term relationships with the necessary service providers, i.e. especially tour operators. The following example gives some detailed insights on how financial incentives can be used to ensure that the tourism product is still accessible.

> **Example 45: Egypt's Charter Flight Support Programme**
> Charter flights are the classical symbol of a package holiday. They enable tour operators to develop efficiently and with a comfortable degree of flexibility, programs to bring tourists to destinations which are seldom sufficiently covered by scheduled flights. Tourist destinations can suffer significantly from the absence of flight connections once charter flight companies decide to discontinue their services. Such a decision is often taken following a negative event, in view of the uncertain demand for the destination.
>
> Following the attacks of 11 September 2001 on the United States, Egypt immediately realized that these attacks would have a strong negative impact on its tourism. As predicted, it was soon hit by a stream of cancellations from European countries. The Ministry of Tourism together with the Egyptian Tourism Federation designed and implemented a 10-step Recovery Plan which included, among other initiatives, an especially innovative plan called the 'Charter Flights Support Programme'. This programme was soon considered to be a prime factor in the fast recovery of Egypt.

The 'Charter Flights Support Programme' was implemented as from 15 November 2001. It was designed to subsidize charter flight operators so that they bear no risk of losing money even if they kept their flights posted for sale until the last minute, as long as they could fill 50 per cent of the seats (65 per cent for some markets).

The support programme was provided via the payment of a fixed sum per empty seat, depending on the flight time and within a specific range of flights seat capacity, as follows:

Flight time	under 2 hours	2–4 hours	over 4 hours
Support sum per empty seat	80 €	150 €	200 €

The eligible range of occupancy in flights was the following:

	All Egyptian Airports (except Cairo & Taba)	Taba Airport
Flights arriving from all points except UK and Scandinavia	min. 50%–max. 79%	35%–79%
Flights arriving from UK and Scandinavia	min. 65%–max. 94%	50%–94%

The effects of the programme showed rapidly: tourist arrivals from traditional but non-resilient markets grew by reasonable rates in direct response to the Charter Flight Support Program: United Kingdom (9.5%), Germany (2.1%) and Spain (28%). Within a year, Egypt regained the prior rates of tourist arrivals. Egypt was thus able to maintain the routes of access to its destinations despite the international difficult circumstances. Far less money than anticipated was finally spent on empty seats. This also demonstrated that the initially expected fear of the tourists was overestimated. Nevertheless, if the availability of seats had not been ensured that way, tourists would have had no chance to access the tourism product, i.e. the destination Egypt.

The 'Charter Flight Support Programme' shows how an innovative approach within the product policy and the necessary imagination can be of great value in times of crisis.

For destinations that were mainly dependent on scheduled flights, this problem of accessibility did not exist in the past. However, there was a so-called reputation problem, i.e. it was important for the destination that not only the national carrier but also a well-known airline from the source market was serving the route. Thus, the well-known brand of this airline could be used toward the potential tourists from the source market. This was not only a signal of quality for the flight but also proof that the destination was valuable enough to be served with regular flights.

This changed with the SARS crisis in Asia. Australia suddenly realized that it heavily depended on flights with stop-overs in major Asian cities such as Singapore, Hong-Kong or Bangkok and these cities were now avoided by tourists as much as possible as a consequence of SARS. The government of Australia tackled this problem systematically by identifying and evaluating alternative stop-overs and direct flights from the most important source markets to Australia in the event of a new outbreak of SARS.

Scheduled flights

189

7.2.3 Personnel

The personnel of the affected organization are not only its 'ambassadors' under normal circumstances but they also make an important contribution towards success if a negative event occurs. This applies in two different ways: on the one hand, towards ones' own customers as the tourism product is marked, to a great extent, by the human contact between the provider and consumer of the service; and, on the other hand, towards the wider social environment for which personnel are an important contact point.

In both areas, personnel's statements and behaviour are paid particular attention to after a negative event. Inconsistencies in official announcements are perceived immediately. Because it has to do with employees, their behaviour and comments are classed as being in accordance with the facts. For this reason, it is important to create and convey guidelines for these unusual situations. In this way, actions that do not conform to corporate goals, if not avoided, are at least less probable. An adequately developed corporate culture, which turns out to be the guidelines for behaviour in unpredictable situations, is also beneficial. It ensures that the organization's fundamental principles and values are internalized. A developed corporate culture thus fosters the conformity of the individual employee's reactions with the organization's reaction.

Corporate culture

> **Example 46: It Could Have Happened Anywhere but I am Glad it Happened in Hawaii**
>
> The impact of a negative event on a tourist's impression of a destination can be substantially changed if he receives the adequate support and assistance.
>
> Roy Stanton from Sydney (Australia) was assaulted in September 2003 during his holidays in Hawaii. Three attackers hit him so strong on the forehead that he was left unconscious. Later, he could no longer remember the details of the attack or the attackers. But he was left with a strong wound on the forehead, a broken nose, a broken tooth and two other damaged ones.
>
> Once in the hospital and after leaving the Emergency Room, Roy promptly received the apologies on behalf of the State of Hawaii, from both the Lt. Governor and the Prosecuting Attorney's Office. But what became even more important to Roy, as it would be to any other tourist or victim, was the immediate assistance that was given to him by the Visitor Aloha Society of Hawai'i (VASH): Two volunteers were without delay sent to him on behalf of the VASH to help him in all matters and to make his 'extended stay' (from 5 days to 3 weeks) as pleasant as possible, in his actual condition. They assisted him in running through all the paper work, looking after his daily accommodation, meals, transportation, they even provided for entertainment in this difficult time. Roy Stanton felt cared for from the beginning. Besides the immediate government's reaction, he felt that the VASH had given him, at all times, the necessary company, comfort and support that a tourist needs in a foreign land.
>
> Back in Australia and despite these unfortunate circumstances, Roy Stanton became one of the best Ambassadors of Hawaii's hospitality. Although he was assaulted and had to face further difficulties upon his return, he declared: *'It could have happened anywhere but I am glad it happened in Hawaii.'* He had felt reassured and was thankful for the selfless services and unfailing attention that were provided to him by the VASH.

VISITOR ALOHA SOCIETY OF HAWAI'I
"O KE ALOHA KE KULEANA O KAHI MALIHINI"
(Love is the Host in Strange Lands)

Since its establishment in the year 1997, the VASH has provided assistance to 6000 visitors victimized by crime or adversity. It is referred to by Hawaii's police department, hospitals and other institutions and administrations. The people working for VASH are volunteers. Their training and missions are made possible because of financial support from the government and donations that businesses, organizations and individuals graciously provide.

However, providing information for employees is also important. It must be ensured that they are constantly kept informed during the active and post-active phase about important circumstances. This aspect is frequently neglected and information provision is carried out in a predominantly exterior-oriented manner. In this way, the company lessens its chances. Experience confirms that employees develop, as a rule, a high and positive relationship to the company in times of crisis. This predestines them for a credible multiplier function.

However, switchboard employees and guards, who are paid great attention due to their exposed position and help to form first impressions, should not be disregarded. One should also note that it is important to understand above all, in a situation of crisis, the implications of one's own actions and to be able to estimate the effect on the system as a whole. This aspect of company-wide thinking and acting becomes more important, the greater the spatial distance is, since it can complicate the exchange of information and coordination. Companies such as McKinsey, which rate the understanding among their employees highly and have a number of branches around the globe, organize

Group interactions in times of stress
Teamwork and communication of intentions are important factors for successful interaction in times of stress. This was confirmed by the GIHRE project which was initiated as a consequence of the Birgenair airplane crash in the Dominican Republic.
Source: Sexton (2004)

regular national sporting events, for example, to bring their employees together. This is especially often the case in tourism. Therefore, special training sessions, which impart this company-wide perspective and the regular transfer of employees, are possibilities to improve the situation. In addition to these measures, which should not be understood as the exclusive task of crisis management but as part of normal management exercises should be used to prepare for crisis situations (see also Section 6.3).

In brief, it remains to be ascertained that personnel are one of the most important instruments of crisis management. With it, the spheres of activity, can, like with no other instrument, be targeted in a differentiated, reliable and in a dialogue-oriented manner. Because they make an important contribution to the success of crisis management, training and practice measures should be correspondingly comprehensive.

7.2.4 Guaranteed services

A particular characteristic of a crisis situation is that the consumer's ability to assess the tourism services on offer is decreased. This is even more relevant because the tourism product, as has repeatedly been illustrated, is a belief and trust product. Apart from the fundamental problems of assessing the service on offer, there is the difficulty of estimating the actual consequences of a negative event on the product.

All consumers, regardless of their product experience, are affected by this restriction on assessment ability. For this reason, measures must be taken that lessen the risk of a tourist making a mistake. The organization's commitment in the form of guaranteed services, for example, belongs to this category. In general, this is understood as promises and regulations that the supplier gives to a service and through which he assures the perfect condition of the goods on offer. Two messages are conveyed to the consumer by means of this method:

1. The customer is assured that potential damage will, in part, be reimbursed.

2. It is documented that the guarantee provider is convinced of the service he is offering.

For these reasons, the use of guaranteed services is, above all, suitable for consumers in the orientation and travel decision phases. Guarantees should be especially implemented more quickly for those products for which the competitive advantage does not come from their basic benefits. Due to the great number of choices available, a quick alternative reaction on the part of the consumer should be assumed. The guaranteed service must not be recoverable or documented in order to be understood as such by the consumer. The principal reaction in the form of a proactive handling strategy or the long presence in difficult markets is already a signal to the consumer. The final design of the guaranteed services and the strength of the obligation depend very much on the type of event as well as on the accompanying circumstances.

In comparison to most instruments, the guarantee has the advantage that it quickly makes an instrument available that can be traded with immediately after a negative event has occurred. Nevertheless, this should not tempt those responsible into implementing the instrument too early. Before its use, the company must be completely convinced of the quality of the guaranteed service. An assurance that cannot be fulfilled would not only trigger legal and economic

Examples of Guarantees

- The Sandal Hotels in the Caribbean offer to their clients the 'Blue Chip Hurricane Guarantee'. If the holiday is affected by a hurricane, the guest receives as compensation a free replacement vacation at any Sandals or Beaches Resort for the same duration as the one originally booked regardless of how many days were affected.

- Air China offered to their clients in 2003 the payment of compensation if they became infected by SARS on one of their flights. The company had this guarantee reinsured.

- The government of Thailand offered in 2003 to every tourist a sum of 100 000 US$ if he was infected by SARS during a stay in Thailand. This guarantee was also reinsured.

consequences in the sense of paying the promised compensation but would also lead to a serious loss of reputation.

Example 47: The TUI Statement of Guarantee – Customers' Confidence in Charter Airlines

German tour operators used to have various charter airlines under contract and usually did not guarantee the employment of one specific airline for one specific flight or destination. This circumstance formed part of each contract between tour operator and client and was also published in the catalogues. The right to change airlines without the customers' approval and knowledge provided more flexibility to the tour operators. If for any sudden reason the planned aircraft could not be used for the flight, tour operators had the possibility to use another airline or aircraft and thus avoid the cancellation of the flight. Particularly in the case of long-haul flights, this procedure was the only practical alternative to fulfil one of the clients' primary demands, which was to get to the holiday destination on time.

However, this sub-chartering system was dramatically affected when in 1996 a charter flight crashed, off the coast of the Dominican Republic, leaving 189 persons dead (most of them German). An Alas Nacionales Boeing 767, which was originally earmarked for the flight but was not ready for use, was replaced with a Birgenair Boeing 757 which crashed shortly after its departure. A very emotional discussion followed the accident. German tourists started feeling insecure towards charter airlines with rather unknown brand names and they tried to avoid using them.

The tour operator TUI realized this problem immediately and issued a *Statement of Guarantee* only two days after the disaster, which was distributed to travel agencies. In this Statement, TUI listed all cooperating charter airlines and guaranteed to only use the listed companies, even in the necessary case of replacement. This quick reaction helped to regain some of the customers' confidence.

Translation:

TUI Statement of Guarantee

TUI guarantees the employment of selected airlines.

Quality on a high level: When selecting our airlines we put high demands on security standards and maintenance servicing. Therefore we employ only the below named airlines. If, because of any unforeseen reason, a short-term change of carrier is necessary, we guarantee that we will only select aircrafts of the listed airlines or of other renowned scheduled airlines.

TOURISTIK UNION INTERNATIONAL

Karl Born
Executive Board, Tourist Service
Special Tour operators

Nobert Munsch
Executive Board, Distribution

TUI employed airlines which are also named in the catalogues:

Aero Lloyd, Air Berlin, Air Europa, Austrian Airlines, Britannia, Condor, Cross Air, Deutsche BA, Eurowings, Futura, Germania, Hamburg Airlines, Hapag-Lloyd, Lauda Air, LTU, Luxair, Martinair, Sobelair, Spanair, Sun Express, Transavia, Virgen Express, Viva Air.

Airlines with which TUI operates for selected destinations:

Air Malta, Air Transat, Air Via, Arkia, Croatia Airlines, Eurocypria, LOT, Novelair, Portugalia, Royal Air Maroc, Tunis Air.

Other renowned scheduled airlines are also employed.

Questions for review and discussion

- For which destinations the question of product accessibility is of special importance?
- Why and how are guarantees helping?
- What role do personnel play within the instruments of crisis management?
- What is the first task of product development?
- What possibilities are offered through combined effects?

Suggestions for further reading

World Tourism Organization (1994), *Aviation and tourism policies: balancing the benefits*, Routledge, London.

World Tourism Organization (1997), *Tourist Safety and Security*, WTO, Madrid.

7.3 Price policy

Objectives

- To be aware of the peculiarities of the price policy
- To realize the importance of price structure policy
- To value the different possibilities of the price progression policy in relation to its advantages and usefulness
- To assess the financial incentives for the distribution channels

Key terms and concepts

- Price structure policy
- Price progression policy
- Scenery effect
- Prestige goods
- Price discrimination

- Special offers, last minute offers
- Discounts
- Commissions
- Cancellations and changes of bookings

The object of price policy is the fixing of sales prices. This includes price policy decisions in the narrower sense as well as condition policy measures. In this way, price structure and price progression policies can be distinguished.

7.3.1 Price structure policy

The task of the price structure policy is the establishment of price structures for product and company areas. This establishment has a strategic function and takes into account that price essentially influences the product's position in the consumer's perceptions. Price structure policy decisions, therefore, are not taken lightly. Inasmuch, such decisions should initially be seen as given within the framework of crisis management. Under normal marketing circumstances, all operative price-political measures must be set in motion in the spectrum claimed by price structure policies. Only in this way can repercussions and consumer irritations be avoided.

If the question is investigated in depth as to what is the scope of price policies, it can be established that pricing is a suitable instrument for reducing the consequences of increased risk awareness. In principle, it offers the opportunity to stimulate and keep demand constant. Provided that operative price decisions are taken within the given price structure policy spectrums, no problems arise. However, it remains questionable whether a temporary abandonment of this corridor is understood by consumers in the case of a negative event and has no long-term negative effect to bear on the product's position.

Experiences confirm that a temporary and limited break from the price structure policy framework is possible. For example, the sale of high-price prestige goods, which were damaged in an accident – if this has to do with damage to the packaging, not to the core product – does not noticeably disturb the product positioning. This is, on the one hand, influenced by the fact that the distribution channels separate customers of the 'defective' prestige product from regular customers. On the other hand, potentially inconsistent target groups cause no problems as in most cases consumption takes place privately and separately.

However, this is different in tourism. Whilst here the division of customers in the act of buying appears possible, problems arise, at the latest stage, in the act of consumption. Because the tourist is normally in contact with other tourists during the trip or at least perceives them, he assesses their simultaneous presence as consistent with his ideas and expectations. This interaction effect among tourists can be described as the 'scenery effect'. If the 'scenery' does not correspond to expectations, the guest's well-being is affected. This is even more so, the higher ranking the product positioning, i.e. the social value, is.

However, the actual consequence occurs not in the affected well-being but in negative word-of-mouth propaganda. In extreme cases, this can even be media reports that describe the destination as being in decline. Therefore, in tourism – in contrast to the previously described case of damaged goods – a generally cautious handling of pricing instruments is advisable. From a strategic point of view, it is therefore to be recommended that a short-term profit loss is preferable to a foreseeable long-term disturbance or the destruction of the experience value strategy. This is even more important as tourism is becoming more and more dependent on experience values and a cheap image is difficult to correct at a later stage. If, therefore, operative price policies that exceed the given spectrum are pursued, it must at least be ensured that conforming target groups are reached and inconsistencies are excluded.

7.3.2 Price progression policy

Price progression policies incorporate operative pricing decisions, which, under normal circumstances, should shift in the framework given by the price structure policy. The practical task of operative price establishment in crisis management is the minimization of the effect that negative events have on demand. The relevant scope is, at least in the medium term, given by breakeven aspects. For a cost leadership strategy, this is lower than for a differentiation strategy. On the other hand, the necessity of consistency with the strategy places fewer restrictions on cost leadership than a differentiation strategy. Regardless of the competitive strategy pursued, the affected organization is interested to keep financial costs as low as possible. In a first step, therefore, it should be attempted to vary those elements of the total price that attract more consumer attention. For the tourism area, it can be assumed that tax, airport taxes, safety fees, etc., are those elements of the total price considered less whereas flight tariffs and hotel accommodation are generally paid more attention.

All price changes are interpreted as a signal from the affected company not only by the customers but also by all the other spheres of activity. Depending on the event and the wider circumstances, the price change can be classed more or less as an admission of guilt. This unfavourable interpretation makes it clear that, in cases of doubt, pricing action must be accompanied by the use of other instruments.

7.3.2.1 Price discrimination

Price discrimination describes measures within price progression policies that require different prices for goods that are exactly the same. The established price differences are greater than the cost differences, provided that they even exist. The different possibilities for price discrimination are related to conditions that can be of a spatial, temporal or customer-oriented nature.

Price discrimination opportunities are fundamentally limited by the fact that customers served differently when the service was sold could meet each other again when they go on the holiday. Price and service comparisons are usually made then. If different prices for the same service become visible, this leads to a loss of trust in the service supplier and has dissatisfaction as a consequence. In spite of this limitation, the use of price discrimination is possible because holidays cannot always be compared with one another due to there being a number of different features.

From a temporal point of view, price discrimination can be considered in two parts. On the one hand, various prices can be demanded depending on the point in time in which the product is consumed (travelling time). This form of price discrimination is extensively unproblematic because it is justified by varying demand and is excluded from tourists who were served differently meeting with one another at the destination. On the other hand, the price can differentiate depending on when the holiday is booked (booking time). Here, incentives are offered to encourage people to book early. Therefore, the late booking behaviour often observed in a crisis can, in part, be counteracted. However, this approach is problematic as the employment of the price instrument is advanced in time. Besides, most clients speculate on a low demand and therefore expect further price concessions, especially last minute offers. Finally, the insecurity in concerning the consequences of the negative event still remains. More problematic, however, is the fact that the simultaneous use of a service offered at different prices cannot be ensured, thus causing a 'scenery effect'. For this reason, a combined use with other marketing instruments is to be recommended.

Spatial price discrimination offers products at different prices in geographically different markets. These variants are offered if the event is perceived differently by various source markets. The linguistic barrier counteracts a direct price and service comparison. But even the frequent spatial separation of these customer groups in the destination allows this form of price discrimination to appear successful as long as behaviour between the groups is not perceived to be too contradictory and the 'sceneries' must no longer be consequently classed as consistent.

Customer-oriented price discrimination is geared to the different function and personal characteristics of the consumer. To a certain extent, this differentiation can also be classed as suitable. This applies,

---

Temporal price discrimination

In practise few innovative approaches are available in the area of temporal price discrimination. One example worth mentioning is the way the tour operator 'Neckermann Reisen' used in 2004 a second set of pricelists. The price for the different tourism services was binding in the first published pricelist until 31 March. While publishing this first pricelist, it was guaranteed that the customer would receive a reimbursement of the difference in case the price published in the second pricelist was lower. The early-booking client would get in any case the best price available.

Nevertheless, in case of major uncertainties related to the tourism product even this approach must be combined with other instruments to be effective.

Travelling time

Booking time

Linguistic barriers

Linguistic barriers between central European and Spanish guests were an important reason why RIU Hotels decided to apply the spatial price discrimination for its establishments in 2003 – a year in which tourism demand was strongly influenced by worldwide terror and the war in Iraq.

above all, if the criteria that form the basis of differentiation correspond to the importance of the sphere of activity. Familiarization trips, for example, which grant price advantages to travel agency employees, can be seen from this perspective. Towards those multipliers, such offers express the interest that the product service is evaluated. In addition, these price differences are understandable for non-affected customers because a relationship between the reason for price discrimination and the target group is discernible. Besides this, customer-oriented price discrimination is always then recommendable if linked to previous services or meeting certain requests, especially if these help to avoid the 'scenery effect'. This can be among other things the amount of time necessary to obtain the product (through the decision of avoiding advisory services and only offering self-service, people are attracted with a larger time budget), the status of the person (student or retired) or only the membership in an association such as the automobile clubs. In all these cases the price discrimination is more likely to be accepted.

7.3.2.2 Special offers

Special offers describe lowering of the selling price for a short period of time. These actions refer to certain commodities for which demand must be increased. Special offers are very popular in tourism. They are used especially if the product no longer appears saleable and threatens to expire. In crisis management, the negative event is the original cause of the special offer. Inasmuch, price admissions refer to difficulties arising when selling the services. Under these circumstances, the aim is to sell the available services before their expiry. An indication of the extent of the discount arises from opportunity costs. Above all, however, the discount is determined by the estimated elasticity of the demand as well as the time remaining before the service expires.

The frequent use of special offers has the negative consequence of getting the consumer used to them. This has already been empirically proved to be true for the case of irregular use. It is even more critical if the consumer does not see a specific reason for these special offers. This normally suggests a careful use of special offers. However, this effect is less dramatic in the case of a negative event as the special offer is justified by the incident. In this way, the probability that future expectations of further 'regular' special offers will be encouraged is judged to be low.

In the last days before expiry special offers are frequently described as last minute offers. The advantage of last minute sales is the availability of a separate sales track, which has established itself in the past few years. The use of airport sales points, specialized travel agencies and the Internet appeals to a price-sensitive group of customers. For these customers, the need to travel and the price are at the fore; the concrete service offer is of less interest. Another advantage arises from the precision with which the segment can be targeted with these sales methods. This avoids costly coverage waste and also irritations in the customer segment. However, the impact of the 'scenery effect', which might occur while using the tourism product service, cannot be ruled out. Therefore, special offers are also as instruments of crisis management an effective instrument for increasing sales. They are, above all, suitable for selling services shortly before their expiry. The reason for the special offer given by the negative event prevents people from becoming accustomed to it. Limits on special offer policies can be seen where they would have a negative effect on product positioning.

Example 48: The 'Thank You' Campaigns

'Thank You Campaigns' are a recent example of innovative and well-elaborated marketing campaigns combining price elements with communication measures and tackling the emotional sphere of the clients.

In the case of the Indonesian airline Garuda, the 'Thank You' campaign included an important component of price policy. The campaign's aim was to recover from the effects of SARS and the Bali attacks, which scared travellers and made them avoid airplanes. The airline chose to launch this campaign in New Zealand, on the occasion of its 15th anniversary. Garuda thanked New Zealanders for their continuous confidence and support in the airline, particularly during the recent difficult events. Garuda expressed its appreciation in a practical way that brought immediate benefits to its customers: It offered a 15 per cent discount on all its flights departing from Auckland to Bali, Jakarta, Singapore and China, among other destinations. The campaign was also designed to lay the foundation for future travel to Bali as a hub for travel throughout Asia. This combination of a 'Thank You' message together with the reduced fares not only pleased clients but avoided bad signalling impacts of a lower price and the scenery effect.

Following the tragic attacks on commuter trains in Madrid (Spain) on 11 March 2004, the Community of Madrid also launched a 'Thank You' campaign. The aim was to show its appreciation for the many expressions of solidarity that were received following the attacks. This 'Thank You' campaign was run in the main European and American newspapers and was addressed on an individual basis to Germany, the United Kingdom, Portugal, France, Italy and the USA. The message was simple and eloquent 'Thank You'. A smaller message appeared under it saying 'Madrid will never forget the displays of solidarity and support from all (…) following the attacks of last 11 March'. Although this campaign was only a communication campaign, it also used the emotional element and was able to reach people's feelings in its major tourism source markets.

As may be seen from these examples, 'Thank You' campaigns are a useful instrument to keep up with the supporters and clients in difficult times. It can be expected that the number of these campaigns will increase in the future as they tackle one of the most important human feelings: gratitude.

7.3.3 Condition policy

As a subsection of price policy, condition policy describes a supplier's systematic behaviour towards his customers in all areas – apart from the previously described price area – which can be the object of contractual agreements about service remuneration. In concrete, this has to do with the formation of discounts, commissions and terms of payment. In light of the following considerations, these condition policy instruments can be used towards end consumers as well as service mediators.

7.3.3.1 Discounts and commissions

In a general sense, discounts are understood as reductions to the listed price which, according to various criteria such as quantities, points in time and functions, can be aimed at retailer levels and, from a loyalty point of view, at consumers. Commissions are the remuneration to a middleman for transacting a piece of business or performing a service. Similar to discounts, commissions are calculated as percentages on the value of the service provided and graded according to comparable criteria. Commissions are useful if the final level of the sales organization achieves no ownership of the goods.

Towards the group of travel agents, the affected service provider has, by means of the temporary raising of commissions, the opportunity to give an additional incentive for sales efforts. This is advantageous from two points of view: on the one hand, through the creation of the set of commissions the concrete obstacles, which are the result of a negative event, can be dealt with. The payment of commissions, which compensate for the additional expense incurred to the travel agent as a result of a negative event, means that an incentive to maintain sales efforts can be given. On the other hand, this price-political behaviour keeps the sales price stable for the end consumer. In this way, the previously described 'scenery effect' is avoided. It can be assumed that these measures prove to be especially suitable in the post-active phase. They ensure, in a subtle way, that attention is paid to the product again but, at the same time, avoid the 'flogging' of the product.

Reward miles

Lufthansa airlines used this kind of additional incentive after the attacks of 11 September 2001 in the USA. The miles required to receive flight awards went down by 33 per cent while at the same time the sales price for those flights was kept stable. This way the airline was not only able to provide additional incentives to fly but also reduced the amount of miles on the accounts of the frequent flying customers during a period of lower occupancy.

Of the discount possibilities for end consumers, loyalty discount is, above all, of interest under these circumstances. These are understood as supplier discounts that are granted for the preferred purchase of their services. Loyalty discounts are often used even under normal circumstances and are expressed in airline bonus systems. The particular importance that these systems enjoy can be traced back to the fact that the attainment of bonus points is no longer tied exclusively to flights. In the meantime, bonus points can be attained by using a number of tourism and non-tourism services. Advantageous in the use of bonus miles is the uncoupling of air miles from the price. On the one hand, this means that even if the same service is more expensive, a preference over competitor products is created due to air miles. On the other hand, even a service that is not as well perceived as a competitor's but costs the same can be made marketable by air miles. Moreover, this effect is intensified by the fact that, in the majority of cases, the cost is not carried by the recipient of the air miles. In this case – predominant in business trips –, air miles change is preferable to a price change. At the same time, however, it must be ensured that the incentive created in the sense of a bonus is effectively communicated to the consumer who takes the decision.

7.3.3.2 Cancellations and changes of bookings

The opportunity to change or cancel a holiday or tourism service booking is not a peculiarity of crisis management. Nevertheless, it cannot be denied that this instrument within the crisis management is of particular importance for customers. The legal possibilities that exist for the tourist have already been considered in-depth taking various contractual conditions into account (see also Section 3.1.5). What is interesting at this point is the aspect of instrument if this cannot be traced back to a legal obligation.

In practice, the active use of the booking change and cancellation apparatus can be increasingly observed. The reason for this is the tour operator or service supplier's wish to adhere to the agreed travel contract. However, the long-term aim of which is to become known as a preferred service provider in the future also explain this behaviour.

With the offering of changes of bookings, the tour operator regularly offers the client a change of destination or parts of the packages booked. With the offer of cancellations the client is able to cancel the whole trip free of charge. Both, cancellations and changes of bookings are as a rule limited to certain periods of time and the affected regions.

Two points are worth noting when it comes to cancellations and changes of bookings which are voluntarily offered and free of charge: first, the isolated behaviour of a tour operator has a considerable signal effect on the consumer's attitude towards the competitors. If a company begins to offer the opportunity to change or cancel bookings, this puts considerable pressure on its competitors. This is derived from the fact that, by granting this correction, this implies recognition of the influence the negative event has on the product. Second, these measures are very costly and quickly lead to a change in the consumer's expectations. All in all, therefore, use of booking change and cancellation instruments should be well considered and active use is advised against.

The possibility of change

The possibility of changing purchased goods is seen in our service-oriented society as an important point to increase customer loyalty and is considered to improve the sales of goods. This is regularly the case since the probability of sales increases as much as the risk of a wrong purchase is reduced.

The possibility of change is however problematic in tourism. More than with other goods, the tourism product must be sold in time as it expires over time. This devaluation of the tourism product has to be borne by another party, if an already sold product is returned by the client as it is regularly the case in the event of a cancellation or a change of bookings.

Diagram 39: Cancellation charges of selected tour operators

Marsans (E)		Airtours (GB)		Nouvelles Frontières (F)		TUI (D)		Thomas Cook (D)[5]	
Days	%	Days	%	Days	%	Days	%	Days	%
>15	[1]	>55	Deposit	>30	35€ [3]	>30	20	>29	20
		55-29	50 [2]	30-22	25 [4]	30-23	25	29-22	25
15-11	5 [1]	28-22	70 [2]			22-16	35	21-15	35
10-3	15 [1]	21-8	90 [2]	21-8	50 [4]	15-9	50	14-7	55
2-1	25 [1]			7-3	75 [4]	8-3	65	6-1	65
afterwards	100 [1]	afterwards	100 [2]	afterwards	100	afterwards	80	afterwards	90

As of November 2005 and all days before departure. (1) To be added are always handling fees of at least 8 € and cancellation charges, if any. The latter varies based on the conditions of the service providers contracted and can reach up to 100 per cent. Thus, these cancellation charges play a significant role but are rather difficult to compare (2) or deposit if greater (3) per person (4) minimum 35€ (5) depends on mode of transportation, in this case hotel / flight package.

7.3.3.3 Terms of payment

The terms of payment mainly regulate consumer and travel agent payment obligations. As far as the consumer is concerned, this has to do with deposits; for the tour operator, payment obligations towards its service providers. These can vary in their amount as well as their due date. From the point of view of crisis management, a change in terms of payment is only sometimes suitable. If the deposit due date or amount changes for the travel service booked, the consumer's sense of risk is only compensated to a certain extent. The cost of the change does not justify its use, particularly as other instruments can achieve better effects. The effect on travel agents can be classed as similarly low where a change to terms of payment is hardly worth the special sales efforts. Here also, other instruments, such as commissions, achieve a better result. For this reason, the terms of payment instrument are of little importance for crisis management.

Questions for review and discussion

- What is the purpose of the price structure policy?
- What are the risks of repeated special offers?
- What makes the use of reward miles recommendable?
- What should be taken into account when defining the commissions for travel agents after a negative event?
- Name the different forms of price discrimination.
- Explain the scenery effect.

Suggestions for further reading

Dolan, R.J. and Simon, H. (1996), *Power Pricing: How Managing Price Transforms the Bottom Line*, The Free Press, New York.

Ritchie, B. and Crouch, G. (1997), 'Quality, price and the tourism experience', in *Quality Management in Tourism* (AIEST (ed.)), AIEST, St. Gallen, pp. 117-139.

Nagle, T. and Holden, R. (2002) *The strategy and tactics of pricing: a guide to profitable decision making*, Prentice Hall, Upper Saddle River, NJ.

7.4 Distribution policy

Objectives

- To be aware of the peculiarities of distribution channels during times of crises
- To be able to define and create incentives and supportive measures for the distribution channels
- Understand the possibilities of distribution channels outside the tourism industry

Key terms and concepts

- Distribution channels
- Direct and indirect distribution
- Travel agents
- Push and pull strategy
- Club travel

The objects of distribution policy are agreements and regulations regarding the route that the products take to get to the customer. A significant peculiarity of tourism sales is that it has to do, not with the sales of a tangible product, but with the sale of a service promise. The customers themselves must travel to the location of the service provider to redeem them of this promise.

Seen from a general point of view, the tasks of distribution policy are of a more strategic nature, comparable to the determinations of price structure policy. Consequently, these decisions must be accepted as fundamentally fixed. Thus, in the following considerations, the effects these determinations have and the action scope allowed for distribution-political crisis management measures are of interest.

Diagram 40: Influences on distribution methods

Decision level	Complexity	Information, advice, confirmation potential	
High involvement Inexperienced in travel Much time Economical	Individual travel Many integral parts Long distance Expensive	Personal advice and sales Moderated, empathy High competence	**high**

	Standardised package
	  holiday
	Mainly transport and
	  accommodation
	Medium distance		

Low involvement Experienced in travel Little time	Only transport or only accommodation Relatively cheap	No advice Impersonal Immoderate Limited competence	**low**
Customer	**Product**	**Distribution channel**	

Source: Adapted from Regele and Schmücker (1998)

The determination whether the tourism product will be sold in a direct or indirect manner is one of these fundamental distribution-political decisions. Whilst direct sales take place between service providers and consumers without interposition from other trade levels, indirect sales choose intermediates. Which of the two forms is finally preferred is decided by the peculiarities of the customer and the product. In Diagram 40, they are placed in relation to one another.

The design of the distribution system, however, is not just the decision between direct or indirect distribution. It must also determine whether primary or secondary distribution organs, from within or outside the tourism sector, will take on sales tasks. Diagram 41 gives an overview of the sales forms available for distribution-political decisions.

Diagram 41: Tourism distribution channels

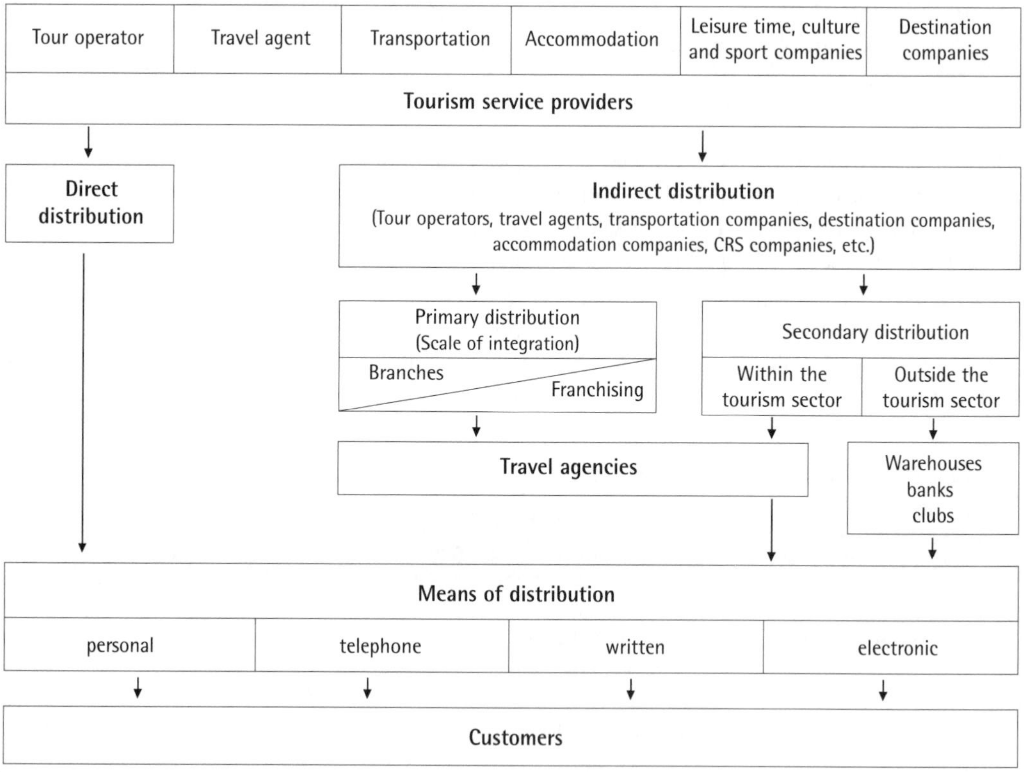

Tour operator	Travel agent	Transportation	Accommodation	Leisure time, culture and sport companies	Destination companies
Tourism service providers					

Direct distribution

Indirect distribution
(Tour operators, travel agents, transportation companies, destination companies, accommodation companies, CRS companies, etc.)

Primary distribution
(Scale of integration)

Branches / Franchising

Secondary distribution

Within the tourism sector	Outside the tourism sector

Travel agencies

Warehouses banks clubs

Means of distribution

personal	telephone	written	electronic

Customers

Source: Adapted from Freyer (1997)

7.4.1 Direct distribution

Direct sales are traditionally dominating in domestic tourism where the majority of bookings take place directly between consumers and service providers. An increased interest in direct sales on the part of the service provider can also be ascertained. This becomes possible because the tourist's travel experience is gradually increasing. Another favouring factor is that many tourism services are considered to be standard services and cause only a low object-specific involvement. Cost considerations are also part of this. The otherwise normal commission payment is omitted due to the omission of the travel agent. Moreover, direct customer contact is becoming more and more important for many service providers. This is the only way in which they can be in a position to generate relevant behaviour and customer data that is becoming more and more decisive in competitive markets.

One of the most important findings within the context of a negative event was that consumers have a suddenly increasing need for information. This is – as has already been illustrated – most suitably fulfilled by a differentiated statement (see also Section 7.1.3). The direct sales method must withstand these two requirements.

For the area of domestic tourism, the activities of direct sales are accompanied by personal attendance from the beginning. In this way, in the actual crisis phase, it is possible to provide customers with information immediately. Because this takes place directly and without third-party interposition, questions can be answered in a competent, differentiated and problem-oriented manner. As a result, the opportunity exists for the customer to paint a relatively precise picture of the circumstances and their consequences. Whether or not this is finally successful is decided by a number of other factors to which reputation belongs to a large extent (see also Section 7.5.2).

This is settled differently in the case of the increasing direct sales of standard tourism products. The fundamentally low need for information on the part of tourists as well as cost pressures results in the use of electronic distribution instruments. They are designed for semi or fully automatic handling of sales. Therefore, it becomes clear that, within the framework of preventive crisis management, organizational precautions must be taken more into account as in the case of the less automated sales of domestic tourism. The aim of the actions must be the creation of flexibility potential that is normally swamped by the rationalization of sales channels but becomes necessary in order to be able to handle the increasingly individual information needs.

7.4.2 Indirect distribution

Retailers or wholesalers are used to sell services in indirect sales. If these intermediaries are legally and economically independent, this is known as 'secondary distribution'. If, on the other hand, it has to do with the company's own branches, this is described as 'primary distribution'. A number of other integration levels exists between these poles, which include cooperations and franchising, among others.

A fundamental advantage that indirect distribution has over direct distribution is already under normal circumstances a better opportunity to sell products that require an explanation. Travel agency employees can immediately respond to customer's questions and needs. This opportunity to inform and advise is also significant in times of crisis. The travel agency's concrete function changes depending on the travel phase in which the tourist is at that moment. Customers, who have already taken a concrete travel decision, ask for specific information about the condition of the product. Here, the travel agency must be able to inform and act both in a competent and trustworthy manner. To do this, it requires appropriate information and support from the service provider. Practice has shown that this is a critical phase. On the one hand, the information provided increases considerably and consequently so does the cost for the travel agency. The commission obtained by the sale is reduced by these additional advices and sales activities. This indicates the need for action and modification of the commission instrument. A service provider trying to maintain a booking can, therefore, introduce a special commission for bookings that are not cancelled and, at the same time, create an additional incentive for the travel agency. On the other hand, many travel agencies are also interested to maintain a good relationship with their client. Consequently, loyalty to the service provider diminishes and often a tendency to give in instead of counteracting the customer's insecurity can be observed.

From these findings, it can be ascertained that the following are required for successful acting on the part of the travel agency:

Interest: This exists from a personal and economic point of view. The more strongly the sales are integrated with the service provider, the lower the necessity of creating separate economic incentives.

Ability: The service provider must provide the trade with appropriate information in order to be able to inform customers in a trustworthy manner.

However, if the customer is still in the orientation phase, there is a different problem. It has already been ascertained that destination images can be influenced before visiting a travel agency to such an extent that the product is not actively named anymore. From the point of view of the affected service provider, the opportunity of the sales talk must be used so that the ousted alternative is taken into consideration again. This requires in addition to the above-mentioned points:

Quality: There is no real negative effect on the product.

Opportunity: The customer's latent need can still be identified.

It is especially difficult to ensure the interest of travel agencies if sales are only integrated to a minimal degree. Specifically in this case, it is important that the service provider seeks contact with the customer and, in this way, exerts influence over the travel agency. The aim of this behaviour, also described as a **Pull strategy**, pull strategy, can be the activation of consumers who are encouraged to search for more information. In addition, it can be attempted to convey the necessary information directly to the customer in order to maintain or re-establish the preference for the product. Which of the two objectives should be striven for in times of crisis depends on the event, the degree the product is affected and the cooperation with the travel agency. In the first case, it is above all important that travel agencies have the appropriate information at their disposal.

Push strategy The push strategy suitably supports this objective. In this case, the travel agency is the target of the marketing efforts, for which reason this is also called trade marketing. Service providers use all marketing instruments, especially sales promotion and condition policy, to motivate the travel agency into greater sales efforts (see also the opportunities for higher commissions stated in Section 7.3.3.1).

As these comments make clear, indirect sales offer the opportunity to advise the customer extensively even when negative events occur. However, the solution of the travel agency information problem is important in the same way as incentives are in secondary distribution. Therefore, it is recommendable to use a mixture of push and pull strategies as well as to use in the post-active phase the opportunities trade marketing offers.

7.4.3 Sales in areas outside the tourism industry

Along with the previously discussed sales forms, distribution channels outside the tourism industry are increasingly gaining in significance. This is of interest also in crisis management from two points of view.

A frequent characteristic of tourism products offered by means of this sales method is the uniqueness of the product on offer. Church groups, banks and sports or automobile clubs temporarily include these holidays in their offers. In most cases, a repetition of the offer is not striven for and the scope of offers is possibly limited only to this product. Through the use of this sales method, service providers come into contact with groups of customers ready to go on holidays and who frequently have a preference for this sales channel. This preference has partly to do with the other people going on the trip. If the offer is not taken at this point in time, there is only a small chance of being able to undertake this trip again with the same group of people.

However, preference for this sales method can also be the result of great trust in the intermediary. Consequently, a reputation transfer can be used while selecting this distribution channel. If the service provider is successful in convincing the intermediary, who is foreign to the industry, of the good condition of the product, the intermediary functions as a guarantor for his clientele. As a result, the efforts can be minimized and price-political concessions can be made. The particular value of this distribution channel for crisis management lies in the accessibility of consumers otherwise scarcely considered to be potential customers and in the trust that the supplier enjoys.

Uniqueness

Great trust

Questions for review and discussion

- Name the advantages of direct distribution.
- What is meant by a push strategy?
- What prerequisites must be met by the travel agencies for successful management in times of crises?
- What advantages are results of the sales in areas outside the tourism industry?

Suggestions for further reading

Buhalis, D. (2003), *eTourism: Information technology for strategic tourism management*, Prentice Hall, Harlow.

7.5 Communication policy

Objectives

- To distinguish crisis communication from risk communication
- To understand the peculiarities and requirements of crisis communication
- To realize the possibilities and risks of unusual attention
- To consider the peculiarities of crisis communication with the different target groups
- To understand the importance of pictorial information
- To evaluate the operational readiness and usefulness of the different measures of communication policy

Key terms and concepts

- Risk communication
- Crisis communication
- Credibility
- Image
- Pictorial information
- Promotion
- Media communication
- Sales promotion
- Familiarization trips
- Participation in trade fairs
- Sponsoring

The principle task of communications policy is to convey information with the aim of influencing and guiding consumer behaviour, opinions and expectations. Traditional interpretations see consumers in the sales market as being the target audience of the communications policy. But even under normal circumstances, a larger communication sphere can be assumed, which incorporates at least part of the wider social environment and employees of the organization. Whilst the consideration of the wider environment is under normal circumstances still a choice – the advantages of integrated communications have already been indicated (see also Section 3.1.1) – the inclusion of the wider environment as a communication sphere is inevitable when a negative event occurs.

7.5.1 Risk vs. crisis communication

Within the context of negative events, two basic types of communication can be distinguished: risk communication and crisis communication. Risk communication pursues a long-term approach, the aim of which is the building of trust and understanding within the context of risks. At the same time, it can also aim at drawing attention to risks that would otherwise not be taken into consideration. Crisis communication, on the other hand, begins suddenly. It describes the attempt, after a negative event has occurred, to minimize its consequences with the instruments of the communication policy and steer to such an extent that credibility is retained for product re-launch activities.

If the activity phases of both communication forms are considered, risk communication lies in the pre-event phase whilst crisis communication is only employed after the onset of the negative event, above all, in the active phase.

Diagram 42: Risk vs. crisis communication

Pre-event phase	Pre-active phase	Active phase	Post-active phase
Risk communication	Crisis communication		

7.5.1.1 Risk communication

Because it takes place in the pre-event phase, risk communication has a preventive character. It is part of the considerations already dealt with which have to do with the strategic handling of negative events. It is used with the aim that the events will be avoided or their consequences will be lessened. Risk communication, which aims to avoid negative events, is of use in tourism where the tourist himself comes into question as the trigger of a negative event. On the one hand, careless tourists should be prevented from entering into risk by explaining risks and dangers. This way it can also be assumed that other potential tourists, who do not see the negative event as the result of careless behaviour, will not be scared off.

Example 49: Risk and Fun

Snowboarders more than any other winter sport enthusiasts, enjoy unprepared slopes. Especially young snowboarders have a desire for freedom and adventure, although they often hardly know how to manoeuvre their board. This becomes more important taking into account that, while doing so, they move in mountain areas where years of experience are normally required to evaluate the dangers.

As reaching all these people for training is an impossible task, the Austrian Ministry for Social Affairs together with the association 'Healthy Austria' and the Austrian Club of Alpinists initiated the project 'Risk and Fun'. Under this project, a focus is made on the training of the opinion leaders in the Snowboarder scene, the so-called 'peers', with the aim of enabling them to make a competent terrain and weather analysis. It is intended, as a consequence, to influence first their own risk behaviour and finally that of the other snowboarders.

Picture: jwiegand

209

The training consists of a five-day course with experienced mountain guides and 'Risk and Fun' trainers, who are also passionate snowboarders and have years of experience in free-ride and deep snow runs. Towards the end of the season all trained peers are invited to a 'chill out' to keep the links between them up-to-date.

On the other hand, tourists should be encouraged to take on responsibility if it has to do with general risks, for example, such as criminal infringements. In this case, the aim of risk communication is to explain to tourists how to undertake precautionary measures. Because knowledge of general risks in the destination is low for most tourists, the responsibility of the destination's authorities and the service provider to undertake such a form of risk communication is generally pointed at (WTO, 2002d; WTO, 1994c; WTO, 1989).

Picture: Signboard warning of possible pick-pocketing at the entrance of Geneva airport (Switzerland).

Example 50: Preventive Measures – The Bahia Tourist Protection Booklet

The Brazilian state of Bahia established back in 1991 the Tourist Protection Police Force (DELTUR), the first of such kind in Brazil to tackle the problem of crime against tourists. Besides its normal functions as a police force, DELTUR produces and widely distributes a booklet to all tourists visiting the State. In eight pages, this booklet provides tourists with information on how to protect themselves, what to do and not do in certain situations and the telephone numbers and addresses of those institutions that can help them.

Brochure: DELTUR

210

Another type of risk communication aims at changing the acceptance of risks. For this, the initiation of a risk dialogue between the organization and the public is recommended. The aim of this communication process is an increase in risk acceptance and a reduction of conflict potential. This form of communication has only limited significance in tourism. At the same time, its fundamental approach has to be viewed critically. Luhmann (1993) for example, indicates that the declining acceptance of risk can be traced back to the loss of confidence. This can be balanced not by communication but only by authority. This authority, which should be understood as ability for the further explanations, aims to avoid additional communication in a time of information overload. Consequentially, it cannot be substituted by communication.

7.5.1.2 Crisis communication

Crisis communication is a form of communication that is suddenly initiated and is dependent on a negative event occurring. Whether it is initiated straight after the event or is slightly delayed, that is, when the active crisis communication comes into play, is decided by the chosen crisis handling strategy. Its reactive or proactive nature has already been dealt with (see Section 5.3). Crisis communication itself, on the other hand, has a defensive character. The initiative for this communication does not come from the affected company or organization; it is caused by the event. This defensive aspect is the same independent of whether or not the organization was prepared for the crisis.

Defensive character

Crisis communication is also different from normal communication due to its increased quantitative and qualitative requirements. Quantitative requirements increase because, on the one hand, there is an increased need for information on the part of those interested in the organization and, on the other hand, because the circle of those demanding information is increasing. From that point of view, crisis communication is also mass communication, which is much more than media communication. The greater qualitative requirements on communication are the result of the particular attention that is paid to the organization. This makes logical, precise and contradiction-free communication necessary, at least during the crisis.

Quantitative and qualitative requirements

Although the defensive character of crisis communication cannot be removed by preparation, being familiar with the particular quantitative and qualitative demands influences whether or not communication is classed as panic or planned communication. Objects of the following discussions are the instruments of the communication policy with regard to the particular demands of crisis communication.

7.5.2 Temporal and content aspects

Crisis communication must take particular demands into account that result from the situation and are different from normal communication tasks. Especially, situations with unusual events are judged by the recipient to be complex. Therefore, the first contextual task of the communication policy lies in the creation of understanding and transparency. This explanation of the context essentially contributes to the credibility of the organization. If decisive information is not successfully conveyed, the objective facts and the rationality become less important and the organization's chances of influencing the information process are diminished.

Temporal

Seen from a temporal point of view, the following sequence arises within the first 24 hours:

Time since occurrence	Situation	Measures of the organization
0-1 hour	• All press organs intend to be the first ones to report about the event • Contradictory reports about the event • Fears about the consequences are mentioned	• Alert members of the crisis committee / advisory group • Inform public authorities • Inform external personnel with public contact (telephone operators, gatekeepers, security staff) • Only if necessary disseminate message to the press 'we are assessing the situation'
1-3 hours	• The situation becomes clearer • First eyewitnesses report about what happened • First comparisons to similar situations are made • First speculations about possible damages and victims	• Short briefing for staff members, use later the intranet • First press release and activation of the emergency website (see Example 54) and emergency telephone numbers (Section 7.5.6.1)
3-6 hours	• Questions about the why are asked • Experts are used to give answers to those 'why's'	• Convocation of the first press conference (see Section 7.5.6.4)
6-24 hours	• Intensive background stories are prepared • Discussion forums / blogs are opened on the web • Statement from associations • Statement from public authorities • The print media reports widely about the event	• First video and telephone conferences with important business partners such as tour operators, travel agency chains, cooperations of travel agencies and associations • First contact with the ministries of foreign affairs of the important source markets

Content

For a proactive handling strategy the following emphasis is typical from a content point of view:

1. Firstly, is the portrayal of the event, for which any kind of speculation must be avoided. It is followed by the declaration of responsibility and affectedness of the organization. Here, it should be underlined that the incident is taken so seriously that it is the highest level of authority that is responsible and manages the situation.

2. In the next step, decisions and measures introduced to cope with crises should be described. In this way, the company's own competence is underlined and contributes to the company being considered, also in the future, as the most important interviewee. It is recommendable to visualize, already at an early stage, the facts and measures (see Section 7.5.5). In the case of events of international importance this includes the use of maps to illustrate distances.

3. Additionally, it remains to explain further measures that are the result of current experiences and serve to avoid future repetitions. Because the event must not necessarily be attributed to the company's own sphere of responsibility, it is recommendable to emphasize the general problems, which form the background of the incident. In this way, the assessment of a shipping disaster, for example, turns out differently if it is seen within the context of the overload of shipping routes. It might also be opportune to mention at this point the investments that are already being

212

carried out in the affected area to minimize the risks. A contribution to a more objective risk assessment by the public and interested stakeholders is also made, if the affected organization is showing how other, independent institutions assess the benefits of those investments – in terms of lowering the risk – in comparison to other efforts.

4. For the later post-active phase it is important to report on the implementation of the recovery measures as well as on the first and ensuing achievements. Those news reports would normally fall into the category of common product announcements that are seldom used by the media. However, as the media finds a very strong interest in rounding up stories in a sense of 'do you remember?', these kinds of reports find their way into the news

> **Risk comparisons**
>
> Comparing risks is dangerous and often counterproductive. This is especially true for the comparison of likelihoods of events that can happen at other locations.
>
> The explanation of the reasons why a destination decided to invest into certain measures of risk prevention and not into others are, depending on the circumstances, helpful to describe the responsible handling of risks. This is especially so, when those risk assessments (cost-benefit analysis) are made by independent and recognized institutions such as the Harvard Centre for Risk Analysis.

and can be used to communicate to potential clients that the products are now available again.

Furthermore, it must be considered that crisis communication is at all times, conclusive, precise and without contradiction (see also more detailed discussion in Section 7.5.3). As these qualitative requirements are especially difficult to handle because of their growing quantity, all communications and press releases must be stored. Only in this way is it possible to ensure consistency during a longer period.

The content and moment at which information is made available is also determined by information obligations that a company must fulfil. In tourism, information relationships with customers prevail. Tour operators in Germany, for example, take on particular responsibility for their customers. They have a general information obligation to their customers and must make all information important for the realization of the trip available. A limit can be seen in the area that is attributed to general life risk. The phase between the conclusion of a travel contract and the start of the holiday is of particular importance. During this phase, the tourist should, without restriction, be made aware of all particular occurrences at the destination that could influence the holidays. These are, for example, changes in beach quality, natural catastrophes and oil pollution (Strangfeld, 1993).

Information obligations

Finally, it should also be taken into account that communication content can have legal consequences. Above all, in communication measures that admit mistakes or make apologies, it should be checked whether they lead to claims of recourse (Avenarius, 1995. For this reason Berger, Gärtner and Mathes, 1989, advise against it). Therefore, the use of such communication content should be avoided in the initial time-critical phase. Apologies should only be made under careful consideration in the medium and long term. On the one hand, it is completely uncertain whether the recipient of the information will take them on positively. On the other hand, there is the danger that, if they occur when media representatives are present, a shortened reproduction outside the context will have the opposite effect to the action in mind.

Legal consequences

7.5.3 The reputation aspect

Reputation has an important function for a company even under normal circumstances. Depending on the organization's reputation, marketing activities, especially actions covered by communication policies, are assessed differently. Reputation is not something fixed, it develops gradually. It is the result of the organization's past actions and communications. If these past actions were similar and credible in their nature, a positive reputation would be assumed. This credibility is an important asset. Nevertheless, its unique value only appears in critical situations. It can then help, like no other instrument, to reduce insecurity and accompany communicative actions with trust. Considered more precisely, credibility is important for crisis communication in two ways: first, it exerts influence over the selection and assessment of information sources; second, it influences the way in which the recipient assesses information.

At a particular moment after the negative event, the media begins to investigate the topic and demand information. At the beginning of this information process, the affected company is the first of the information sources to be consulted. It is only later in the course of media coverage that a transfer process occurs, which calls on a wider circle of information sources. This transfer process can be accelerated by the affected organization. Implausible actions as well as implausible statements contribute to journalists quickly making use of unofficial sources and other information providers. In this way, not only the opportunity of being the first to comment on events is wasted but emotional coverage is encouraged.

It is especially this emotional coverage that is a disadvantage for the company. If the company loses credibility in the eyes of media representatives, media reports concentrate more on inconsistencies within statements than on the actual content of the communication. In order to make this implausibility clear even to media consumers, the contradictions are portrayed in a polemic and exaggerated manner and possibly even contrived. Because this is a common consequence of implausibility or inconsistency in information policies, it must be paid great attention. Moreover, credibility is important in the affected organization's direct relationship to the various spheres of activity. From this point of view, it has a longer and wider perspective. Longer, because it is geared towards both past experiences and the future effect of the information on the recipient. Wider, because it is a result of the whole spectrum of information, which is drawn upon to paint a picture of the circumstances.

This offers opportunities because not every unfavourable media report is of consequence. At the same time, it makes clear the necessity for the affected organization to act circumspectly from a future perspective. Even longer after the phase in which the negative event is the object of media coverage and totally independent of this, credibility influences the success of the marketing measures now implemented. If this credibility is missing in the various spheres of activity, constructive suggestions and changes have no chance of success. The remaining possibilities should be estimated as just as low. Mostly, they boil down to the purchase of more external credibility in which trustworthy institutions or people must be active on behalf of the organization. This is not only lengthy and costly but also very uncertain regarding its success (see also Section 7.5.10).

Seen as a whole, a positive reputation is a type of crisis insurance. It lessens consequences and contributes to gaining attention of the company's point of view.

7.5.4 Possibilities and risks of unusual attention

A potential consequence of negative events is that the affected organization unwillingly becomes the focus of general interest. The accompanying communication processes are unusual for them and can incorporate both possibilities and risks. One possibility is doubtless great attention. If this is the case in normal circumstances, that consumer interest is only achieved with difficulty by means of communication instruments, information is then demanded – without further help from the organization. Expressed in another way, the information market changes from a saturated market with a surplus offer, in which communication must be paid for, to a market with a surplus of demand. If, in addition, it is taken into account that consumers only take notice of 2 per cent of general media and 5 per cent of advertising information due to information overload, one can have an idea of the value of this change (Kroeber-Riel, 1993a). The possibility, therefore, is a medium- and long-term increase in the degree of aided and unaided recall, which would otherwise be connected to considerable financial expenditure for the affected organization.

Example 51: The Changes of the Recall

The tour operator Öger Tours became in 1996 subject of the unusual attention of the media as a charter flight with 189 people on board, most of them clients of the tour operator, crashed into the sea shortly after take-off from the Dominican Republic.

Up to then, Öger Tours, a midsize tour operator, had a rather limited aided recall among the German population. As market research from the time before the accident demonstrated, the company reached only an aided recall of 6.8 per cent, leaving the company far behind other known and competing tour operators in the German market.

This changed after the accident. Already in August 1996 Öger Tours reached an aided recall in the German population of 64 per cent. As results from the following year showed, this was not a temporal change in recall. The aided recall of Öger Tours with 61 per cent remained high.

Tour operator	Aided recall (%)
Neckermann Reisen	82
TUI	70
Jahn Reisen	45
Fischer Reisen	40
Alltours	37
Hetzel Reisen	35
Dertour	31
ITS	31
Ameropa	26
Transair	20
Öger Tours	6.8

Source: Süddeutsche (1996)

Sources: Jacobs (1996), Hildebrandt (1997)

Because, however, it has to do with a negative event, an influence on image is also connected with this recall increase. The direction and strength of this change is determined by the relationship between product and event, previously described under image transfer, as well as by the organization's current actions.

Therefore, two cases are conceivable:

- The increased degree of aided and unaided recall is accompanied by a negative, that is to say disadvantageous, image change. In this case, it must be attempted to identify and lessen the negative connotations related to the event. If this is successful, it is possible to profit in the long-term from the increased aided and unaided recall. This was the case, for example, when an aircraft belonging to Lauda Air crashed in Thailand. Responsible and circumspect behaviour in the crisis situation and after it meant that negative effects on the company's image were kept to a minimum. Fiedler (1994) even describes how the measures taken created a winning sympathy for the company.

- Less frequent than the first case but just as possible are simultaneous positive image changes brought about by the event itself. For example, it was possible to demonstrate that the Austrian wine scandal influenced positively the image dimensions 'traditional wine country' and 'variety of brands' (Peschke, 1986). These positive changes have to be identified and taken care of in the long-term in order to be able to draw benefit from the incident. However, an immediate concentration on the reduction of the connotations related to the event, like in the first case, which accompany even this positive image change, should take place.

Example 52: The Risks of Calls for Donations

Donations to help more unfortunate people or those who suffer hard times are a very old human custom.

These donations were important in areas which had little to do with tourism. However, in the recent past, the significance of donations for the tourism sector increased. This has had secondary effects. Theuerkorn (2004) demonstrated, with the case of the century floods which affected larger areas of central Europe in August 2002, that donations were helpful for the local population and for the reconstruction of the infrastructure but that they also had negative effects. The continuous and especially hard breaking core messages of those calls for donations extended the phase of suffering and were in direct contradiction to the recovery efforts of the tourism companies and destination organizations.

A similar situation was observed in the case of the many Asian countries affected by the Tsunami in 2004, which depended to an even higher degree on tourism. Despite a wave of donations which was hardly seen before, most tourism organizations in the region were rather sceptical about how this money could help them. The Phuket Tourism association (Indonesia) went as far as to say:

'It is, of course, very kind of people to provide donations to various organizations. Instead of dropping money in a donation box and staying at home, however, it would be more helpful now to bring your money yourself and spend it here as a normal tourist'

Other risks are rooted in the form of the communication process. Multi-stage communication processes not initiated by the company occur and replace the normal communication relationships. Once triggered, these cannot be controlled exclusively by the affected company. The independent communication processes make it difficult to estimate the effect that the marketing apparatus finally has.

Diagram 43: Three-actor model

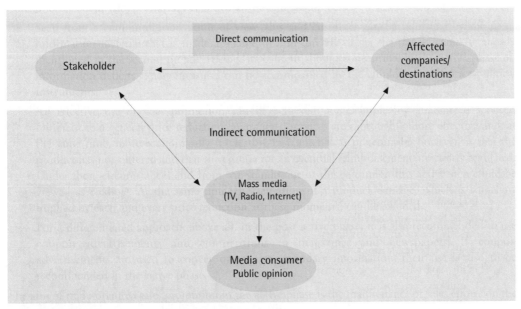

Almost always, if other social groups take part in this communication process, the three-actor model known from conflict research applies. Its peculiarity is that communication takes place on two levels, of which one is direct communication between the participants and the other is indirect communication via the mass media. The latter serves only to influence public opinion in the sense of its own standpoint and not to discuss objectively. High rhetorical abilities are an important prerequisite for the affected company in order to have a positive influence on this process.

7.5.5 Pictorial vs. text information

Under normal circumstances, an important determination of the mixture of pictorial and textual communication is also important for the different aspects of crisis communication. As it was already mentioned, negative events only become discernible by the interposition of the media if they are not experienced on a personal level. If an incident becomes worth reporting, it is spread by print, acoustic or audio-visual media. At the same time, it can be observed that audio-visual media is the more dominant, for which reason television is described as sensationalizing.

This circumstance can be traced back to various influences:

1. The high proportion of pictorial information means that television makes information perception easier. Instead of a sequential information perception like with text information, information is perceived holistically by means of pictorial information which requires less cognitive effort. This becomes especially clear if it is considered that an average recipient of information needs 1.5 to 2.5 seconds to perceive a picture of medium complexity whilst, in the same space or time, he comprehends only 10 words (Kroeber-Riel, 1993a).

2. The recipient of the information develops a different relationship to textual information than he does to pictorial information. He trusts the latter more because he believes he has seen everything with his own eyes, therefore, pictures are subject to little logical intellectual control. This is also confirmed by empirical investigations, according to which, television was considered by over half of those questioned to have a relatively high level of credibility. Newspapers and radio followed at a distance, their relative credibility only being acknowledged by 1 in 6 (Berg and Kiefer, 1992; Berger, Gärtner and Mathes, 1989).

3. As well as being informative in nature, pictures convey a high proportion of emotional stimuli which can hardly be conveyed in words. This is where the danger of negative news coverage lies as the emotional effect on recipients occurs whether they have high or low involvement. This effect could be clearly observed for example, during the mishandling of prisoners in Iraq in 2004 and in the conflict of Nestle baby food in which audio-visual media played an extraordinary role in conveying feelings.

4. Finally, apart from these aspects of quicker perception, greater credibility and more intense emotional activation, pictures also make it easier to remember an event. In concrete terms, this means that a negative event communicated by means of audio-visual media, especially if it is conveyed in the form of moving rather than static pictures, is remembered for a longer time.

Visual impressions

Pictures / visual impressions are important for the media. During the media opening tour during the ITB 2005 the destinations affected by the Tsunami were subject of high interest. Destinations have to know how to use these 'unique' opportunities of unusual attention for an effective product presentation.

If these findings are transferred to the appropriate employment of instruments, there is much to favour the use of pictorial communication even in times of crisis. In the past, important arguments, especially the availability of information channels and the flexibility of the necessary instruments, undoubtedly spoke out against its use. In the active phase, communication was restricted to verbal communication preferably in the form of press releases. However, the use of the Internet avoids these restrictions. Pictorial information, even in the form of video sequences, can be made available early and without much preparation time. Extensive use should be made of these possibilities from the very beginning because they are an important crutch for credible communication.

7.5.6 Communication with different target groups

Crisis communication includes elements of public relations as well as customer communication. On the one hand, it performs a public relations function, the aim of which is to create a positive and benevolent atmosphere for the organization, principally among the wider spheres of activity. On the other hand, crisis communication also has concrete sales objectives that are normally reserved for advertising or sales promotion.

The aim is to fulfil, in the most differentiated way possible, the tourists' increased need for information in the orientation, decision and holiday phase as well as in the wider spheres of activity. These measures can be carried out with the inclusion of the media, in a direct or indirect manner.

7.5.6.1 Communication with customers

Direct communication between the affected organization and interested parties offers many advantages. It allows individual needs and questions to be dealt with very precisely. That way it fulfils the necessity for a differentiated employment of the instruments as already discussed. In addition, this form of communication reduces the filtering and distortion of information by third parties. The extent that this kind of communication can reach and the time to make the instruments available, were in the past reasons to concentrate on media communication and recommend – similar to the preparation for the media – to prepare thoroughly for these special circumstances. The following table lists important and typical documents which should be prepared and kept available by the organization for direct customer communication.

Diagram 44: Documents to be prepared (Clients)

1.	Develop website for emergency situations and translate if necessary
2.	Prepare a list with golden rules on how to handle clients in stressful situations (maximum 2 pages) so that they can be updated easily
3.	Prepare call-in hotline questionnaire
4.	Develop practical guidelines for the operators of the emergency phones (maximum 2 pages)
5.	Prepare typical questions and respective answers and advices for telephone operators
6.	Develop practical guidelines for the email operators (maximum 2 pages)
7.	Prepare typical questions and respective answers as auto texts for email operators
8.	Develop customer information letter for actual and booked (future) guests

Emergency telephone numbers are particularly important. They are used regularly by affected organizations and destinations. The preparations do not only ensure that a sufficient number of operators will be available but also that the affected clients, relatives and potential clients are separated from the regular telephone traffic of the organization. Depending on the type and scope of the event, other organizations or state institutions follow suit and they make emergency telephone numbers available.

Emergency telephone

As well as conveying information, this form of direct communication with customers helps to cope with emotional problems that often arise among those directly or indirectly affected by the negative event. In addition, it ensures the accessibility or presence of the responsible organization. This demonstrates that the organization is still 'in charge' and controlling the situation. The fulfilment of both these needs makes an important contribution towards avoiding long-term damage to those affected (Butollo, 1990; WTO, 1994d). Another advantage is the possibility of questioning callers and assessing their concerns to draw conclusions as to further measures to be taken and the content of the communication.

Identify interfaces

Many organizations are surprised about the unusual way of being contacted in times of crises. Often the interested people get in contact with the organization for the first time or the typical ways of contact are jammed. It is for this reason recommendable to systematically identify the different 'interfaces' an organization can have for the information seeker. Using telephone books, telephone information services, search engines, associations, etc., can identify interfaces in the forerun and, if necessary, be corrected.

Example 53: Call-In Hotline Questionnaire

The following sample shows how a telephone conversation could be structured. The answers are, whenever possible, directly typed into a computer.

Thank you for calling. We appreciate your interest. How can we help you?

1. **Identify caller's concerns**

   _____

2. **If they want general information, inform them.**
   The status of the situation is:
   The (DISASTER) occurred at _____
   (Time, place, area affected) _____
   Damage includes:
   Injured _____ Dead _____ Cost of damages _____

Facilities that are open include: (provide list of resorts and attractions that are open)

Facilities that are not yet open, but are expected to be reopened within a week are: (give list)

Facilities that will be closed for an extended period of time are: (give list)

Would you mind if we ask you a few questions so that we may send you more information about our area upon further recovery?

Name _____

Address _____

Phone (if appropriate) _____

Where did you see or hear about our Call-in-Hotline? _____

Do you have a confirmed reservation in the area and will you still be coming? _____

Thank you for calling.

Source: Based on WTO (1998b)

In the last few years, the Internet has started to play such an important role in crisis communication that it is difficult to imagine how organizations were able to handle these situations without it. Using the website opens the possibility to offer to all interested people information which in its scope could not otherwise be kept available and directly accessible. This refers to background information that can place the event in a temporal and topical context as well as up-to-date news. The latter can now, through the Internet, be made available directly, continuously, without delay and without the intervention of the 'middleman' media. Moreover, all the advantages of pictorial communication can be made use of. This applies both for static and moving pictures that can be made available in the form of complete video sequences. Webcams can also offer a very good opportunity to let the interested customer verify how the situation actually is in the destination (see also Example 55). This is especially true for the active time of a crisis when the tourism product was not affected and for the post-active phase, i.e. once the product is in good condition again. Without interference or obligation, the customer might take control of the camera, zoom into places of interest and choose the moments of verification. The problems of trust and belief, which are inherent to the tourism product, can in this way be reduced significantly.

Using emails offers nearly the same advantages as using emergency phones. While the latter should be primarily used for those directly affected by the negative event, since the advantage of speaking to someone helps to better overcome the emotional difficulties and might be a time advantage if professionally handled, emails are a very flexible tool which is not only open to direct customer communication. Firstly, emails do not require a direct counterpart. Once sent, the other part feels that he has communicated his problem to the organization. It then only depends on the organization when this turns into a contact, i.e. a reply is given to the problem. If the person is directly affected, an individual reply can be given. If it is a general request, auto texts can be used and detailed information given about the different parts of a question. Even the use of computer programmes, as described earlier, analysing the content of the emails and generating automatic replies helps to reduce the impact for the affected organization (see Section 4.2.2.5). However, for email communication as well as for emergency phones it should not be forgotten that an increase in direct communication with customers requires more flexibility on the part of the affected organization. This has to do on one hand with properly trained staff. Besides the personal qualifications already mentioned (see Section 6.3) they must be prepared to deal with the peculiarities of crisis communications. It is for example common in crisis situations, that both channels of communication are not only used by affected customers but also by those interested in what happened. This includes the curious public but sometimes also the press. It is at the same time necessary to also take care that personal and sensitive information is not passed on to externals who could take advantage of this confidentiality.

On the other hand there are additional organization and infrastructure measures to be considered while using the Internet. Among them is the development of emergency websites for different basic scenarios already before a negative event happens. This increases the reaction speed enormously (for the typical parts of such a website see Example 54 and Example 55). In this manner and already at a very early stage, the address of the website can be announced to the general public through a press release. Furthermore, it is important to analyse whether the hosting server is likely to be affected by negative events and whether other backup servers in other regions are available and accessible for staff updates. A recent reminder of how important this point is was Hurricane Katrina in 2005, which left many internet servers in the affected region in the USA unavailable.

Website

Webcams

Emails

Trained staff

Backup servers

221

Message Boards and Blogs

The need of communication during a crisis is high. Weblogs are following the idea of message boards (Picture: R. Newell) and extend them even further into the sphere of classical media. Flickr.com and Moblog.co.uk (Picture: A. Stacey) were two very highly used weblogs after the London bombings in 2005 that published first hand impressions that cell phone users had taken with their cameras.

Customers and people directly affected are also interested in publishing their impressions and interacting with the wider public. This form of publishing is no longer controlled by third parties and has reached with weblogs a speed which often makes them the first hand sources of information.

Solidarity and Support

People who before the negative events had little in common might form new groups as a consequence. This has to be taken into consideration and can offer new opportunities (see Example 44).
Picture: werenotafraid.com

Whether it was the Iraq war, the Tsunami catastrophe 2004 in Asia or the bombings in London in 2005, weblogs reported faster and with more first hand impressions than the traditional media or even than the affected organizations. In the case of the London bombings, the first pictures taken in the subway with the cameras of cell phones were sent to specialized weblogs for cell phone pictures and published within 30 minutes. It is difficult to say which of the weblogs will take the lead in reporting and building a forum for the discussion of those affected and those 'interested to know' or i.e. potential customers. The affected organization should be in any case prepared to deal with those stakeholders, understand their functioning well (that includes realizing their enormous information power besides the traditional media) and to offer reliable information. Weblogs often become information platforms and forums for solidarity and support, as it happened in the case of London.

Example 54: Luxair's Webpages after the Accident of November 2002

On 6 November 2002, a Luxair Fokker 50 flying from Berlin to Luxembourg crashed in heavy fog conditions a few minutes before its landing. It left twenty passengers dead and only two people survived (the captain and one passenger). It was the first accident for the company, which had been operating for more than 40 years within Europe. It was also the first time that this type of aircraft was affected.

Some 60 minutes after the accident, the company changed the presentation of its website on the Internet. It replaced the homepage with its classical banners and promotion by a special page providing all the details and news of the accident. The page was simple and concentrated on textual information. The text that the Internet journalist drafted was approved within minutes by the CEO and was made available immediately worldwide. It was directed both at the customers and relatives of those involved in the accident as well as to the media. The page was permanently updated with new and more detailed information. It also gave details and maps of the places where the various press conferences would be held.

Making this information available through the Internet reduced the amount of calls to the emergency numbers from people who had no relatives involved in the accident. In that sense it narrowed the emergency communication to those most important at that moment but also provided extremely detailed information to normal clients of the company who also had an enormous interest in keeping themselves informed about the accident.

The web pages which had some 36 000 accesses on the first day, more than ten times higher than in normal situations, worked without problems during these difficult moments. Due to the reduction of unnecessary graphics on this page, the data volume remained only slightly higher than usual. The communications department of Luxair which had the overall responsibility for this webpage had one person permanently assigned to update the page with information. At the same time 10 other people were attending emergency telephone numbers.

Two days after the accident, the emergency homepage was replaced by the classical homepage of the company although with a prominent link to the former emergency homepage, which became as from then a sub-page.

The Luxair Homepage during the day of the accident and the regular homepage.

Example 55: The PTA Tourism Recovery Centre

Phuket is Thailand's biggest island and a major tourism destination. At first it was mainly visited by Europeans but then it rapidly became also very popular among Asian tourists. On 26 December 2004 the destination was hit by a devastating tsunami which caused some 300 000 victims across different regions of the Indian Ocean. Many foreign tourists were among the victims.

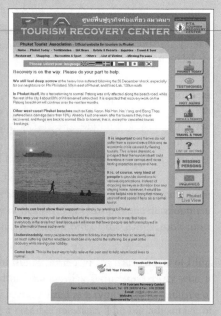

The Phuket Tourism Association established shortly after the Tsunami, the website of the PTA Tourism Recovery Centre, which was a central element in the communication strategy of the destination with its clients and the relatives of the victims. This way the function of a central information and contact point was provided with consistent and comprehensive information. Furthermore, the individual tourism service providers were assisted in this manner and thus relieved in their communication efforts.

As the pictures show, the website was characterized by its clear structure. Relatives and friends of the victims were redirected to specific web pages for missing persons and victims. The central communication focal point could be contacted by email and a reply was guaranteed within 24 hours.

Furthermore, the website offered a clear overview of the actual developments and the recovery measures in the destination. Links to all the different hotels and tourism service providers were

given but only activated once the service became available again. Until then, the service provider remained only listed inactively.

Intensive use was made of the website for all kinds of pictorial information, which allowed a short and terse communication. Nearly all pictures were labelled with the date of the picture to guarantee authenticity and actuality. Furthermore, pictures and statements about the situation of actual guests in the destination were published in their respective mother tongues. A webcam was added later to the website which gave interested users a first hand impression of the situation and allowed them to direct the cameras view along the Phuket beachside.

7.5.6.2 Communication with staff members

Communications with the staff is of great importance. However, this is often not taken enough care of in situations of crisis when the main focus of the communication efforts is directed towards the external spheres of activity.

The internal communication efforts towards the staff should in the first place provide a clear situation overview, explain the actual measures taken by the organization, other external partners and the public authorities as well as include a clear statement of intention for the own organization. This statement should be regularly reminded and recalled and if necessary be updated. That way all staff members, even those not directly involved in the crisis coping activities, can evaluate whether their individual actions are in line with the overall aim and intention of the organization.

Depending on the size of the affected organization different groups can be distinguished which can be addressed individually.

Diagram 45: Measures of internal communications

Target group	Measure
All employees	• Special page on the **Intra**net page • Password protected **Internet** page • Hotline for employees' questions • Email update • Message board for up-to-date messages and press clippings
For decision makers	• Password protected **Intra**net page • Password protected **Internet** page • Telephone- and video conferences • Email update • Press clippings
For retirees	• Password protected **Internet** page • Retiree associations • Email updates • Special telephone numbers with daily updated recorded announcements

In general, management must realize that staff members are one of the most important assets and permanent ambassadors of the organization (see also Section 7.2.3). The issues of concern and questions of staff members are therefore and because of the obligation to ensure their well-being, paid special attention to. However, it must also be taken into account that especially in times of crisis there is information which must be considered very sensitive and which, if published, could cause considerable harm to the organization and its credibility. In this case, despite the legitimate interest staff members might have, no comments should be made to inquiries of this kind.

7.5.6.3 Communication with tour operators and travel agents

Tour operators and travel agents have a different and extended want for information than normal customers. This includes for example that tour operators have in many countries legally founded information obligations to their customers. Also their contractual obligations, higher entrepreneurial risk, monitoring competitors and interest to maintain customer relations, make additional decisions necessary.

If the communication measures are to be of use, they must be prompt, comprehensive and credible. Above all, they must allow the tour operator to assess the situation as objectively as possible. That includes that the influence of the various product areas is illustrated and explained in the same way as the measures introduced. Ideally, affected destinations intend to contact their most important partners within the first 6-24 hours. Telephone or videoconferences are the most suitable instruments for this kind of communication. In comparison to the alternative individual conversation, these instruments save plenty of time and allow a first coordination process among the interested parties.

For the information to the end consumer through the tour operator or travel agent, the use of standardized messages is recommendable and should be supported by pictorial information (such as maps of the affected area, pictures...). It is also and especially important in the early phase following the negative event, that business partners are offered the possibility to link to the website of the affected organization or destination, where the end consumer is kept up-to-date. In this way the service providers and the destinations ensure a fast and consistent information supply.

Familiarization trips

Familiarization trips have been used intensively as an instrument by the countries affected by the Tsunami in 2004. As in this crisis, regions which actually had not been hit by the Tsunami were perceived as affected, these trips were designed to inform and correct these perceptions and were aimed at high-level journalists, tour operators and travel agents. However, while doing so it must be ensured that they are not mixed within the same group – too different are the information necessities and working styles.

Briefing of the 800 participants of the Mega Familiarisation Trip in Thailand in March 2005. The participants came from the important source markets of Europe, South-East Asia, China, Australia and Japan.

Moreover, it should be considered that tour operators and travel agents have a personal interest in keeping the consequences of a negative event to a minimum. They also often have their own ideas as to how problems can be handled. In order to consider these ideas and needs, the affected service provider should strive for dialogue-oriented communication. It is to be recommended that in this dialogue, if possible, always the highest management levels are involved. This allows for extraordinary decisions to be taken faster. Furthermore, credibility and interest in those measures introduced and those to be taken in the future are in this way effectively documented. Ideally, these information efforts are appropriately accompanied by direct product assessments – the so-called familiarization trips. This applies to the active phase, if it concerns the assessment of potential damage, as well as to the post-active phase, if the measures already carried out are to be assessed (see Section 7.5.8).

7.5.6.4 Media communication

Mass media communication processes are characterized by various peculiarities, the observation of which is of significance for the affected organization's communication efforts. The principal influence variables of media coverage have already been discussed (see Section 2.2.3). At this point, therefore, those peculiarities that offer control formations for the affected organization are mainly of interest.

In the first place, the importance of quickly making information available must be discussed. Journalists are always under pressure to explain. They have to explain what has occurred and illustrate its consequences to their audience. Therefore, if a journalist puts a question to an organization and it is not answered, he cannot simply leave it at that. Rather, he tries to answer the question himself using alternative sources. If he is able to do this, the organization has wasted a vital opportunity to put forward its own position and influence the communication process. Because, however, not all questions are directed at the organization, it becomes necessary to introduce media monitoring in order to quickly determine which needs are current. The most sensible thing is to implement this monitoring process in the news agencies, as it is their information that is predominantly used by media representatives. If a quick reaction is assumed, this offers the organization the opportunity to present its own point of view before the news is published in the mass media.

Making information quickly available

As many questions follow a certain scheme, especially at the beginning of a crisis, the preparation of documents and statements, which only need to be completed with the specific information, is advised. Diagram 46 lists the most important documents to be prepared for a significant increase in consistency and time advantage.

Diagram 46: Documents to be prepared (Media)

1.	Develop model of a first standby message: 'We are evaluating the situation'
2.	Develop model of a first message to staff confirming the occurrence of the event
3.	Develop model of a first formal press release for communicating that the event has occurred
4.	Prepare typical questions with their respective answers and advice for the first press conference
5.	Prepare a list of golden rules on how to handle media representatives (maximum 2 pages)
6.	Prepare practical advice for the radio interviews (maximum 2 pages)
7.	Prepare practical advice for TV interviews (maximum 2 pages)
8.	Prepare practical advice for print media interviews (maximum 2 pages)
9.	Prepare background and fact sheets on the own organization (location, business segment, title and name of top management, employees, short company history)

Although general aspects of credibility have already been discussed, a further facet of credibility based on the personality of the spokesperson is of great importance for the communication. It is generally agreed that this function should be undertaken centrally and, if possible, by someone at the top management level of the organization. At the same time, however, external aspects and the form of expression determine whether the person and also the content of the communication are seen to be

Credibility

credible. For this reason, it should be determined at an early stage which person is to act as a representative for the organization in this situation.

Normally, the advantage of a relationship of trust already built up with responsible media representatives is pointed at. In this way, thoughtless and rash media coverage should be avoided in times of crisis. Furthermore, this should help to communicate the core messages to the media, which are rarely conveyed by press conferences in situations of this kind so that they include them in their stories. Regularly in those situations, recognition sinks to around one-fourth of the otherwise normal perception. In practice, however, the organization is confronted with several adversities that bring the effectiveness of this behaviour into question. On the one hand, a change of editorial takes place depending on the type of event. Coverage responsibility changes from the previously responsible editorial (e.g. economic editorial) to the editorial in charge of current affairs. Whilst it is still possible to have a relationship with the former, this would appear to be less probable for the latter because, under normal circumstances, the editor has no professional interest in the subject. On the other hand, with regard to electronic media, the number of independent television and radio journalists who sell their reports to broadcasters is constantly increasing in the same way as the change frequency of teams or their employees is increasing. Therefore, if a relationship of trust is to be established, it should be related to the organization rather than to a person.

The organization also has legal and economic ways of controlling the media. Legal possibilities include corrective statements, omission claims and damage claims, which mean that both material and immaterial damage can be asserted. A prerequisite for the implementation of such claims, however, is that the organization is able to prove a journalist's culpable behaviour and at the same time provide evidence that there is a contextual link between the report and the damages. As a rule, this is difficult. Econo-

---

New Sources

The need to report quickly and the competing sources of information especially weblogs, force the traditional media to use new ways to obtain information. All major news channels use journalists who observe the different weblogs but also encourage users to send their pictures and comments directly to their newsrooms.

Picture: BBC webpage on 21 July 2005. The picture shows the part of the webpage where visitors were invited to send their direct contributions to the broadcaster.

mic opportunities available as a reaction are, on the other hand, numerous and include, for example, advertising boycotts as well as the use of rival media organizations. Whilst economic methods can be implemented without causing further sensation, the use of legal methods requires careful reflection. It must be considered whether unchallenged archiving is not preferable to the danger of lengthy negative coverage.

It can be concluded that the contact with the mass media requires a certain amount of practice and should not take place if the company is unprepared. An analysis of the principal peculiarities and mechanisms of media communication is recommendable even before a crisis occurs. This at least ensures that the situation will be dealt with in a prudent and targeted manner. However, this is not a guarantee of success. Consistent behaviour combined with a reputation acquired over a period of time are the most effective instruments for balanced media coverage.

7.5.7 Advertising

Advertising describes efforts to influence the behaviour of the recipient of information using certain methods of communication. Under normal circumstances, this is a known attempt to induce customers to buy or consume a product, that is, sales advertising. However, the intention of advertising, that is, to convey information and control behaviour, can aid every set corporate goal, including crisis management.

> **Hong Kong Advertising**
>
> The promotional slogan 'Hong Kong will take your breath away' was changed immediately after the appearance of SARS into 'There's no place like Hong Kong'.

It can be assumed that certain advertising measures have been introduced before a negative event has occurred. Consequently, it is the company management's first task to examine the coherence of these advertising decisions. This examination should be carried out under consideration of short- and medium-term corporate goals, which have changed because of the negative event and the situation itself. The often voiced point of view that advertising should be essentially stopped cannot be followed as that way an important communication channel and, consequently, the chance to exert influence would be lost.

In the active phase, the aim of advertising is to convey information. This arises from the fact that, in times of crisis, the affected organization has to deal with information deficits as well as the negative event itself. These information deficits are apparent in the various spheres of activity and are not rectified by the media but in many cases, intensified. In such situations, advertising has the task of transferring information that would otherwise have no chance of being conveyed and would cause damage to the organization's credibility and image if absent or distorted.

Active phase

> **Influential aims of advertising**
>
> Three influential aims of advertising can be distinguished: topicality, emotion and information. That which brings attention to the product, that is the topicality, is a result of the negative event and rules it out as an influential aim. The release of emotional stimuli or the conveying of information about the product remain as influential aims.

For the active phase, advertisements, promotional letters and leaflets are useful advertising tools due to their availability, suitability and cost. Radio and television advertising appear to be suitable in principle but are costly. Their effective use requires, therefore, a six to seven figure budget. For this reason, their practical use is restricted to very large tour operators and destinations or requires innovative approaches (see Example 56).

- During all phases, advertisements in newspapers and magazines prove to be useful advertising tools for conveying information which represents the company line. One advantage is their quick availability which is only restricted by time needed for the writing of the content and the layout of the advertisement. Another advantage is their high coverage and cost effectiveness. Of disadvantage, on the other hand, is the lack of opportunity for differentiation. Consequently, they are of special use for a content which can be the same for all readers of a newspaper or magazine.

Land in Sight!

Humour contributes to relaxation and conveys confidence to the customer. A promotional post card of the city of Pirna following the century floodingin central Europe in 2002 used the slogan 'Land in sight' together with pictures of the flooding and the actual recovery. The poster of Saxony stated 'Saxony - dry again' was designed by the Dresdner Agency for Marketing and Design Ö Grafik and showed two kids wrapped up in towels, linking them to the world famous darling angels leaning on the balustrade at the base of Raphael's painting 'The Sistine Madonna' that hangs in the Dresden Old Masters Picture Gallery in Germany. This image became a representative symbol for Dresden.

- Promotional letters are, to a great extent, suitable for explaining the actual circumstances to, for example, those customers in the pre-holiday phase. They can directly inform the customer of product-political or price-political measures. Apart from the opportunities to select the target groups, the content of the communication can be individualized. This helps to comply with the above-mentioned differentiation necessities for the information, the product on offer or the price. The usefulness of this advertising medium is only restricted by the necessity of keeping the contact addresses ready.

- Leaflets and brochures can relatively quickly impart comprehensive information to potential and current customers as well as other more relevant spheres of activity. A differentiation of the content is only possible if the targeted persons, which are to be informed similarly, can be reached through the same distribution channel of information. These are in principle the distribution channels of the service promise as well as inserts in newspapers and magazines.

To what extent the affected organization is able to achieve its influential goals in a crisis situation by means of informative advertising depends, above all, on whether the information offered to the target person in this situation is relevant and credible.

Example 56: Project Phoenix: PATA's Communications Strategy during the SARS Crisis

The Pacific Asia Tourism Association (PATA) was created more than fifty years ago to provide leadership to the collective efforts of its members, currently more than a thousand and coming from both government (nearly 100 governments, states and city tourism bodies from the Asia-Pacific region) as well as the private sector (carriers, Europe-based tour operators, hotels, etc). Its aim is that of '…enhancing the growth, value and quality of Pacific-Asia travel and tourism for the benefit of its members'.

The advent of SARS in 2003 brought one of the most devastating events of Asia-Pacific, both in terms of human and financial losses. The impact on tourism was almost immediate and had enormous consequences on the tourism industry and the local population. To respond to the need of its members in such difficult circumstances, PATA decided to launch without delay a strong campaign to restore the reputation of Asia-Pacific worldwide and the public's confidence in this region as a travel destination. It also wanted to ensure that the region would be better equipped in the future to deal with the next crisis. The project was called 'Project Phoenix'.

PATA's first objective was to obtain funds to finance the new campaign. This was not an easy task as not all countries felt immediately affected by SARS. However PATA's argument was clear: 'SARS and fear know no borders – the region's problem is your problem'. This became increasingly true and as a result, PATA was able to gather within three weeks 350 000 US$ from 15 NTOs and six key industry players, together with other pledges of in-kind support.

To be able to influence global consumer perception with this modest budget, PATA developed a well-elaborated communication strategy composed of 4 core elements:

1. It started with a massive and pro-active information campaign through press releases, interviews and backgrounders, which explained SARS and clarified its impact and consequences. This was done by working with PATA's premier partners, CNN, BBC World and CNBC, to position PATA as the key authority to which they could turn to for quotes. The result was extensive press coverage and TV exposure.

2. PATA also negotiated as much free ad space and air time as possible. This was made possible through the partnerships PATA already had with CNN, Time and Fortune and also since these also relied on a healthy tourism sector for much of their advertising revenue. A very strong campaign called 'Welcome back' was thus launched.

3. PATA also quickly developed a new website called 'TravelWithPATA.com', that included travel news, features about Asia-Pacific destinations, in-depth guides from Lonely Planet and a special section on travel advisories. This travel advisories' section was linked to Abacu's Travel Smart Asia, which uses iJet Travel Intelligence. It was particularly important as it provided 'an alternative source' of information to the ministries of foreign affairs on health, security, transport, upcoming political protests, natural hazards, etc.

4. Finally, PATA promoted this new website through TV commercials with BBC World (series of eight 60 second vignettes showcasing Phoenix contributors destinations and promoting the website), the National Geographic Channel (30-second spots that directly promoted the website) and the 'SMILES campaign' which used TV to drive traffic to the website and used a printed version to welcome visitors back and to recognize Phoenix contributors.

Altogether, PATA's Project Phoenix campaign of information and promotion reached 216 million consumer households between August and December 2003. Although it is always difficult to determine the impact of such a campaign, it is a good example of how combined efforts, a strategic approach and specific actions can help to overcome a crisis. Demand for hotels and airline seats in the November 2003 - February 2004 period was extremely high. Also destinations affected by SARS found that the rebound came sooner than expected and bounced higher than previously thought.

When Asia-Pacific had to face another crisis a few months later, the bird flu, PATA was immediately able to work on a well developed concept. Right from the beginning and similarly to the SARS crisis, it intensely engaged in direct communications and looked for multipliers of its messages. It distributed key messages to all PATA members, the media, PATA chapters and to a special database of travel industry communications and PR professionals. The core of the messages were hard facts and explanations on the bird flu, its health threat to visitors visiting Asian cities and the risk of catching bird flu by eating cooked chicken or eggs. To avoid distortion at the end-users level, PATA coordinated with IATA and the WHO to ensure as much as possible consistency in the messages. In addition, it distributed updated messages to its members and partners that could be used when talking to the media.

In both cases PATA demonstrated the importance of good background information, coordination, credibility and consistency for an efficient communication strategy. If those points are considered, even smaller organizations with a rather limited budget can be in the position to react efficiently in crisis situations.

Post-active phase

Whilst, in the active phase, tactical advertising has to even out bottlenecks, in the post-active phase, strategic influential objectives of product positioning are once again brought to the fore. This deployment of the advertising instruments does not have any crisis-specific peculiarities. It uses the same measures and instruments as under normal circumstances. It is worth mentioning here that strategic influential objectives could have changed as a result of the negative event. On the one hand, they could prove themselves to be fundamentally unsuitable and make a repositioning necessary. On the other hand, the aimed or held positioning could still be sensible, for which reason advertising measures must be directed towards the recovery of this position. Consequentially, before initiating activities in the post-active phase, a fundamental assessment of the actual and desired positioning must take place. If this is not done, advertising activities can cause lasting damage.

7.5.8 Sales promotion

The aim of sales promotion is the creation of unique, non-recurring additional incentives to purchase the product. They should immediately encourage sales. Apart from communicative measures, sales promotion includes other marketing elements that belong to price, product and distribution policy. Sales promotion actions are frequently used in tourism especially to balance fluctuations in demand under normal circumstances. Sales promotion actions are also fundamentally suitable for crisis management. However, it must also be noted that the generation of topicality for the product in the active phase is not the aim of sales promotion but rather overcoming the other sales problems. It is only in the post-active phase that the opportunity arises to view topicalization as an aim of sales promotion.

According to the target groups, the following cases of sales promotion can be differentiated:

Consumer-oriented sales promotion is aimed at the end customer.

- Seen from a communication point of view, this end customer can be informed by means of information material that is made available to him directly or via the travel agent. As already mentioned in the section on advertising, its content should concentrate in the active phase on information deficits. These measures can be accompanied by the employment of price-political instruments.

- An effective use of sales promotion can be achieved, for example, by guaranteed services. Different to a general price reduction, guaranteed services are thoroughly more effective and, at the same time, more economically interesting instruments. A prerequisite, however, is that the product has not suffered and that the criteria for an eventual reimbursement are clearly regulated. Under these circumstances and from the standpoint of the consumer, this active step could be viewed as credible. At the same time, the sensation of a product damage, which is somehow implied by each and every price reduction at these moments, can be avoided.

- For a differentiated approach, above all, in the post-active phase, it is also recommended to use coupon advertisements and competitions in magazines and newspapers. If coupon advertisements are used to convey or request secondary information, their use is also to be recommended in the active phase.

The aim of trade-oriented sales promotion in the active phase is the maintenance of sales efforts on the part of the travel agent; in the post-active phase, it is the recovery of previous sales figures.

- Seen from a communication point of view, this includes the preparation of information material with which travel agency employees can provide customers with correct information. This includes background information as well as information to help argue the case with customers. It is important that this is quickly made available because travel agency employees are normally the first refuge for customers. Financial incentives should also accompany these actions in order to support the particular strain of the additional information work.

- Apart from training, through which the sales assistant is prepared to handle specific problems, familiarization trips are of much use in the post-active phase. The latter offers the possibility to assess the product itself and to be comprehensively informed unlike any other instrument. Familiarization trips are always useful if product changes can only be communicated with difficulty as with events that trigger a slowdown in demand due to a perceived security situation.

Motivation and ability should increase with sales promotion aimed at the own sales personnel.

- The incentives are numerous and include both monetary and prestige benefits. These can be in the form of a competition or can be gained by fulfilling certain requirements. Training measures aim to prepare solutions for particular sales problems in the same way as trade-oriented sales promotion. To what extent such measures are necessary for destinations, which address the staff of their tourism offices, and tour operators depends on the corporate culture. If there is already a high identification with the corporate goals, this type of sales promotion action has no additional motivation success.

Sales promotion is a useful instrument offering a broad variety of creating incentives. The specialty, different to the other instrument of the communication policy, is the generation of a direct incentive to purchase the product. Nevertheless, it should be noted that these incentives are created in such a way that they are understood as a logical consequence of the negative event and help to overcome specific sales problems. In this way, it is ensured that, for all market segments, the additional incentive is understood and the organization's credibility is not harmed.

> ### Example 57: Make it Singapore!
>
> As the world globalizes and communications are made easier, international meetings become increasingly frequent. They are generally held in attractive tourism destinations or international hubs and bring together a large number of professionals interested in attending events where opinion leaders are likely to discuss key issues relating to their field of activity. Often, these participants never thought of visiting this destination and therefore these meetings bring a unique opportunity to discover it.
>
> Singapore was considered for more than twenty years Asia's top convention city and for five years in a row, one of the top-five convention cities in the world. The high-level business culture that had been developed there attracted innumerable fairs, conventions and meetings from all over the world. In 2003, however, Singapore was strongly hit by the SARS epidemic that spread throughout Asia. In very little time, the number of international meetings decreased dramatically.
>
> To regain its high-quality image and attract once again both tourists and international events, the Singapore Tourism Board launched, jointly with the Singapore Exhibition & Convention Bureau, the 'Make it Singapore!' campaign. This sales promotion campaign was aimed at congress organizers and offered an attractive basket of incentives to entice key decision-makers to hold their events in Singapore. These incentives differed on whether the event was for instance a convention, a corporate meeting, an exhibition and so on. These are some examples:
>
> Conventions:
>
> * Eligibility criteria: Minimum 400 visitor nights, minimum stay of 2 consecutive nights in Singapore, confirmed before 31 December 2005 and held before 31 December 2007;
> * Incentives: Financial support (for bidding costs to secure new events in Singapore), up to 30 per cent financial support for organizers (for speaker support, overseas marketing costs, management fee of professional conference organizers), non-financial support and hotels (same incentives as for exhibitions), for confirmed events (1 complementary room for every 25 rooms confirmed, up to a maximum of 5 rooms for the duration of the event, room upgrades for VIPs (up to 3 rooms), late check-out, etc.), with airlines (mutually beneficial commercial arrangements based on net flown revenue generated by organizers).
>
> Exhibitions:
>
> * Eligibility criteria: Minimum 1000 foreign exhibition visitors, minimum 50 per cent foreign exhibitors, minimum 1000 sqm of net exhibition space, first time held in Singapore, confirmed before 31 December 2005 and held before 31 December 2007;
> * Incentives: Financial support (up to 30 per cent for overseas exhibitor and visitor promotion support, buyer or speaker support, foreign journalist support); non-financial support (facilitation to secure exclusive venues, of immigration clearances, publicity, etc.), for site inspections (2 complementary rooms for up to 3 nights each for decision-makers); discount of food bill for welcome or opening reception at the official hotel/venue where the event is being held, special rates for set-up and tear-down days, among others.

With this initiative, the Singapore Tourism Board was able to reach out to the organizers of major events in a very efficient manner and achieved the promotion of their destination to important opinion leaders. The word-of-mouth helped to spread among friends and colleagues, the complete recovery of Singapore and its once-again exceptional conditions for international events.

By the end of 2004, more than 159 events from very different fields of activity had been confirmed for 2005-2009 including the 2006 annual meetings of the International Monetary Fund and of the World Bank, 2005 International Olympic Committee meeting, World Trade Organization Ministerial Conference, ITMA Asia 2005, to name a few.

7.5.9 Fairs

Fairs are one of the most important forums for tourism service providers to present their products. Some of the most important international tourism fairs are the Internationale Tourismus Börse (ITB) in Berlin (Germany), the World Travel Market (WTM) in London (United Kingdom) and the Feria Internacional de Turismo (FITUR) in Madrid (Spain). They are attended by both trade visitors and the general public.

Diagram 47: Important International Tourism Fairs

Fair	Period	Exhibitors	Trade visitors	Journalists	Total visitors
World Travel Market (WTM)	November	5 000	26 000	2 700	46 000
Feria Internacional de Turismo (Fitur) – International Tourism Trade Fair	End of January	11 000	93 000	7 300	202 000
Borsa Internazionale del Turismo (BIT) – International Tourism Exchange	February	5 000	100 000	6 000	147 000
Internationale Tourismus Börse (ITB) – International Tourism Exchange	Beginning of March	10 400	84 000	7 300	142 000
Moscow International Travel&Tourism Exhibition (MITT)	End of March	2 500	70 000[1]	100	98 000

Figures for 2004/2005. 1) Statement made for 2002, out of 111 000 visitors.

Fairs are, for the active and post-active phase of crisis, central platforms for the exchange of news, product presentations and background interviews. The personal contact allows an improved communication and the individual clarification of possible problems. This form of contact is especially important during the active phase of a crisis. In this phase it is important to take into consideration that the stand and the activities of the affected organization or destination are looked at with special interest. The number of people approaching the stand of the affected organization or destination and requesting information can be much higher than during normal times. It must also be noted that both the trade visitors and end consumers are much more involved than normal and are therefore more interested in factual information.

Press representatives at the Maldives booth during ITB 2005.

Destinations and organizations affected by negative events often use fairs also to get in contact with the press. The most suitable approach is through press conferences which regularly take place during international tourism fairs. However, due to the large number of exhibitors, there is a shortage of time slots available. Furthermore, the best days and hours are generally taken already a long time ahead, often agreed at least 12 months in advance. As a result, organizations and destinations that regularly hold press conferences at these events have better chances to present their information as the bookings are already made. Nevertheless, depending on the importance of the event and the organization, these press conferences can also be arranged outside the fairgrounds or even directly in the booth. However, distances and installations are not optimal and therefore these options need to be evaluated more carefully.

Fairs are in general an effective and cost-efficient instrument to reach the different target groups. As a rule, there is enough exposition space available to even arrange for short-term participation. Nevertheless, as mentioned before, regular participation in these fairs is more advantageous as planning is time consuming and the success of a fair participation is highly influenced by the experience with the particular event. If a presentation cannot be arranged during the fair, at least a personal visit should be considered to contact important business partners.

7.5.10 Sponsoring and product placement

Sponsoring is based on the principle of the exchange of services between the sponsor, who provides a previously defined sum of money or payment in kind, and the recipient. People, groups and organizations as well as events can be sponsored.

The use of sponsoring in crisis management can take on various forms. If we consider the person or group of people being sponsored, they should ensure the personalization of the product already under normal circumstances. If we go back to the person sponsored before the onset of the negative event, they can use in the active phase their persuasive effect and credibility to declare their continuing support for the product. These measures transfer trust, which is convenient for reducing the perceived increased risk. A variation which complies with these requirements is the use of celebrities who spent their holidays in the destination before the crisis and who now stand up for it either by declaring that they will continue to spend their holidays in the destination or with their active participation in the recovery efforts.

More problematic, on the other hand, is the inclusion of people who only commence their activity after the crisis has already begun. Because the intention of the sponsor is obvious, this offers a starting point for public criticism. Therefore, late inclusions should only occur in exceptional circumstances. This includes the case when due to their lack of credibility, people with high public standing become active for the organization.

Example 58: Prominent Faces – Helping to Get Up Again

It is known that sponsoring helps to promote a product. Less often practised, because quite more risky, is the use of prominent figures when it comes to overcome negative events or even long lasting negative images. Hillary Rodham Clinton, then a first Lady and now a Senator from New York, visited in 1999 the city of Palermo, the Sicilian capital (Italy), which had been struggling with the negative image of a Mafia stronghold. During her visit she did everything to underline that she believed that this city should be considered a safe tourist destination. The press echo proved the success of this visit for the destination with many positive articles on the 'securer destination' or 'The Renaissance of Italy'.

Another example of using prominent faces was the advertisement campaign launched by Lufthansa after the September 11 attacks on the United States. Understanding that the restraint of customers to fly was more emotional than rational, they used personalities with a high public credibility in their 3-month campaign. The company's strategy was honoured by a higher-than-average result.

Advertisements in 2001 with the former Minister of Foreign Affairs of Germany, Hans-Dietrich Genscher, the CEO of Siemens, Dr. Heinrich v. Pierer and the former President of Germany, Prof. Dr. Roman Herzog.

The sponsoring of events is an encouraging variant, for example, for destinations affected by negative events. Depending on the size and significance of the event, the accompanying media coverage gives rise to national or international interest. In this way, the destination becomes an indirect integral part of media coverage. Moreover, it offers the possibility to target specific market segments based on the appropriate thematic selection of the sponsored event. Much more important than this addressing of a specific segment is, however, the thematic selection from the point of view of communication content. If the participants or event themes have a beneficial relation to the desired communication goals, an effective indirect communication can, therefore, be produced. This is subject to little intellectual control from recipients because it is taken on in passing and, therefore, subconsciously. Therefore, providing the event is successful, positive news coverage is very probable.

Diagram 48: Time frame for selected events of interest for the wide public or opinion leaders in tourism

Events	Frequency	Decision before the beginning of events	Further length of time before the decision[1]
Olympic Games	every 4 years	7 years	2-4 years
FIFA Soccer World Championship	every 4 years	6 years	2-4 years
UEFA-European Championship	every 4 years	6 years	1 year
General Assembly of the World Tourism Organization (WTO)	every 2 years	2-4 years	6 months
Meeting of the Executive Council of the World Tourism Organization (WTO)	twice a year	2-6 months	1-6 months
Annual meeting of the German Association of Travel Agents and Tour Operators (DRV)	annually	1-2 years	1-3 months
Annual Conference of the Pacific Asia Travel Association (PATA)	annually	2 years	3 months
Annual Meeting of the World Travel & Tourism Council (WTTC)	annually	1 year	2 months
American Society of Travel Agents (ASTA) World Travel Congress	annually	5-8 years	1-4 years
Annual Meeting of the International Association of Scientific Experts in Tourism (AIEST)	annually	1 year	1-6 months

1) Those lead times are average minimum times. Due to national preparations they can take much longer.

However, if the risks do not appear to be controllable, the establishment of such exposed events should be avoided. This became clear at the sponsored American Society of Travel Agents (ASTA) conference in Manila in 1980, which was attended by 6000 American travel agency employees. A bomb attack against the Philippine President Marcos at this event caused long-term damage and a decline in visitor numbers rather than the intended promotion of tourism (Hall, 1994).

Ideally, these measures take place in the post-active phase once the product changes that might have been necessary are completed. In this way, an undesired analysis of the negative events can be avoided as much as possible, but cannot be ruled out completely. This is often already ensured by the lengthy application periods that exist for this type of event. Generally, it can be found that the more exposure an event enjoys, the more in advance the event is assigned to a destination. Nevertheless, recent events have also shown that there is a second rule existing. The more devastating an event is and the more emotional the reaction becomes, the higher the likelihood that an event is moved to the location. The latter was confirmed for instance, by the organization of the 'World Economic Forum' which, as a consequence of the attacks of 11 September 2001, was held in New York City (USA) instead of Davos (Switzerland) where it was originally planned, and the extraordinary meeting of the Executive Council of the World Tourism Organization in Phuket (Thailand) just two months after the Tsunami catastrophe in December 2004.

Concerning the number of events to be selected, it should be considered that one major event is sufficient to inform about the completion of product measures or to revive the destination. However, if the crisis made a new positioning necessary, the sponsoring of smaller- and medium-sized events over a longer period of time should be aimed for.

Product placement, that is, the placing of a product in a non-promotional part of a medium, is another instrument available within the communication policy.

First, films are of great significance in the arrangement and establishment of realms of experience. Second, as a rule, stimulation is carried out unobserved and by means of credible communicators. The main problem after negative events is the enormous length of time necessary to produce a film before it reaches the audience. It is also difficult to find a producer with an adequate script who accepts this product placement. Only if the content is of quality, the film reaches the market segment aimed at and, if it becomes successful, it can be assumed that the film helps the destination indirectly. As the following example demonstrates there are coincidences and other possibilities to use films while coping with crises.

Example 59: Movies in the Recovery Strategy

Movies are very useful instruments in the recovery strategy of a destination as they stimulate the tourist's interest for the destination. Since pictures are the most effective tool to influence people's perception – more than text messages – and that following a crisis customers are overwhelmed by negative impressions they have seen in the media, it is important to compensate and correct these impressions. Movies can in this sense easily transmit these positive connotations and have the advantage of primarily telling a story and only indirectly featuring the destination. This way they very effectively bypass the cognitive control of the viewer.

However, using movies in a recovery strategy is difficult to plan as producing them requires a lot of preliminary lead-time. The trilogy 'Lord of the Rings', whose first part 'The Fellowship of the

---

Ring' was launched in Summer 2001 in the United States, and the following parts at intervals of twelve months, was an extremely helpful tool for the recovery of New Zealand as a tourist destination after the SARS crisis. The impact of these movies on New Zealand was significant and helped place New Zealand in the international spotlight. As Andrew Adamson, a New Zealander film director, admits 'The Lord of the Rings ended up being a huge commercial for New Zealand.'

But preparations for the films had already started many years ago, long before the SARS outbreak began to affect New Zealand's industry and especially its tourism sector. It was in the mid 90s that Director Peter Jackson came up with the idea of filming Tolkien's Hobbit trilogy and in 1998 the film rights were purchased by New Cinema Line. Location finding started to take place in 1998 and shootings began finally in August 1999. They were completed 18 months later, in December 2000.

It is clear that this long preliminary lead-time makes it difficult to use films for instant crisis management as they cannot be activated spontaneously or flexibly. For example, the development of the specialized software programs for the special effects of the 'Lord of the Rings' took more than two years.

Avoiding this time disadvantage and still making use of the important imaginary effects of films to promote a destination is nevertheless possible based on 'star-power.' Using a celebrity who is positively related to the destination because of films or is recognized as a typical representative of his country can offer the opportunity of transmitting a credible message. The big advantage of employing a famous personality is that in the event of a crisis he or she can be activated for commercials quickly. A prominent example is the Hong Kong campaign 'Live it, love it' featuring action film star Jackie Chan greeting visitors in several languages and inviting them to his home-country. The Hong Kong Tourism Board launched this worldwide tourism marketing campaign in September 2003, two months after the territory was declared SARS-free, to rebuild visitors' confidence and encourage tourists to return to Hong Kong. The 16 million US$ 'Live it, love it' campaign included television, print and radio advertising.

Questions for review and discussion

- Explain the possibilities and risks of unusual attention for the affected destination or organization.
- How do you evaluate the usefulness of movies in the recovery strategy?
- Describe the quantitative and qualitative peculiarities of crisis communication.
- How important is credibility for crisis communication?
- What is the aim of advertisement in the active phase?
- How do you evaluate sponsoring with people who initiate their activity when the crisis has already begun?

Suggestions for further reading

Beeton, S. (2005), *Film-induced Tourism*, Channel View Publications, Clevedon.

Beirman, D. (2003), *Restoring Tourism Destinations in Crisis*, CABI Publishing, Wallingford.

Siegenthaler, P. (2002), 'Hiroshima and Nagasaki in Japanese Guidebooks', *Annals of Tourism Research,* 29(4), pp. 1111-1137.

World Tourism Organization (1997), *Tourist Safety and Security*, WTO, Madrid.

World Tourism Organization (1998), *Handbook on Natural Disaster Reduction in Tourist Areas*, WTO, Madrid.

8   The future of crisis management

Crisis management has only recently become a main centre of attention for tourism research. Some of the reasons are that the tourism industry has a relatively short development history and that the economic importance that the tourism sector has achieved over the past decades is still mostly unrecognized. Looking back, the tourism sector was also spared from major crises during times of steady growth and, whenever these occurred, it recuperated relatively fast, especially from small incidents.

Despite of this, the significance of crisis management has increased for those involved actively in the tourism industry. A non-ending chain of negative events has challenged the sector over the last years. It has reminded us of its vulnerability and that crisis management cannot and should no longer be ignored, neither by destinations nor tourism companies.

Like any other business activity, crisis management also depends on careful planning and on a thorough understanding of the underlying factors and relations that cause crises. When this understanding is missing, unnecessary situations and crises, which could have often been avoided or at least limited in their scope, evolve. The consequences of this are then not only to be borne by the customers and the tourism companies but have in addition wider effects on the whole economy and society.

Many crises, especially in the tourism sector, originate and are consequences of the perceived problems of destinations and tourism products and are seldom the result of material or objective deficits. These situations can only be avoided and coped with strategic and operational measures of marketing. For this reason, marketing instruments were extensively discussed in this book. Nonetheless, it is important not to forget that marketing instruments strongly depend on creativity, both during normal times and in times of crisis. The presentation of these instruments cannot therefore be complete. The aim was rather to illustrate the different possibilities to shape, combine and use the instruments, which can on this basis be further developed.

The value of crisis management is manifold. On the one hand it ensures the sustainable development of tourism and avoids unnecessary difficult situations. On the other hand it allows destinations, which were so far excluded from this development because of structural, social, political and other problems, to participate in tourism. This is especially true for many developing nations that choose tourism development to alleviate poverty in their countries. In principle this is a very promising approach as many of these countries have unique cultural and natural attractions, which are important for a successful tourism development. However, it has to be taken into account that structural problems, which are also often found in these countries and have already existed for many years, cannot be easily eliminated. Thus, for countries that are potentially more exposed to negative events, a professional and preventive crisis management is particularly necessary.

From the perspective of tourism service providers, especially tour operators, crisis management will soon become an integrative part of the service bundle of a package holiday as part of a quality strategy. Factors such as unknown languages, unawareness of the visited country, foreign currencies and unfamiliar customs were once important reasons to choose a package holiday. Nowadays, however the increasing travel experience of tourists has questioned these advantages and caused a decline in this form of travel. Taking this into account and going back to the original idea of a package holiday to go on a trip with an easy mind, crisis management has become as a result a useful complementary service that a tour operator can offer. As with travel insurances, clients are prepared to pay a premium for keeping this service available, although they hope not to have to face a situation where they might need it. Despite the usually unpleasant feelings related to the term 'crisis', customers are starting to value crisis management and the efforts that are undertaken in this area by tour operators. This changing attitude underlines the growing importance of crisis management for the future.

Bibliography

Adams, W. (1986), 'Whose lives count?: TV coverage of natural disasters', *Journal of Communication*, 36(2), pp. 113-22.

Ahmed, S. (1986), 'Understanding residents' reactions to tourism marketing strategies', *Journal of Travel Research*, 25(2), pp. 13-18.

Ahmed, Z. (1991), 'The influence of the components of a State's Tourist Images on Product positioning strategy', *Tourism Management*, 12(4), pp. 331-340.

Ahmed, Z. (1996), 'The need for the Identification of the Constituents of a Destination's Tourist Image: A Promotional Segmentation Perspective', *Tourism Review*, 51(2), pp. 44-57.

Ansoff, H. I. (1981), 'Managing Surprise and Discontinuity – Strategic Response to Weak Signals', *Zeitschrift für betriebswirtschaftliche Forschung*, 28(1), pp. 129-152.

Anson, C. (1999), 'Planning for Peace. The Role of Tourism in the Aftermath of Violence', *Journal of Travel Research*, 38(1), pp. 57-61.

Apostolopoulos, Y., Leivadi, S. and Yiannakis, A. (eds.) (1996), *The Sociology of Tourism*, Routledge, London.

Ashworth, G. J. and Goodall, B. (1990), *Marketing Tourism Places*, Routledge, London.

Autonomy (2005), *Understanding the Hidden 80%*, Autonomy, Cambridge.

Avenarius, H. (1995), *Public Relations*, Wissenschaftliche Buchgesellschaft, Darmstadt.

Aziz, H. (1995), 'Understanding attacks on tourists in Egypt', *Tourism Management*, 16(2), pp. 91-95.

Bar-On, R. (1990), 'The effect of international terrorism on international tourism', in *Terror in the Skies* (A. Lewis and M. Kaplan (eds.)), ISAS, Jerusalem, pp. 83-104.

Becheri, E. (1991), 'Rimini and Co – The end of a legend?: Dealing with the algae effect', *Tourism Management*, 12(3), pp. 229-235.

Beerli, A. and Martín, Josefa D. (2004), 'Factors Influencing Destination Image', *Annals of Tourism Research*, 31(3), pp. 657-681.

Beeton, S. (2001), 'Horseback Tourism in Victoria, Australia. Cooperative, Proactive Crisis Management', *Current Issues In Tourism*, 4(5), pp. 422-439.

Beeton, S. (2005), *Film-induced Tourism*, Channel View Publications, Clevedon.

Beirman, D. (2003), *Restoring Tourism Destinations in Crisis*, CABI Publishing, Wallingford.

Berg, K. and Kiefer, M. (eds.) (1992), *Massenkommunikation*, Nomos, Baden-Baden.

Berger, R., Gärtner, H. and Mathes, R. (1989), *Unternehmenskommunikation*, Gabler, Frankfurt am Main.

BGHZ (100, 185), *Entscheidungen des Bundesgerichtshof in Zivilsachen* [Official Case Reporter of the German Federal Court in Civil Matters], 100, pp. 185-189.

Bhattarai, K., Conway, D. and Shrestha, N. (2005), 'Tourism, Terrorism and Turmoil in Nepal', *Annals of Tourism Research*, 32(3), pp. 669-688.

Bieger, T. (2002), *Management von Destinationen*, 5th edn., Oldenbourg, München.

Bieger, T. and Boksberger, P. (2004), 'Krise oder Strukturbruch', in *Risiko und Gefahr im Tourismus* (D. Glaeßer and H. Pechlaner (eds.)), Erich Schmidt Verlag, Berlin, pp. 271-291.

Blake, A. and Sinclair, M. T. (2003), 'Tourism Crisis Management. US Response to September 11', *Annals of Tourism Research*, 30(4), pp. 813-832.

Boltz, D. (1994), *Konstruktion von Erlebniswelten*, Vistas, Berlin.

Born, K. (2004), 'Mit dem Krisendruck umgehen', in *Risiko und Gefahr im Tourismus* (D. Glaeßer and H. Pechlaner (eds.)), Erich Schmidt Verlag, Berlin, pp. 91-99.

Boush, D. and Loken, B. (1991), 'A process-tracing study of brand extension evaluation', *Journal of Marketing Research*, 28(1), pp. 16-28.

Brändström, A. (2001), *Coping with a Credibility Crisis: The Stockholm JAS Fighter Crash of 1993*, Crismart, Stockholm.

Braun, O. and Lohmann, M. (1989), *Die Reiseentscheidung*, Studienkreis für Tourismus, Starnberg.

Bruhn, M. and Meffert, H. (1995), *Dienstleistungsmarketing*, Gabler, Frankfurt am Main.

Brunt, P. (1997), *Market Research in Travel and Tourism*, Butterworth-Heinemann, Oxford.

Brunt, P., Mawby, R. and Hambly, Z. (2000), 'Tourist victimisation and the fear of crime on holiday', *Tourism Management*, 21(4), pp. 417-424.

Buckley, P. and Klemm, M. (1993), 'The decline of tourism in Northern Ireland – the Causes', *Tourism Management*, 14(3), pp. 184-194.

Buhalis, D. (2003), *eTourism: Information technology for strategic tourism management*, Prentice Hall, Harlow.

Bundestagsdrucksache No. 8/786 (1977), *Entwurf eines Gesetzes über den Reiseveranstaltungsvertrag*, Bundestag, Bonn.

Butollo, W. (1990), 'Krisen-Psychologie', *Süddeutsche Zeitung*, 15/16 September.

Callander, M. and Page, S.J. (2003), 'Managing risk in adventure in tourism operations in New Zealand: a review of the legal case history and potential for litigation', *Tourism Management*, 24(1), pp. 13-23.

Caribbean Hotel Association/Caribbean Tourism Organization (1998), *Hurricane Procedures Manual*, CHA/CTO, Barbados.

Carmouche, R. and Kelly, N. (1995), *Behavioural Studies in Hospitality Management*, Chapman & Hall, London.

Carter, S. (1998), 'Tourist's and traveller's social construction of Africa and Asia as risky locations', *Tourism Management*, 19(4), pp. 349-358.

Cassedy, K. (1991), Crisis *Management Planning in the Travel and Tourism Industry*, PATA, San Francisco.

Cavlek, N. (2002), 'Tour Operators and Destination Safety', *Annals of Tourism Research*, 29(2), pp. 478-496.

Chakravarti, D., MacInnis, D. and Nakamoto, K. (1990), 'Product category perceptions, elaborative processing and brand name extension strategies', in *Advances in Consumer Research Vol. 17* (M. Goldberg, G. Gorn and R. Pollay (eds.)), Association for Consumer Research, Provo UT, pp. 910-916.

Chesney-Lind, M. (1986), 'Visitors as victims: crimes against tourists in Hawaii', *Annals of Tourism Research*, 13(2), pp. 167-191.

Clift, S. and Grabowski, P. (eds.) (1997), Tourism and Health: *Risks, Research and Responses*, Cassell, London.

Coface (2004), *Risque Pays 2004*, Sedec, Paris.

Cohen, E. (1988), 'Tourism and AIDS in Thailand', *Annals of Tourism Research*, 15(4), pp. 467-486.

Coles, T. (2003), 'A Local Reading of a Global Disaster. Some Lessons on Tourism Management from an Annus Horibilis in South West England', *Journal of Travel and Tourism Marketing*, 15(1), pp. 173-216.

Control Risks (2004), *Risk Map 2005*, Control Risks Group, London.

Corke, J. (1993), *Tourism Law*, 2ⁿᵈ edn., Elm Publications, Huntingdon.

Coshall, J. (2005), 'Interventions on UK Earnings and Expenditure Overseas', *Annals of Tourism Research*, 32(3), pp. 592-609.

Cossens, J. and Gin, S. (1994), 'Tourism and AIDS: The Perceived Risk of HIV Infection on Destination Choice', *Journal of Travel & Tourism Marketing*, 3(4), pp. 1-20.

Cothran, D. and Cothran, C. C. (1998), 'Promise or political risk for Mexican tourism', *Annals of Tourism Research*, 25(2), pp. 477-497.

Council of the European Communities (1990), *Council Directive 90/314/EEC of 13 June 1990 on package travel, package holidays and package tours,* EEC, Brussels.

Cushnahan, G. (2004), 'Crisis Management in Small-Scale Tourism', *Journal of Travel and Tourism Marketing,* 15(4), pp. 323-338.

De Sausmarez, N. (2004), 'Implications for Tourism and Sectoral Crisis Management', *Journal of Travel and Tourism Marketing*, 15(4), pp. 217-232.

Des Kilalea (1987), 'Marketing to the affluent: natural treasure attracts repeat business', *Advertising Age,* 58, pp. 12-13.

Dolan, R.J. and Simon, H. (1996), *Power Pricing: How Managing Price Transforms the Bottom Line,* The Free Press, New York.

Downs, J. and Paton, T. (1993), *Travel Agency Law*, Pitman, London.

Drabek, T. E. (1995), 'Disaster Responses within the Tourism Industry', *International Journal of Mass Emergencies and Disasters,* 13(1), pp. 7-23.

Drosdek, A. (1996), *Credibility Management,* Campus, Frankfurt am Main.

Dunwoody, S. and Peters, H. P. (1993), 'Massenmedien und Risikowahrnehmung', in *Risiko ist ein Konstrukt* (Bayerische Rückversicherung (ed.)), Knesebeck, München, pp. 317-341.

Dyllick, T. (1992), *Management der Umweltbeziehungen*, Gabler, Frankfurt am Main.

Eckert, H. W. (1995), *Die Risikoverteilung im Pauschalreiserecht,* 2ⁿᵈ edn., Luchterhand, München.

Elliott, J. (1997), *Politics and Public Sector Management,* Routledge, London.

Eugenio-Martin, J.L., Sinclair, M.T. and Yeoman, I. (2005), 'Quantifying the Effects of Tourism Crises: An Application to Scotland', *Journal of Travel and Tourism Marketing,* 19(2/3), pp. 23-36.

Fakeye, P. and Crompton, J. (1991), 'Image differences between prospective, first-time, and repeat visitors to the Lower Rio Grande Valley', *Journal of Travel Research*, 29(2), pp. 10-16.

Fasse, F.-W. (1995), *Risk-Management im strategischen internationalen Marketing*, Steuer-und Wirtschaftsverlag, Hamburg.

Faulkner, B. (2001), 'Towards a Framework for Tourism Disaster Management', *Tourism Management*, 22(2), pp. 135-147.

Fesenmeier, D. and MacKay, K. (1996), 'Deconstructing destination image construction', *Tourism Review*, 51(2), pp. 37-43.

Fiedler, S. (1994), 'Kommunikation zur Krisenvermeidung und -vorsorge', in *Erfolgsfaktor Krise* (R. Gareis (ed.)), Signum-Verlag, Seedorf, pp. 211-235.

Fink, S. (1986), *Crisis Management: Planning for the Inevitable,* American Management Association, New York.

Floyd, M. F., Gibson, H., Pennington-Gray, L. and Thapa, B. (2003), 'The Effect of Risk Perceptions on Intentions to Travel in the Aftermath of September 11 2001', *Journal of Travel and Tourism Marketing*, 15(2/3), pp. 19-38.

Forschungsgemeinschaft Urlaub und Reisen (FUR) (2002), *Entwicklung der touristischen Nachfrage vor dem Hintergrund der Terroranschläge und deren Folgen,* FUR, Kiel.

Frechtling, D. (2001), *Forecasting Tourism Demand: Methods and Strategies*, Butterworth-Heinemann, Oxford.

Freyer, W. (1995), *Tourismus*, Oldenbourg, München.

Freyer, W. (1997), *Tourismus* – Marketing, Oldenbourg, München.

Freyer, W. and Schröder, A. (2004), 'Terrorismus und Tourismus – Strukturen und Interaktionen als Grundlage des Krisenmanagements', in *Risiko und Gefahr im Tourismus* (D. Glaeßer and H. Pechlaner (eds.)), Erich Schmidt Verlag, Berlin, pp. 101-113.

Frömbling, S. (1993), *Zielgruppenmarketing im Fremdenverkehr von Regionen*, Lang, Frankfurt am Main.

Fuchs, M. (1995), *Erlebniswelt Bundesländer*, Diploma thesis, Vienna 1993, quoted after Mayerhofer, W. (1995), Imagetransfer, Service Fachverlag, Wien.

Führich, E. (2002), *Reiserecht*, 4th edn., C.F. Müller, Heidelberg.

Galtung, J. and Ruge, M. (1965), 'The structure of foreign news', *Journal of Peace Research*, 2 (1), pp. 65-91.

Gammack, J. (2005), 'Tourism and Media', *Annals of Tourism Research*, 32(4), pp. 1148-1149.

Gartner, W. and Shen, J. (1992), 'The impact of Tiananmen Square on China's tourism image', *Journal of Travel Research*, 30(4), pp. 47-52.

Gee, C. and Gain, C. (1986), 'Coping with crises', *Travel & Tourism Analyst*, 1(4), pp. 3-12.

George, R. (2003), 'Tourist's perceptions of safety and security while visiting Cape Town', *Tourism Management*, 24(5), pp. 575-585.

Gialloreto, L. (1988), *Strategic Airline Management: the Global War Begins*, Pitman, London.

Glaeßer, D. (2001), 'Krisenmanagement im Tourismus – Was ist angesichts der aktuellen Vorfälle zu tun', in *Terrorismus versus Tourismus* (H. Bähre (ed.)), Integron, Berlin, pp. 9-15.

Glaeßer, D. (2002a), *Crisis management – what has this crisis taught us, Report presented to the Second Meeting of the Tourism Recovery Committee of the World Tourism Organization in Berlin, Germany,* WTO, Madrid.

Glaeßer, D. (2002b), 'Crisis management in air transport and tourism', in *Air Transport and Tourism* (P. Keller and T. Bieger (eds.)), AIEST, St. Gallen, pp. 121-142.

Glaeßer, D. (2004), 'Krise oder Strukturbruch?', in *Risiko und Gefahr im Tourismus* (D. Glaeßer and H. Pechlaner (eds.)), Erich Schmidt Verlag, Berlin, pp. 13-27.

Glaeßer, D. and Pechlaner, H. (eds.) (2004), *Risiko und Gefahr im Tourismus*, Erich Schmidt Verlag, Berlin.

Gold, J. R. and Ward, S. V. (eds.) (1994), *Place Promotion: the Use of Publicity and Marketing to Sell Towns and Regions,* Wiley, Chichester.

Gómez Martín, M.B. (2005), 'Weather, Climate and Tourism: A Geographical Perspective', *Annals of Tourism*, 32(3), pp. 571-591.

Gomez, P. (1981), *Modelle und Methoden des systemorientierten Managements*, Haupt, Bern.

Goodall, B. and Ashworth, G. (1987), *Marketing in the Tourism Industry: the Promotion of Destination Regions*, Routledge, London.

Goodrich, J. N. (2002), 'September 11, 2001 Attack on America: A Record of the Immediate Impacts and Reactions in the USA Travel and Tourism Industry', *Tourism Management*, 23(6), pp. 573-580.

Grönvall, J. (2000), *Managing Crisis in the European Union: The Commission ND 'Mad Cow Disease'*, CRISMART, Stockholm.

Gu, Z. and Martin, T. (1992), 'Terrorism, seasonality and international air tourist arrivals in Central Florida', *Journal of Travel & Tourism Marketing*, 5(1), pp. 3-15.

Gutiérrez, C. and Bordas, E. (1993), 'La competitividad de los destinos turísticos en mercados lejanos', in *Competitiveness of Long Haul Tourist Destinations* (AIEST (ed.)), 35, AIEST, St. Gallen, pp. 103-211.

Haedrich, G. (1993), 'Tourismus-Management und Tourismus-Marketing', in *Tourismus-Management* (G. Haedrich et al. (eds.)), de Gruyter, Berlin, pp. 33-43.

Haedrich, G. (1998a), 'Kommunikationspolitik', in *Tourismus-Management* (G. Haedrich et al. (eds.)), de Gruyter, Berlin, pp. 379-403.

Haedrich, G. (1998b), Destination marketing – Überlegungen zur Abgrenzung, Positionierung und Profilierung von Destinationen, *Tourism Review*, 53(4), pp. 6-12.

Hahn, D. (1979), 'Frühwarnsysteme, Krisenmanagement und Unternehmensplanung', *Frühwarnsystem, ZfB-Ergänzungsheft* 2, pp. 25-46.

Hall, C. M. (1994), *Tourism and Politics*, John Wiley & Sons, New York.

Hall, C. M. (1995), *Tourism and Public Policy*, Routledge, London.

Hall, C. M., Timothy, D. J. and Duval, D. T. (2004), *Safety and Security in Tourism*, Haworth Press, New York.

Hartman, C., Price, L. and Duncan, C. (1990), 'Consumer evaluation of franchise extension products', in *Advances in Consumer Research Vol. 17* (M. Goldberg, G. Gorn and R. Pollay (eds.)), Association for Consumer Research, Provo UT, pp. 120-127.

Hätty, H. (1989), *Der Markentransfer*, Physica, Heidelberg.

Hauser, T. (1994), *Krisen-PR von Unternehmen*, FGM Verlag, München.

Heath, E. and Wall, G. (1992), *Marketing Tourism Destinations: a Strategic Planning Approach*, Wiley, New York.

Hellenthal, M. (1993), *Policy Study of Traveller Safety – Confidential Report for the World Travel & Tourism Council*, WTTC, London.

Hildebrandt, K. (1997), 'Öger Tours geht in die Offensive', *FVW International*, 18(19), pp. 20-21.

Hilton, D. and Slugorski, B. R. (1986), 'Knowledge based causal attribution: the abnormal conditions focus model', *Psychological Review*, 93(1), pp. 75-88.

Hindley, G. (1983), *Tourists, Travellers and Pilgrims*, Hutchinson, London.

Hinterhuber, H. and Ortner, S. (2004), 'Risikomanagement als nicht-delegierbare Führungsaufgabe', in *Risiko und Gefahr im Tourismus* (D. Glaeßer and H. Pechlaner (eds.)), Erich Schmidt Verlag, Berlin, pp. 191-207.

Hoffman, B. (1998), *Inside Terrorism*, Victor Gollancz, London.

Höhn, R. (1974), *Das Unternehmen in der Krise*, Verlag für Wissenschaft, Wirtschaft und Technik, Bad Harzburg.

Hollinger, R. and Schiebler, S. (1995), 'Crime and Florida's tourists', in *Security and Risks in Travel and Tourism (Proceedings of the International Conference at Mid Sweden University)*, Mid Sweden University, Östersund, pp. 183-215.

Holzmüller, H. and Schuh, A. (1988), 'Skandal – Marketing', in *Umweltdynamik* (H. Frank, G. Plaschka and D. Rößl (eds.)), Springer, Wien, pp. 17-47.

Horner, P. (1996), *Travel Agency Practice*, Longman, London.

Huan, T.C., Beaman, J. and Shelby, L. (2004), 'No-Escape Natural Disaster: Mitigating Impacts on Tourism', *Annals of Tourism Research*, 31(2), pp. 255-273.

Huang, J.H. and Min, J.C.H. (2002), 'Earthquake devastation and recovery in tourism: the Taiwan case', *Tourism Management,* 23(2), pp. 145-154.

Hultkrantz, L. and Olsson, C. (1995), 'Chernobyl effects on domestic and inbound tourism in Sweden', in *Security and Risks in Travel and Tourism (Proceedings of the International Conference at Mid Sweden University),* Mid Sweden University, Östersund, pp. 37-74.

Hurley, J. (1988), 'The hotels of Rome', *The Cornell H.R.A. Quarterly,* 29(2), pp. 71-79.

Inglis, D. and Holmes, M. (2003), 'Highland and Other Haunts: Ghosts in Scottish Tourism', *Annals of Tourism Research,* 30(1), pp. 50-63.

Ingold, A., McMahon, U. and Yeoman I. (eds.) (2000), *Yield Management: Strategies for the Service Industries,* 2nd edn., Continuum, London.

Intergovernmental Panel on Climate Change (2001), *Climate Change 2001: The Scientific Basis,* Cambridge University Press, Cambridge.

Ioannides, D. and Apostolopoulos, Y. (1999), 'Political Instability, War, and Tourism in Cyprus: Effects, Management, and Prospects for Recovery', *Journal of Travel Research,* 38(1), pp. 51-56.

Jacobs, H. (1996), 'Öger Tours', *FVW International,* 18, p. 15.

Jeck-Schlottmann, G. (1987), *Visuelle Informationsverarbeitung bei wenig involvierten Konsumenten* (Dissertation), Universität Saarbrücken, Saarbrücken.

Jossé, G. (2004), *Strategische Frühaufklärung in der Touristik,* Dt. Univ.-Verlag, Wiesbaden.

Jungermann, H. (1991), 'Inhalte und Konzepte der Risikokommunikation', in *Risikokontroversen* (H. Jungermann, B. Rohrmann and P.M. Wiedemann (eds.)) Springer, Berlin, pp. 335-354.

Jungermann, H. and Slovic, P. (1993a), 'Charakteristika individueller Risikowahrnehmung', in *Risiko ist ein Konstrukt* (Bayerische Rückversicherung (ed.)), Knesebeck, München, pp. 89-107.

Jungermann, H. and Slovic, P. (1993b), 'Die Psychologie der Kognition und Evaluation von Risiko', in *Risiko und Gesellschaft* (G. Bechmann (ed.)), Westdeutscher Verlag, Opladen, pp. 167-207.

Kaas, K. P. (1990), 'Marketing als Bewältigung von Informations- und Unsicherheitsproblemen im Markt', *Die Betriebswirtschaft,* 50(49), pp. 539-548.

Kahn, H. and Wiener, A. (1967), *Ihr werdet es erleben,* Molden, Wien.

Kaspar, C. (1989), 'Systems approach in tourism: the Saint Gall Management Model', in *Tourism Marketing and Management Handbook* (S.F. Witt and L. Moutinho (eds.)), Prentice-Hall International, Hemel Hempstead, pp. 443-446.

Kaspar, C. (1991), *Die Tourismuslehre im Grundriss,* 4th edn., Paul Haupt Verlag, Bern.

Kelders, C. (1996), *Unterstützung strategischer Entscheidungsprozesse,* M&P, Stuttgart.

Keller, P. and Smeral, E. (1998), 'Increased international competition: new challenges for tourism policies in European countries', in *Faced with Worldwide Competition and Structural Changes: What are the Tourism Responsibilities of European Governments?* (WTO (ed.)), WTO, Madrid, pp. 1-24.

Kemmer, C. (1995), 'Resident and visitor safety and security in Waikiki', in *Security and Risks in Travel and Tourism (Proceedings of the International Conference at Mid Sweden University),* Mid Sweden University, Östersund, pp. 75-83.

Kerstetter, D. and Cho, M.H. (2004), 'Prior Knowledge, Credibility, and Information Search', *Annals of Tourism Research,* 31(4), pp. 961-985.

Kirsch, W. and Trux, W. (1979), 'Strategische Frühaufklärung und Portfolio-Analyse', *Frühwarnsystem, ZfB-Ergänzungsheft 2*, pp. 47-69.

Kleinert, H. (1993), 'Kommunikationspolitik', in *Tourismus-Management* (G. Haedrich et al. (eds.)), de Gruyter, Berlin, pp. 287-300.

Köhler, R. and Böhler, H. (1984), 'Strategische Marketing-Planung', *Absatzwirtschaft*, 27(3), pp. 93-103.

Konert, F. J. (1986), *Vermittlung emotionaler Erlebniswerte*, Physica, Heidelberg.

Konrad, L. (1991), *Strategische Früherkennung*, Universitätsverlag Brockmeyer, Bochum.

Kotler, P. (1984), *Marketing Management*, 5th edn., Prentice Hall, Englewood Cliffs.

Kotler, P., Haider, D. and Rein, I. (1993), *Marketing Places*, The Free Press, New York.

Kotler, P., Bowen, J. and Makens, J. (1999), *Marketing for Hospitality and Tourism,* 2nd edn., Prentice Hall, Englewood Cliffs.

Krampe, G. and Müller, G. (1981), 'Diffusionsfunktionen als theoretisches und praktisches Konzept zur strategischen Frühaufklärung', *Zeitschrift für betriebswirtschaftliche Forschung*, 33(5), pp. 384-401.

Kreikebaum, H. (1993), *Strategische Unternehmensplanung*, Kohlhammer, Stuttgart.

Kreilkamp, E. (1998), 'Strategische Planung im Tourismus', in *Tourismus-Management* (G. Haedrich et al. (eds.)), de Gruyter, Berlin, pp. 287-324.

Kreilkamp, E. (2004), 'Strategische Frühaufklärung im Rahmen des Krisenmanagements im Tourismusmarkt', in *Risiko und Gefahr im Tourismus* (D. Glaeßer and H. Pechlaner (eds.)), Erich Schmidt Verlag, Berlin, pp. 13-27.

Krippendorf, J. (1991), *The Holiday Makers: Understanding the Impact of Leisure and Travel*, 2nd edn., Heinemann, Oxford.

Kroeber-Riel, W. (1986), 'Erlebnisbetontes Marketing', in *Realisierung des Marketing* (C. Belz (ed.)), Verlag Auditorium, St. Gallen, pp. 1137-1151.

Kroeber-Riel, W. (1992), *Konsumentenverhalten,* Verlag Vahlen, München.

Kroeber-Riel, W. (1993a), *Strategie und Technik der Werbung*, Kohlhammer, Stuttgart.

Kroeber-Riel, W. (1993b), *Bildkommunikation*, Vahlen, Stuttgart.

Krystek, U. (1979), *Krisenbewältigungs-Management und Unternehmungsplanung* (Dissertation), Justus Liebig-Universität, Giessen.

Krystek, U. (1987), *Unternehmungskrisen*, Gabler, Wiesbaden.

Krystek, U. and Müller-Stewens, G. (1992), 'Grundzüge einer Strategischen Frühaufklärung', in Strategische Unternehmensplanung, *Strategische Unternehmensführung* (D. Hahn and B. Taylor (eds.)), Physica-Verlag, Heidelberg, pp. 337-364.

Kupsch, P. (1973), *Das Risiko im Entscheidungsprozeß*, Gabler, Wiesbaden.

Laws, E. and Buhalis, D. (eds.) (2001), *Tourism Distributions Channels: Practices, Issues and Transformations*, Continuum, London.

Lebrenz, S. (1996), *Länderimages,* Josef Eul Verlag, Lohmar.

Lehto, X. Y., O'Leary, J.T. and Morrison, A.M. (2004), 'The Effect of Prior Experience on Vacation Behavior', *Annals of Tourism Research*, 31(4), pp. 801-818.

Leimbacher, U. (1992), *Krisenplanung und Krisenmanagement*, Zentralstelle für Gesamtverteidigung, Bern.

Lennon, G. (1999), 'Marketing Belfast as a tourism destination', *Tourism*, 47(1), pp. 74-77.

Lennon, J. and Foley, M. (1999), 'Interpretation of the Unimaginable', *Journal of Travel Research,* 38(8), pp. 46-50.

Lennon, J. and Foley, M. (eds.) (2000), *Dark tourism: the attraction of death and disaster,* Continuum, London.

Lepp, A. and Gibson, H. (2003), 'Tourist Roles, Perceived Risk and International Tourism', *Annals of Tourism Research,* 30(3), pp. 606-624.

Leslie, D. (1999), 'Terrorism and Tourism: The Northern Ireland Situation – A look behind the Veil of Certainty', *Journal of Travel Research,* 38(1), pp. 37-40.

Linde, F. (1994), *Krisenmanagement in der Unternehmung: eine Auseinandersetzung mit den betriebswirtschaftlichen Gestaltungsaussagen zum Krisenmanagement,* Verlag für Wissenschaft und Forschung, Berlin.

Luhmann, N. (1993), *Risk: A Sociological Theory,* de Gruyter, New York.

Luhmann, N. (2005), *Risk: A Sociological Theory,* Aldine Transaction, New Brunswick, N.J.

MacKay, K.J. and Fesenmaier, D.R. (1997), 'Pictoral Element of Destination in Image Formation', *Annals of Tourism Research,* 24(3), pp. 537-565.

Maier, J. and Kadner B. (2004), 'Der Klimawandel als Krisenfelder und Anpassungsstrategien im bayrischen Alpenraum und speziell im Mittelgebirge', in *Risiko und Gefahr im Tourismus* (D. Glaeßer and H. Pechlaner (eds.)), Erich Schmidt Verlag, Berlin, pp. 143-154.

Mansfeld, Y. (1995), 'Wars, tourism and the 'Middle East' factor', in *Security and Risks in Travel and Tourism (Proceedings of the International Conference at Mid Sweden University),* Mid Sweden University, Östersund, pp. 109-128.

Maslow, A.H. (1943), 'A Theory of Human Motivation', *Psychological Review,* 50(4), pp. 370-396.

Mason, P., Grabowski, P. and Du, W. (2005), 'Severe acute respiratory syndrome, tourism and the media', *International Journal of Tourism Research,* 7(1), pp. 11-21.

Mathes, R., Gärtner, H.-D. and Czaplicki, A. (1991), *Kommunikation in der Krise,* Institut für Medienentwicklung und Kommunikation, Frankfurt am Main.

Mathes, R., Gärtner, H.-D. and Czaplicki, A. (1993), 'Krisenkommunikation Teil 1', *PR Magazin,* 24(11), pp. 31-38.

Mayerhofer, W. (1995), *Imagetransfer,* Service Fachverlag, Wien.

Mazanec, J. (1989), 'Consumer behavior in tourism', in *Tourism Marketing and Management Handbook* (S. Witt and L. Moutinho (eds.)), Prentice Hall, Hertfordshire, pp. 63-68.

McLellan, R.W. and Foushee, K. (1983), 'Negative Images of the United States as Expressed by Tour Operators from Other Countries', *Journal of Travel Research,* 22(1), pp. 2-5.

McQuail, D. (2005), *McQuail's Mass Communication Theory,* 5th edn., Sage Publications, London.

Mercille, J. (2005), 'Media Effects on Image: The case of Tibet', *Annals of Tourism Research,* 32(4), pp. 1039-1055.

Meyer, W. (1981), 'Das Image von Dänemark als Urlaubsland', in *Reisemotive, Länderimages, Urlaubsverhalten* (Studienkreis für Tourismus (ed.)), Studienkreis für Tourismus und Entwicklung e.V., Ammerland/Starnberger See, pp. 141-157.

Middleton, V. and Clarke, J. (2001), *Marketing in Travel and Tourism,* 3rd edn., Butterworth-Heinemann, Oxford.

Mileti, D. and Sorensen, J. (1987), 'Determinants of organizational effectiveness in responding to low probability catastrophic events', *The Columbia Journal of World Business,* 22(1), pp. 13-21.

Miller, G. A. and Ritchie, B. W. (2003), 'A Farming Crisis or a Tourism Disaster? An Analysis of the Foot and Mouth Disease in the UK', *Current Issues in Tourism,* 6(2), pp. 150-171.

Mitroff, I. and Pearson, C. (1993), *Crisis Management,* Jossey-Bass, San Francisco.

Mitroff, I. and Pearson, C. (1996), *The Essential Guide to Managing Corporate Crises,* Oxford University Press, Oxford.

Money, R.B. and Crotts, J.C. (2003), 'The effect of uncertainty avoidance on information search, planning and purchases of international travel vacations', *Tourism Management*, 24(2), pp. 191-202.

Morgan, N. and Pritchard, A. (2000), *Advertising in Tourism and Leisure*, Butterworth-Heinemann, Oxford.

Moutinho, L. (ed.) (2000), *'Strategic Management in Tourism'*, CAB International, Wallingford.

Mühlbacher, H. and Botschen, G. (1990), 'Benefit-Segmentierung von Dienstleistungsmärkten', *Marketing ZFP*, 12(3), pp. 159-68.

Müller, H., Kramer, B. and Krippendorf, J. (1991), *Freizeit und Tourismus* (Berner Studien zu Freizeit und Tourismus 28), Forschungsinstitut für Freizeit und Tourismus, Bern.

Müller, H. and Flügel, M. (1999), *Tourismus und Ökologie* (Berner Studien zu Freizeit und Tourismus 37), Forschungsinstitut für Freizeit und Tourismus, Bern.

Muthukrishnan, A. and Weitz, B. (1991), 'Role of product knowledge in evaluation of brand extension', in *Advances in Consumer Research Vol. 18* (R. Holman and M. Solomon (eds.)), Association for Consumer Research, Provo UT, pp. 407-413.

Nagle, T. and Holden, R. (2002) *The strategy and tactics of pricing: a guide to profitable decision making*, Prentice Hall, Upper Saddle River, NJ.

Nelson Jones, J. and Stewart, P. (1993), *Practical Guide to Package Holiday Law and Contracts*, 3rd edn., Tolley Publishing, Croydon.

Niehuus, M. (2001), *Reiserecht*, Dt. Anwaltverlag, Bonn.

Oelsnitz, D. (1993), *Prophylaktisches Krisenmanagement durch antizipative Unternehmensflexibilisierung*, Verlag Josef Eul, Lohmar.

Okumus, F. and Karamustafa, K. (2005), 'Impact of an Economic Crisis', *Annals of Tourism Research*, 32(4), pp. 942-961.

Okumus, F., Mehmet, A. and Arasly, H. (2005), 'The impact of Turkey's economic crisis of February 2001 on the tourism industry in Northern Cyprus', *Tourism Management*, 26(1), pp. 95-104.

Opaschowski, H. (1995), *Freizeitökonomie*, Leske und Budrich, Opladen.

Pacific Asia Travel Association (2003), *Crisis – It Won't Happen To Us*, PATA, San Francisco.

Page, S.J., Bentley, T. and Walker, L. (2005), 'Tourist Safety in New Zealand and Scotland', *Annals of Tourism Research*, 32(1), pp. 150-166.

Park, W., Lawson, R. and Milberg, S. (1989), 'Memory structure of brand names', in *Advances in Consumer Research Proceedings Vol. 16* (T. Srull (ed.)), Association for Consumer Research, Provo UT, pp. 726-731.

Pearce, P. L. (1982), *The Social Psychology of Tourist Behaviour*, Pergamon, Oxford.

Peattie, S., Clarke, P. and Peattie, K. (2005), 'Risk and responsibility in tourism: promoting sun-safety', *Tourism Management*, 26(3), pp. 399-408.

Perrow, C. (1992), *Normale Katastrophen*, Campus, Frankfurt am Main.

Peschke, G. (1986), 'Der Skandal', in *Jahrbuch der Werbung* (E. Neumann et al. (eds.)), Econ, Berlin, pp. 21-23.

Peymani, B. and Felger, S. (1997), 'Angst vor der großen Stornowelle', *FVW International*, 18(26), pp. 1-4.

Phipps, D. (1991), *The Management of Aviation Security*, Pitman, London.

Phuket Tourism Association (2005), *Come back to Phuket!*, Press release, PTA, Phuket, 18.01.2005.

Pikkemaat, B. and Peters, M. (2004), 'Alpine Katastrophen als Impuls für Innovationen im Tourismus', in *Risiko und Gefahr im Tourismus* (D. Glaeßer and H. Pechlaner (eds.)), Erich Schmidt Verlag, Berlin, pp. 323-336.

253

Pizam, A. and Fleischer, A. (2002), 'Severity versus Frequency of Acts of Terrorism: Which has a Larger Impact on Tourism Demand', *Journal of Travel Research*, 40(3), pp. 337-339.

Pizam, A. and Mansfield, Y. (eds.) (1995), *Tourism, Crime and International Security Issues*, Wiley, New York.

Pizam, A. and Mansfield, Y. (eds.) (1999), *Consumer Behavior in Travel and Tourism*, Haworth Press, New York.

Pizam, A. and Sussmann, S. (1995), 'Does Nationality Affect Tourist Behavior?', *Annals of Tourism Research*, 22(4), pp. 901-917.

Pohl, H. (1977). *Krisen in Organisationen* (Dissertation), Universität Mannheim, Mannheim.

Poirier, R.A. (1997), 'Political Risk Analysis and Tourism', *Annals of Tourism Research*, 24(3), pp. 675-686.

Porter, M. E. (1998a), *Competitive Advantage*, Free Press, New York.

Porter, M. E. (1998b), *Competitive Strategy*, Free Press, New York.

Poustie, M., Ross, J., Geddes, N. and Stewart, W. (1999), *Hospitality and Tourism Law*, International Thomson Business Press, London.

Poynter, J. (1989), *Foreign Independent Tours: Planning, Pricing and Processing*, Delmar, Albany.

Prideaux, B. (2004), 'The Need to Use Disaster Planning Frameworks to Respond to Major Tourism Disasters: Analysis of Australia's Response to Tourism Disasters in 2001', *Journal of Travel and Tourism Marketing*, 15(4), pp. 281-298.

Prideaux, B., Laws, E. and Faulkner, B. (2003), 'Events in Indonesia: exploring the limits to formal tourism trends forecasting methods in complex crisis situations', *Tourism Management*, 24(4), pp. 475-487.

Priel, A. and Peymani, B. (1996), 'Angestrebtes Rekordjahr in weiter Ferne', *FVW International*, 17(18), p. 50.

Pümpin, C. (1980), *Strategische Führung in der Unternehmenspraxis*, Schweizerische Volksbank, Bern.

Raffée, H., Sauter, B. and Silberer, G. (1973), *Theorie der kognitiven Dissonanz und Konsumgüter-Marketing*, Gabler, Wiesbaden.

Raich, F., Pechlaner, H. and Dreyer A. (2004), 'Risikowahrnehmung in touristischen Destinationen', in *Risiko und Gefahr im Tourismus* (D. Glaeßer and H. Pechlaner (eds.)), Erich Schmidt Verlag, Berlin, pp. 217-228.

Reason, J. (1974), *Man in Motion: the Psychology of Travel*, Weidenfeld and Nicolson, London.

Regele, U. and Schmücker, D. (1998), 'Vertriebspolitik im Tourismus', in *Tourismus-Management* (G. Haedrich et al. (eds.)), de Gruyter, Berlin, pp. 405-445.

Reilly, A. (1987), 'Are organizations ready for crisis?', *Columbia Journal of World Business*, 22(1), pp. 79-88.

Richter, L. (1992), 'Political Instability and Tourism in the Third World', in *Tourism and the Less Developed Countries* (D. Harrison (ed.)), Wiley, New York, pp. 35-46.

Richter, L. (1999), 'After Political Turmoil: The Lessons of rebuilding Tourism in Three Asian Countries', *Journal of Travel Research*, 38(1), pp. 41-45.

Richter, L. and Waugh, W. (1986), 'Terrorism and Tourism as Logical Companions', *Tourism Management*, 7(4), pp. 230-238.

Ries, K. and Wiedmann, K.-P. (1991), *Risikokommunikation als Problemfeld des Strategischen Marketings*, Institut für Marketing, Universität Mannheim, Mannheim.

Ritchie, B. (2004), 'Chaos, Crises and Disasters: A Strategic Approach to Crisis Management in the Tourism Industry', *Tourism Management*, 25(6), pp. 669-683.

Ritchie, B. and Crouch, G. (1997), 'Quality, price and the tourism experience', in *Quality Management in Tourism* (AIEST (ed.)), AIEST, St. Gallen, pp. 117-139.

Ritchie, B.W., Dorrell, H., Miller, D. and Miller, G. (2004), 'Crisis Communication and Recovery for the Tourism Industry: Lessons from the 2001 Foot and Mouth Disease Outbreak in the United Kingdom', *Journal of Travel and Tourism Marketing*, 15 (2), pp. 199-216.

Ritchie, B. and Goeldner, C. (eds.) (1994), *Travel, Tourism and Hospitality Research: a Handbook for Managers and Researchers,* 2nd edn., Wiley, New York.

Robinson, M., Evans, N. and Callaghan, P. (eds.) (1996), *Tourism and Culture: Image, Identity and Marketing,* Business Education Publishers, Sunderland.

Roehl, W. S. and Fesenmaier, D.R. (1992), 'Risk Perceptions and Pleasure Travel: An Exploratory Analysis', *Journal of Travel Research,* 30(4), pp. 17-26.

Romeo, J. (1991), 'The effect of negative information on the evaluations of brand extensions and the family brand', in *Advances in Consumer Research Vol. 18* (R. Holman and M. Solomon (eds.)), Association for Consumer Research, Provo UT, pp. 399-406.

Rubio-Ayache, D. (2004), *Droit du tourisme,* Éditions BPi, Clichy.

Ryan, C. (1993), 'Crime, violence, terrorism and tourism: an accidental or intrinsic relationship?', *Tourism Management,* 14(3), pp. 173-183.

Ryan, C. (1995), *Researching Tourist Satisfaction: Issues, Concepts, Problems,* Routledge, London.

Ryan, C. and Page, S. (eds.) (2000), *Tourism Management: Towards the New Millennium,* Elsevier, Oxford.

Sailer, R. (2001), 'Risk Assessment and Crisis Management for a Winter Tourist Resort - A Case Study', in *ESRI User Conference Proceedings 2001* (Abstracts and Papers presented at the 21st Annual ESRI User Conference, July 9-13, 2001), ESRI, Redlands CA.

Santana, G. (1995), 'Crisis management and the hospitality industry', in *Security and Risks in Travel and Tourism (Proceedings of the International Conference at Mid Sweden University),* Mid Sweden University, Östersund, pp. 148-167.

Santana, G. (1999), 'Tourism: toward a model for crisis management', *Tourism,* 47(1), pp. 4-12.

Sayed el, M. K. (1997), 'The case of Egypt', in *Shining in the Media Spotlight* (WTO (ed.)), WTO, Madrid, pp. 21-25.

Scherler, P. (1996), *Management der Krisenkommunikation,* Helbig & Lichtenhahn, Basel.

Scherrieb, H. R. (1992), 'Qualitäts- und Imagemanagement', *Revue de Tourisme,* 47(3), pp. 11-15.

Scheurer, R. (2003), *Erlebnis-Setting – Touristische Angebotsgestaltung in der Erlebnisökonomie* (Berner Studien zu Freizeit und Tourismus Nr. 43), Forschungsinstitut für Freizeit und Tourismus, Bern.

Schilling, A., Nöthinger, C. and Ammann, W. (2004), 'Naturgefahren und Tourismus in den Alpen – Die Krisenkommunikation bietet Lösungsansätze', in *Risiko und Gefahr im Tourismus* (D. Glaeßer and H. Pechlaner (eds.)), Erich Schmidt Verlag, Berlin, pp. 61-74.

Schönefeld, L. (1994), 'Krisenkommunikation in der Bewährung', in *Unternehmen in der ökologischen Diskussion* (L. Rolke, B. Rosema and H. Avenarius (eds.)), Westdeutscher Verlag, Opladen, pp. 207-222.

Schrattenecker, G. (1984), *Die Beurteilung von Urlaubsländern durch Reisekonsumenten,* Service Fachverlag, Wien.

Schulten, M. F. (1995), *Krisenmanagement,* Verlag für Wissenschaft und Forschung, Berlin.

Schulze, G. (1996), D*ie Erlebnis – Gesellschaft,* Campus Verlag, Frankfurt am Main.

Schweiger, G. (1992), *Österreichs Image in der Welt,* Service Fachverlag, Wien.

Sexton, J. B. (ed.) (2004), *The Better the Team, the Safer the World: Golden Rules of Group Interaction in High Risk Environments: Evidence based suggestions for improving performance,* Gottlieb Daimler and Karl Benz Foundation and Swiss Re Centre for Global Dialogue, Ladenburg and Rüschlikon.

Seyderhelm, B. (1997), *Reiserecht,* Müller Verlag, Heidelberg.

Sharpley, R. (1999), *Tourism, Tourists and Society,* 2nd edn., Elm Publications, Huntingdon.

Sharpley, R. and Sharpley, J. (1995), 'Travel advice – security or politics?', in *Security and Risks in Travel and Tourism (Proceedings of the International Conference at Mid Sweden University)*, Mid Sweden University, Östersund, pp. 168-182.

Siegenthaler, P. (2002), 'Hiroshima and Nagasaki in Japanese Guidebooks', *Annals of Tourism Research*, 29(4), pp. 1111-1137.

Simon, H. (1992), *Preismanagement: Analyse, Strategie, Umsetzung*. Gabler, Wiesbaden.

Skriver, A. (1990), 'Vom Unterhaltungswert von Katastrophen', *E+Z*, 31(4), pp. 15-16.

Smith, D. and Park, W. (1992), 'The effect of brand extensions on market share and advertising efficiency', *Journal of Marketing Research*, 29(3), pp. 296-313.

Smith, V. (1998), 'War and tourism', *Annals of Tourism Research*, 25(1), pp. 202-227.

Sönmez, S. (1998), 'Tourism, Terrorism, and Political Instability', *Annals of Tourism Research*, 25(2), pp. 416-456.

Sönmez, S., Apostolopoulos, Y. and Tarlow, P. (1999), 'Tourism in Crisis: Managing the Effects of Terrorism', *Journal of Travel Research*, 38(1), pp. 13-18.

Sönmez, S., Backman, S. J. and Allen, L. R. (1994), *Managing Tourism Crises,* Clemson University, Clemson.

Sönmez, S. and Graefe, A. (1998a), 'Influence of terrorism risk on foreign tourism decisions', *Annals of Tourism Research,* 25(1), pp. 112-144.

Sönmez, S. and Graefe, A. (1998b), 'Determining Future Travel Behaviour from Past Travel Experience and Perceptions of Risk and Safety', *Journal of Travel Research,* 37(4), pp. 171-177.

Starn, R. (1971), 'Historians and Crisis', *Past and Present*, 52, pp. 3-22.

Steger, U. and Antes, R. (1991), Unternehmensstrategie und Risiko–Management, in *Umwelt–Auditing* (U. Steger (ed.)), FAZ, Frankfurt am Main, pp. 13-44.

Stern, E. (2000), *Crisis Decisionmaking: A Cognitive Institutional Approach (Vol. 6),* The Swedish Agency for Civil Emergency Planning (ÖCB), Stockholm.

Strangfeld, R. (1993), 'Rechtliche Rahmenbedingungen', in *Tourismus-Management* (G. Haedrich et al. (eds.)), de Gruyter, Berlin, pp. 105-131.

Stutts, A. (1990), *The Travel Safety Handbook*, Van Nostrand Reinhold, New York.

Süddeutsche Zeitung (1996), 'So bekannt sind die Reiseveranstalter', *Süddeutsche Zeitung,* 12.03.1996, p. 911.

Teye, V.B. (1986), 'Liberation Wars and Tourism Development in Africa: The case of Zambia', *Annals of Tourism Research,* 13(4), pp. 589-608.

Theuerkorn, S. (2004), *Krisenmanagement in touristischen Destinationen. Zwischen theoretischen Ansätzen und praktischer Umsetzung. Dargestellt am Beispiel Sachsen nach dem Hochwasser im August 2002* (diploma thesis), Katholische Universität Eichstätt-Ingolstadt, Eichstätt-Ingoldstadt.

Thierry, C. P. and Mitroff, I. (1992), *Transforming the Crisis Prone Organization*, Jossey Bass, San Francisco.

Timothy, D. J. (2001), *Tourism and Political Boundaries,* Routledge, London.

Trommsdorff, V. (1975), *Die Messung von Produktimages für das Marketing*, Carl Heymanns, Saarbrücken.

Trommsdorff, V. (1990), 'Image als Einstellung zum Angebot', in *Wirtschaftspsychologie in Grundbegriffen* (C. Hoyos (ed.)), Psychologie Verlags Union, München, pp. 117-128.

Tscharnke, K. (1995), *FVW International*, 17(5), p. 181.

Tschiderer, F. (1980), *Ferienortplanung*, Paul Haupt Verlag, Bern.

Tversky, A. and Kahneman, D. (1974), 'Judgement under uncertainty: Heuristics and biases', *Science,* 185, pp. 1124-1131.

Ullberg, S. (2001), *Environmental Crisis in Spain: The Boliden Dam Rupture* (Vol. 14), The Swedish Agency for Civil Emergency Planning (ÖCB), Stockholm.

Ulrich, H. and Probst, G. (1995), *Anleitung zum ganzheitlichen Denken und Handeln*, Paul Haupt Verlag, Bern.

United Nations Population Fund (2004), *State of World Population 2004: The Cairo Consensus at Ten - Population, Reproductive Health and the Global Effort to End Poverty*, UNFPA, New York.

Uysal, M. (ed.) (1994), *Global Tourist Behaviour*, International Business Press, New York.

Vallois, F. (1995), *International Tourism: an Economic Perspective*, Macmillan, New York.

Vellas, F. and Bécherel, L. (1995), *International Tourism*, Macmillan, New York.

VisitScotland (2005), *Avian Flu: A Pandemic Waiting to Happen (A Briefing Paper)*, VisitScotland, Edinburgh.

Vukonic, B. (1997), *Tourism and Religion*, Elsevier Science, Oxford.

Wahab, S. (1995), 'Terrorism – a challenge to tourism', in *Security and Risks in Travel and Tourism (Proceedings of the International Conference at Mid Sweden University)*, Mid Sweden University, Östersund, pp. 84-108.

Weiermair, K. and Gasser, R. (1995). 'Safety and risk in tourism' in *Security and Risks in Travel and Tourism (Proceedings of the International Conference at Mid Sweden University)*, Mid Sweden University, Östersund, pp. 134-147.

Weinberg, P. and Konert, F.-J. (1985), 'Vom Produkt zur Produktpersönlichkeit', *Absatzwirtschaft*, 28(2), pp. 85-97.

WEU (1995), *Directives on Planning Options and Priorities to the Planning Cell, 6, (Unpublished draft*, 10 April), WEU, Brussels.

Wiedemann, P.M. (1994), 'Krisenmanagement und Krisenkommunikation', in *Krisenmanagement bei Störfällen* (H.J. Uth (ed.)), Springer, Berlin, pp. 29-49.

Wiedemann, P. M. and Schütz, H. (2004), *'Was sollte ein Risikomanager über die Risikowahrnehmung wissen?', in Risiko und Gefahr im Tourismus* (D. Glaeßer and H. Pechlaner (eds.)), Erich Schmidt Verlag, Berlin, pp.75-87.

Wilkinson, P. (1993), *Policy Study of Traveller Safety – Confidential Report for the World Travel & Tourism Council*, WTTC, London.

World Tourism Organization (1980), *Physical Planning and Area Development for Tourism in the Six WTO Regions*, WTO, Madrid.

World Tourism Organization (1985), *Contractual Procedures and the Nature of Contracts for Tourist Services between Tour Operators and their Counterparts in Tourist Receiving Countries as well as Users and Consumers of Tourist Services*, WTO, Madrid.

World Tourism Organization (1989), *Document TOUR/89-DI.9, Interparliamentary Conference on Tourism, Madrid*, WTO, Madrid.

World Tourism Organization (1991a), *Special Report on the Impact of the Gulf Crisis on International Tourism*, WTO, Madrid.

World Tourism Organization (1991b), *Medidas recomendadas para la seguridad en turismo*, WTO, Madrid.

World Tourism Organization (1992), *Manual of Quality, Hygiene and Food Safety in the Tourism Sector*, WTO, Madrid.

World Tourism Organization (1993), *Sustainable Tourism Development*, WTO, Madrid.

World Tourism Organization (1994a), *Marketing Plans & Strategies of National Tourism Administrations*, WTO, Madrid.

World Tourism Organization (1994b), *Document SEC/2/94/BM*, WTO, Madrid.

World Tourism Organization (1994c), *Document SEC/2/94/HEUNI,* WTO, Madrid.

World Tourism Organization (1994d), *Document SEC/2/94/CTO, Crime and Tourism in the Bahamas,* WTO, Madrid.

World Tourism Organization (1994e), *Budgets of National Tourism Administrations,* WTO, Madrid.

World Tourism Organization (1994f), *Aviation and tourism policies: balancing the benefits,* Routledge, London.

World Tourism Organization (1995), *Plan of Action for the WTO/UNESCO Cultural Tourism Programme 'The Slave Route',* WTO, Madrid.

World Tourism Organization (1996a), *Budgets of National Tourism Administrations,* WTO, Madrid.

World Tourism Organization (1996b), *What Tourism Managers Need to Know,* WTO, Madrid.

World Tourism Organization (1996c), *Awards for Improving the Coastal Environment,* WTO, Madrid.

World Tourism Organization (1996d), *Global Distribution Systems,* WTO, Madrid

World Tourism Organization (1997), *Tourist Safety and Security,* WTO, Madrid.

World Tourism Organization (1998a), *Tourism – 2020 Vision,* WTO, Madrid.

World Tourism Organization (1998b), *Handbook on Natural Disaster Reduction in Tourist Areas,* WTO, Madrid.

World Tourism Organization (1998c), *Guide for Local Authorities on Developing Sustainable Tourism,* WTO, Madrid.

World Tourism Organization (1999), Impacts of the Financial Crisis on Asia's Tourism Sector, WTO, Madrid.

World Tourism Organization (2000), *Global Code of Ethics for Tourism,* WTO, Madrid.

World Tourism Organization (2001), *Special Report No. 18, Tourism After 11 September 2001: Analysis, Remedial Actions and Prospects,* WTO, Madrid.

World Tourism Organization (2002a), *Special Report No. 19, Tourism Recovery Committee for the Mediterranean Region,* WTO, Madrid.

World Tourism Organization (2002b), *Special Report No. 20, The Impact of the September 11th Attacks on Tourism: The Light at the End of the Tunnel,* WTO, Madrid.

World Tourism Organization (2002c), *Special Report No. 21, Climbing Towards Recovery?,* WTO, Madrid.

World Tourism Organization (2002d), *Safety and Security in Tourism – Partnerships and Practical Guidelines for Destinations* (Unpublished document), WTO, Madrid.

World Tourism Organization (2003a), *Tourism Recovery Series,* WTO, Madrid.

World Tourism Organization (2003b), *Document CME/24/5(b) Special Support Programme for the Recovery of the Travel and Tourism Industry in the Middle East and North Africa,* WTO, Madrid.

World Tourism Organization (2003c), *Climate Change and Tourism,* WTO, Madrid.

World Tourism Organization (2003d), *Evaluating NTO Marketing Activities,* WTO, Madrid.

World Tourism Organization (2004), *Indicators of Sustainable Development of Tourism Destinations,* WTO, Madrid.

World Tourism Organization (2005a), *Tsunami Relief for the Tourism Sector – Phuket Action Plan,* WTO, Madrid.

World Tourism Organization (2005b), *Tsunami: One Year on – A summary of the implementation of the Phuket Action Plan,* WTO, Madrid.

World Tourism Organization (2005c). *Proposal to Channel Funds for the Economic and Operational Recovery of Small and Medium-Size Tourism Enterprises Affected by the Tsunami,* WTO, Madrid.

World Tourism Organization (2005d), *Document TF2/Project Proposal for the WTO Emergency Task Force,* WTO, Madrid.

World Tourism Organization (2005e), *Document A/16/22 – Recommendations on Travel Advisories,* WTO, Madrid.

World Tourism Organization (2005f), *Document A/16/16 – Actions in favour of the Tsunami-affected countries,* WTO, Madrid.

World Tourism Organization, *Yearbook of Tourism Statistics,* Various Editions, WTO, Madrid.

World Tourism Organization and Asian Development Bank (2005), *An Initial Assessment of the Impact of the Earthquake and Tsunami of December 26, 2004 on South and Southeast Asia,* WTO, Madrid.

World Tourism Organization and United Nations (1994), *Recommendations on Tourism Statistics,* WTO, Madrid.

Yeoman, I., Galt, M. and McMahon-Beattie, U. (2005), ' A Case Study of How VisitScotland Prepared for War', *Journal of Travel Research,* 44(1), pp. 6-20.

Young, W. B. and Montgomery, R. J. (1998), 'Crisis Management and its Impact on Destination Marketing', *Journal of Convention and Exhibition Management,* 1(1), pp. 3-18.

Index